Faster Reading for Business

George D. Spache, Ph.D.
Paul C. Berg, Ph.D.

Faster Reading
for Business

THOMAS Y. CROWELL COMPANY

New York, Established 1834

Dr. Spache is Head of the Reading Laboratory and Clinic and Professor of Education at the University of Florida.

Dr. Berg is Head of the Reading Laboratory and Clinic at the University of South Carolina.

Preface

Several years ago one of us wrote an article on rapid reading which appeared in the Sunday magazine section of about forty newspapers in this country.[1] The response to this brief article was immediate and, to us, amazing. We received several dozen letters every day for months after from adults and young people clamoring for reading instruction. This book was written as a partial answer to the tremendous demand for self-improvement evidenced in these hundreds of letters.

There are a great many reading training manuals for college students but very few, in our opinion, that are intended specifically for the adult in business, industry, or the professions. Those materials originally written for college students are not appropriate for the average adult in content or the type of training they offer. Therefore we planned a reading improvement manual that deals with the kinds of reading matter educated adults attempt and promotes growth of the particular reading skills such individuals need.

We have tried to profit from our experiences as a former psychological consultant to management, and as head of a university reading clinic. Every reading selection, test, and exercise has been tried out in a reading clinic serving almost a thousand college students and adults each year. Each part of the book has been carefully selected to represent the types of reading materials that adults in business encounter. Each reading skill taught is carefully integrated into the complete, multidimensional task we call efficient reading.

We are familiar with the demands upon the time available to the

[1] Spache, George, "You Can Read a Book in Thirty Seconds," *Parade*, May 16, 1954, pp. 4-5.

average business or professional person. Therefore, we have planned this book to be used in half-hour sessions devoted to self-improvement in reading. With the exception of several tests that may require more time, each chapter may be completed in approximately thirty minutes. Thus each portion forms a complete, self-contained unit that can be explored in an interval of time readily accessible to most business people.

Use of the book will result in learning many new and more efficient ways of handling reading materials. You will learn to preview materials quickly to obtain ideas of their general content and to select certain pieces for more detailed reading. You will learn how to skim difficult materials for their main ideas, some details, and their implications and conclusions. You will learn how to read for ideas—the only sound method of reading rapidly. You will learn how to scan materials rapidly—to find, to collate, to organize facts effectively.

We are indebted to many of our friends and colleagues for advice and assistance in preparing these materials. Dr. John R. Martin, of New York City, gave many suggestions concerning content and approaches, based on his long experience as a psychological consultant to management. In obtaining standards for the Flexibility Tests, we are grateful to the following, who used the tests with their reading classes and offered many constructive criticisms: Mrs. Ruth B. Armsby, National Bureau of Standards, United States Department of Commerce; Dr. James I. Brown, University of Minnesota; Miss Frances Cook, Washington, D.C.; Dr. Elsie Dotson, University of Texas; Mr. Edmund N. Fulker, Department of the Air Force; Mrs. E. Laura Hodges, Pittsfield, Massachusetts; Mr. James A. Martin, Middle Tennessee State College; Dr. Esther McConihe and Dr. Rebecca A. Pedersen, Western Reserve University; Mrs. E. Christine Morris, University of Nebraska; Dr. A. J. Pelletieri, University of St. Thomas; and Miss Florence Sherbourne, University of Arkansas.

We would also like to express our appreciation for assistance in preparing the bibliographies from Miss Margaret Enid Knox, Head of the Department of Reference and Bibliography of the University of Florida.

Contents

Faster Reading for Business

1

So You Think You Can Read Well?

What You Will Do
> Discover some facts about the reading skills of the average American

What You Will Learn
> How this book will help you improve your reading

HOW WELL DOES THE AVERAGE AMERICAN READ?

The average American businessman or businesswoman spends approximately fifteen to twenty hours a week reading technical reports, correspondence, trade journals, and the like. Studies of the reading skills of adults show that many are handling their materials about as efficiently as an elementary school child could. A recent article in the *Harvard Business Review* points out that the rate and comprehension of the average businessman is comparable to that of a seventh-grader. Many adults read at a speed of about 200 to 250 words a minute. This rate is not much faster than the speed with which a fluent adult talks. In fact, it is not much faster than if the reader were saying each word aloud. These results are confirmed by hundreds of clinics and reading tests given to management and supervisors in training courses in industry.

One might expect that businessmen of the executive level would certainly utilize reading to keep themselves informed, to broaden their outlook, and to help them in making business decisions. However, several surveys of the reading habits of business executives refute this assumption. The members of management resemble the ordinary

1

American in reading the books of the best-seller lists—that is, if they read at all for recreation. A *Fortune* report estimates that not more than 20 per cent of executives read as many as a dozen books a year on general subjects.[1] A *Harvard Business Review* survey found the reading of businessmen, such as it was, to be almost completely related to management and "practical" books.[2] More than half of the young executives enrolled in the advanced management course at Harvard read virtually no books except textbooks and business reports. As one executive was quoted in *Fortune,* "Reading is not part of the concept of what a businessman is supposed to be or to be doing. The concept is of a man pressed by tangible problems that require tangible solutions. The businessman is a man of action. Reading doesn't fit into this concept." [3]

What is true of businessmen is even more true of other segments of the population. Active reading is carried on only by about 25 or 30 per cent of the population. Only about 10 per cent use a library as often as once a month. Three-fourths of all the books borrowed from libraries are read by less than 5 per cent of the population. Although increasing numbers of books and magazines are published almost each year, the reading of these is confined to a relatively small portion of the entire population. People read what they feel they must, and reading is not a "must" activity for most of them.[4]

WHY DO MANY AMERICANS READ SO POORLY?

Here are the five major causes of poor reading:

1. *Vocalizing.* Lip, or throat, or tongue movements while reading slow you down to a walk. If these movements are present to a serious degree, the adult never learns to read silently any faster than he can talk. Ideally speaking, you should be able to read at rates three, four, or five times as fast as you can possibly talk.

[1] Duncan Norton-Taylor, "Why Don't Businessmen Read Books?" *Fortune,* Vol. XLIX (May, 1954), pp. 115-117.

[2] Edward C. Bursk and Donald T. Clark, "Reading Habits of Business Executives," *Harvard Business Review,* XXVII (May, 1949), pp. 330-345.

[3] Duncan Norton-Taylor, *ibid.,* p. 117.

[4] Lester Asheim, "What Do Adults Read?" in "Adult Reading," *55th Yearbook, National Society for the Study of Education,* Part II, pp. 5-29.

2. *Habit.*   Many present-day adults were trained in their early years in methods that led to slow reading. Guy Buswell's study of the reading habits of children and adults showed that most readers gained little in rate after the fourth or fifth grade. A good many struggled on through high school or college and into adult life with the reading skills of the elementary school child.

For the past few years educators and critics of public education have been engaged in a furious debate over this point. This is probably not the place to review all the arguments pro and con. But there is little question of the fact that a great many adults are thoroughly dissatisfied with their reading skills. Their training did not prepare them to deal easily and fluently with the great mass of reading matter that is part of business and modern life.

3. *Lack of reading experiences.*   Concentration of reading in one difficult field, such as law, science, or business materials, tends to affect reading skills. Those adults who have narrow reading interests, or are forced by the demands of earning a livelihood to overemphasize one kind of reading, often show this in their reading performances. They lack the skills that come from reading a variety of materials in different ways and seldom read with maximum efficiency even in their chosen field.

4. *Limited vocabulary.*   Lack of broad vocabulary knowledge, or of skill in recognition and understanding of new terms, makes rapid, fluent reading almost impossible. Vocabulary deficiency is particularly a handicap in attempting to read in unfamiliar fields.

5. *Lack of flexibility.*   Most adults are almost incapable of using different reading rates for varying materials. They have never been trained in higher-level reading skills such as skimming, previewing, and thorough reading. They tend to read without regard for the structure of the materials, the purpose of their reading, or the possibility of employing different approaches to comprehension.

DO YOU READ THESE WAYS?

These are the characteristics of the slow or poor reader. Check those that apply to you.

Slow Rate Do you:	*Poor Comprehension* Do you:
Move lips while reading	Attempt to read straight through
Whisper to yourself	Struggle along paragraph by paragraph
Read practically word by word	Depend upon memory rather than understanding
Read everything at same rate	Lose place, get confused
"Hear" or "think" each word as you read	Forget what you are reading, have to reread
Read about as fast as you can talk	Find technical materials a tough job
Seldom read an entire book	Become easily distracted by noise, or own thoughts
Prefer magazines and short stories to novels	Fail to recognize humor, satire, or symbolic language
Slow down in recognizing and understanding difficult words	Read only in one or a few fields
Become tired after short periods of reading	Seldom read for recreation

CAN YOU IMPROVE YOUR READING?

Reports from many clinics and reading laboratories show that large, even surprising improvements in rate and comprehension are possible for most adults. These improvements in reading skill often result in dramatic savings in time and money. After a trial course, the New York Mutual Life Insurance Company decided to extend its reading training course to almost all of the sixteen hundred members of its headquarters staff. The officers of this company discovered that the training resulted in saving time on paper work by about 25 per cent. A survey by a St. Paul manufacturing company revealed that a $174,480 savings in management's time could be realized by training 200 of the company's top-level executives in efficient reading. After a reading training course, Monsanto Chemical Company officials estimated that the increased speed and efficiency resulted in an annual saving of over $40,000 in terms of the value of the reading time of their average executive.

Personal gains for the individual are equally significant. Some may even be able to rid themselves of that symbol of the present-day businessman—the briefcase bulging with work to be completed at home. Johnson and Johnson executives and supervisors increased their reading speed from an average of 215 words per minute to 425 words per minute after a seventeen-hour course. Increases as great as 50 to 100 per cent in speed and marked growth in efficiency are often reported. Of course, such gains are an individual matter depending upon the basic causes of the individual's difficulty and the rigidity of his habit of slow reading. Gains in comprehension tend to appear a bit more slowly than those in rate since more than just a change of pace is involved. Comprehension gain means increasing efficiency in handling various kinds of reading matter, learning and using better approaches and more flexibility, and learning to relate purpose to speed and concentration. The evidence is, that with concentrated attention to this problem for five or six weeks, marked improvement is usually achieved.

WHAT THIS BOOK WILL DO FOR YOU

The materials offered in this book have been tried out extensively with college students and adults. Typical of the results obtained from fifteen to twenty half-hour sessions are 30 per cent or better increases in reading rate and increases in comprehension of 20 per cent or better.

Besides helping you to achieve sizable gains in both rate and comprehension, this book will give you many of the other accomplishments of the really skillful reader. It will train you in three or four methods of rapid reading suited to different reading situations. It will train you in a method of reading difficult, technical material more completely and comprehensively. It will give you habits of critical reading—detecting propaganda techniques, recognizing bias and prejudice, weighing and evaluating persuasive writing. It will offer you methods of improving your vocabulary that will work for you the rest of your life. It will offer you suggestions for improving your listening and writing abilities. Finally, it will help you to read more intelligently in statistical and mathematical materials.

This book is not merely a substitute for a reading improvement course you might take at some clinic. It is a reading improvement course in itself. The book differs from most training courses in offering no mechanical or cure-all training devices. Emphasis on direct rather than mechanical approach to reading improvement is supported by the published results of many other reading specialists. Training in efficiency and comprehension, such as that given here, is more effective in producing gains in both rate and comprehension than courses mainly stressing rate.

If you will devote a half hour a day for five or six weeks to learning these techniques you will undoubtedly see appreciable gains in your reading skills.

WHAT THIS BOOK WILL NOT DO FOR YOU

This book will not double your rate of reading in all types of materials. There is no such thing as a general rate of reading that operates in all situations. Improving speed in one reading task does not necessarily generalize to all other reading situations. We are not trying to teach you to read rapidly, and therefore superficially, but how to adapt your rate to the purpose and importance of the materials you are reading. This book will not suddenly enable you to read technical materials you now can't understand. Nor will it enable you to read fluently in unfamiliar fields. Such an ability can only come gradually out of increasing reading experiences. As is true in every other learning situation, you will learn to read fluently in many fields of interest by gradually familiarizing yourself with the vocabulary and concepts peculiar to those fields. Finally, this book will not provide you with the reading background you may not now have. If you are narrowly read, or if you have concentrated your reading in one or two highly specialized fields, this book cannot magically help you to read and enjoy literary materials, for example. This book will, however, suggest ways and means of extending your reading and of finding time to do the kinds of reading you now miss, so that you may gradually broaden your reading interests.

2

How Well Do You Read?

What You Will Do
 Evaluate your reading skills by several tests

What You Will Learn
 Which reading skills you need to improve

   The most practical way of evaluating your present reading skills is by a trial on materials of known difficulty. These materials have been used extensively with college students and adults and standards for the average adult have been established. This formal approach to measurement of your reading skills is time-consuming. But it is much preferable to a simple estimate based on casual reading. Rate and comprehension vary markedly from one type of selection to the next for the average reader. Therefore the material on which an evaluation of reading skills is based must be carefully chosen and used with a sufficient number of individuals to determine its true difficulty and the performances of the average person in reading it.
   In taking each of these tests, try to follow the directions carefully. If you do not take them in the same way as others did, you cannot compare your results with the standards. You will probably need about a half-hour of uninterrupted time to take this first test and score it.

GENERAL READING TEST

   Directions.   This is a test of your skill in general reading. Read the short article in this test in the same way that you ordinarily read any interesting article. Read as rapidly as you can and still understand what you read. When you finish reading, you will be asked to answer questions on the material you have read.

You will need to make an accurate record of the time you take to read this selection. Write the time you began to read on the line *"Begun"* next to the title of the article. As soon as you finish reading, before answering the questions, write down the time you finish on line *"Ended."*

Then begin to answer the questions. Do *not* look back at the article again.

Morale and Productivity [1]   Begun_____

    by Dick Carlson   Ended_____

The greatest of all arts is the ability to create circumstances which cause people to want to produce to the maximum of their capacity in the attainment of common objectives, not because they have to but because they want to.

Productivity is dependent upon a variety of conditions. It involves the product, plant design, flow of work, facilities and equipment, production know-how, methods, procedures and many other engineering factors. In addition to these engineering factors productivity is also dependent upon morale, a willingness to work, and job satisfaction on the part of all employees.

Morale is an attitude of mind, it is the unconscious fragile spirit that permeates the entire organization; it takes a long time to develop it; it is fluid and unstable; it is never permanently established, and it must not be taken for granted.

A recent case study of the Farm Bureau Insurance Companies, Columbus, Ohio, made these observations vividly clear.

Top Management must accept final responsibility for the morale and productivity of the total work force; for employee attitudes, and their willingness to produce; for attaining maximum production with a minimum of stress, strain, and friction; and for the teamwork and loyalty of the total work force.

In order to maintain morale and productivity, it is essential that adequate management controls be established and maintained which will

[1] Adapted from *Systems*, 18, No. 5, May-June, 1954, pp. 4-5. Copyright 1954 by Remington Rand. Used by permission.

assist the president and his board of directors to: (1) project desired results accurately; (2) identify and forecast major trends; (3) determine needs for changes; and (4) detect problems in time to take corrective action before they become critical.

What can top management do to create the climate which causes high morale and productivity? Five steps which will definitely improve morale are:

1. Develop and Publish Objectives and Policies. This takes courage and skill, but whenever men place greater emphasis upon security or the status quo than they do upon opportunity, initiative withers and dies.

2. Create Relationships and Conditions. All executives and supervisors must have pride in their organization, pride in their own jobs, and pride in the accomplishments of their subordinates. Experience proves that the performance of the total work force is directly related to the quality of their supervision.

3. Develop Acceptance. Build up in the minds of first and second line supervision, as well as the top executives, an understanding and acceptance of what the company is attempting to accomplish—a deep conviction about the organization's purposes and objectives.

4. Conduct well-planned and effective meetings regularly (a) at least once a year—all employees; (b) three or four times a year—all supervisory personnel; (c) once a month—all key management personnel; and (d) weekly—top management conferences, as required. It's what happens in the executive sessions of management, when the doors are closed and the chips are down, that makes for real "morale" in the organization.

5. Issue well-designed and interesting publications: (a) company paper—weekly or monthly; (b) management reports to employees—annually or quarterly; (c) reports to owners, members, stockholders, or policyholders—annually; (d) periodicals and special reports as required; (e) handbooks, standard practice instructions; (f) organization manuals, at appropriate levels; and (g) continuous training materials.

Some of the strongest incentives that can be provided by management in the development of employee morale include recognition of individual abilities and interests; opportunity insofar as practicable, proportionate to performance; rewards (non-financial as well as financial) commensurate with performance.

PUT THE PRINCIPLES TO WORK

We can see how some of these viewpoints and principles were put to work by the management of the Farm Bureau Insurance Companies. A preliminary study emphasized the fact that their organization structure had, through the years, like Topsy, "jes' growed." Departments had developed around strong individuals, rather than around major functions. As in other organizations, many problems could be traced in part to an inadequate organization structure.

As soon as the management of these Companies agreed that a revised organization structure was imperative, the question was asked: "Reorganization along what lines?" The answer was, "A structure well designed to accomplish most effectively the over-all objectives of the organization."

Without a definite written statement of company objectives, it is difficult to design a sound organization structure or to develop criteria for appraising the effectiveness of management, except by opinion, guesswork, or individual judgment.

Whenever a company undertakes a reorganization program, it takes courage to let the chips fall where they may. Whenever the careers and the status of top executives are affected in a reorganization program, there is always a grave danger that fundamental principles and major issues will be obscured by self-interest. Unless management has the will and the courage to be completely objective, little improvement can be made.

Good organization, however, is not a cure-all. If any executives are weak, no amount of tinkering with the organization structure is going to solve that problem. Imaginative and capable management is a constant need that doesn't end with the adoption of an organization structure.

After the revised plan of organization was established, the next step was the development and adoption of an executive salary program. This included the design and installation of an executive position classification plan for the grading of more than 700 supervisory and management positions; the establishment of equitable salary ranges for each grade; the classification of all positions affected from the first-line supervisors to and including the president, and the adoption of a systematic program for appraising executive performance, together with a well-organized plan for approving salary increases.

The Companies' next major problem was "growing pains." Based upon the successful experience of two pilot programs, the decision was made to decentralize all operations. Since that time several regional offices have been moved to regional locations, and all the Companies' operations have been completely decentralized into geographic units.

Every one of the moves has gone off like clockwork. Details have been thoroughly worked out in advance by those to be affected. Each of the regional offices has gone through the same kind of staging treatment.

A definite plan has been developed and adopted to assure adequate coordination of all phases of management including line and staff executives, home office, and regional operations.

MANAGEMENT CONTROLS

Concurrently with the decentralization, the Farm Bureau management faced the problem of establishing management controls and reports which would reflect current adherence to established objectives, budgets, and programs for the organization as a whole, the home office staff, and each of the regional offices. This has been accomplished through:

1. Organization Manuals, which outline in writing descriptions of all management jobs, as well as the objectives, functions, responsibilities and criteria for measuring the performance of every major home office and department within the Companies.

2. President's Report to the Board, which summarizes monthly and quarterly the Company's accomplishments of total end results in conformity with over-all objectives and policies as previously approved by the Board.

3. Management Control Reports, which reveal currently the basic information necessary to assure adherence to established objectives and standards by each major department.

The fundamental improvements in operation reveal in part the results of the long-range management improvement program which created the circumstances necessary in order to change the previous trends of decreasing productivity and increasing costs.

I believe that what has been done by these Companies to improve morale and productivity can be done by almost any organization, to the extent that its management will analyze the causes of any unsatisfactory trends in its operations and then apply effective remedial action.

Write down the time you finished reading.

Questions on "Morale and Productivity"

1. What does the writer suggest is the greatest of all arts? (*Check one.*)
   a. Ability to promote a desire in people for maximum production in the accomplishment of common objectives
   b. Ability to create a feeling of need in people to attain common objectives
   c. Ability to create some common objectives which cause people to want to produce
   d. Ability to cause people to produce to the maximum of their capacities

2. Final responsibility for the level of morale in an organization rests with:
   a. top management.
   b. supervisors.
   c. all employees.
   d. personnel department.

3. Well-planned meetings should be held regularly with all employees at least:
   a. once a year.
   b. three or four times a year.
   c. once a month.
   d. twice a year.

4. Supervisory personnel should meet in conference:
   a. three or four times a year.
   b. once a week.
   c. twice a year.
   d. once a month.

5. A detailed management report to employees ought to be issued:
   a. at least once a year.
   b. weekly.
   c. only as a special directive.
   d. monthly.

6. In order to design a sound organizational structure, the first step should be to:

    a. develop it from the judgment of its top executives.

    b. create an "executive position classification plan."

    c. create a written statement of company objectives.

    d. adopt a systematic program for appraising executive performance.

7. The Farm Bureau Insurance Companies have moved organizationally toward:

    a. centralization of operations at the home office.

    b. decentralization of operations to regional locations.

    c. a partial decentralization of operations to regional offices.

    d. less operational control, either centralized or decentralized.

8. A high level of morale in an organization:

    a. may be easily destroyed but quickly rebuilt.

    b. is easily destroyed but rebuilt with difficulty.

    c. may be accepted as relatively permanent, once firmly established.

    d. may be maintained in certain departments while being nonexistent in others.

9. The main idea of this selection is that:

    a. morale among workers is the responsibility of management.

    b. morale is fluid and unstable.

    c. the employee should be made conversant with company objectives and policies.

    d. productivity is directly dependent upon morale.

10. One of the problems mentioned which is common to reorganization is:

    a. the amount of time lost during the changeover.

    b. the expense involved in the changeover.

    c. the appearance of self-interest which tends to defeat the program.

    d. the lack of men within the organization to take over the newly constituted positions.

11. Productivity is influenced largely by:

   a. engineering factors.
   b. the organization of the manufacturing process.
   c. morale and job satisfaction.
   d. morale as well as engineering.

12. The illustration of the Farm Bureau Insurance Companies was well chosen because:

   a. it showed the best way to achieve reorganization.
   b. it began with the reclassification of all managerial positions.
   c. the reorganization followed a number of the author's principles for improving morale.
   d. it demonstrated one way to overcome decreasing productivity and increasing costs.

13. Adequate management controls:

   a. consist mainly of departmental and top management reports to the president.
   b. keep every employee informed of the company's progress.
   c. enable top management to appraise the effectiveness of personnel.
   d. permit top management to evaluate current accomplishment of the company's objectives by all persons and departments.

14. From this article, we may conclude that the author believes:

   a. practically all employees are responsible for morale and productivity.
   b. employee selection and placement are not important elements of morale and productivity.
   c. high productivity is impossible without high morale.
   d. productivity is the direct result of management's success in creating and maintaining morale.

15. Which one of these is *not* included as one of the five essentials of morale?

   a. Clear statement of objectives
   b. Adequate communication between management and employees

    c. Acceptance of the company's purposes and objectives by supervisory and management personnel

    d. A program for handling employee suggestions and complaints

16. Which one of these ideas offered by the author is probably *not* essential for morale in the small business concern?

    a. An effective publications program

    b. A clear statement of objectives

    c. Pride in the company's purposes and objectives

    d. Acceptance of the company's aims by supervisory personnel

To determine your rate of reading, divide the number of minutes you needed to read the article into 1,300, the number of words. Your rate may then be compared with the standards given below.

RATE

Better than 300	Excellent
250 to 300	Very Good
200 to 250	Good
150 to 200	Fair
Below 150	Poor

Now compare your answers with the following correct answers to the sixteen questions.

1. a.	5. a.	9. a.	13. d.
2. a.	6. c.	10. c.	14. d.
3. a.	7. b.	11. d.	15. d.
4. a.	8. b.	12. c.	16. a.

COMPREHENSION

Above 13	Excellent
12 or 13	Very Good
10 or 11	Good
7 to 9	Fair
Below 7	Poor

WHAT DO YOUR SCORES MEAN?

There are four common patterns of reading skill revealed by this general test.

The Slow Reader. This type of reader often secures a rather high degree of comprehension. But reading is a burdensome task for him. He honestly believes that it is necessary to read slowly in order to comprehend thoroughly. Therefore, he tends to read books, articles, newspapers, and magazines, simple or difficult material, all at the same slow rate. He doesn't really read, he studies everything. This attitude is based on a false assumption. Except in quite difficult material, slow reading does not result in better comprehension. In most reading situations, moderately fast reading produces better comprehension of ideas.

The slow reader ignores the various purposes for which different types of reading are undertaken. There is no such thing as fast recreational reading for him, because, in the first place, he doesn't enjoy reading. He seldom reads as a pastime, yet often feels the lack of cultural background that reading might bring him. Such an individual reads accurately, it is true, but he sacrifices time, enjoyment, and breadth of reading in his inflexible emphasis upon getting all the facts.

Fortunately, this is the easiest type of reading difficulty to overcome. Reports from many reading clinics and training courses show that the average slow reader can be helped in a relatively short period. Most slow readers who learn to apply the techniques of rapid reading are able to see improvement in five or six weeks. In this book, chapters 3 to 6 are written particularly for you. You will improve your other skills as well if you use the remainder of the book conscientiously, but you should work hardest with the portion dealing with improvement of rate.

The Fast Reader. There is a type of reader who believes that time is the essence of every reading situation. Good reading is synonymous in his thinking with fast reading, regardless of the purpose for reading or the intrinsic complexity of the material. Such a reader tends to score high in rate but poorly in comprehension. In a way, this individual is just as inflexible as the slow reader. He has only one method of approach —rapid, superficial reading. As we have pointed out, rapid reading does promote a flow of ideas and results in more real understanding than word-by-word reading. But this is true only within certain limits. When speed results in relatively poor comprehension, then that rate is inappropriate. When the material is technical, rapid reading is impractical, unless the reader finds the concepts quite simple.

The glib, overly fast reader wastes as much time as the slow reader, because he gains so little for the amount of effort he has made. This individual must curb his rate to a practical level or until comprehension increases to at least average levels. Chapters 5 to 7 will help the fast reader acquire techniques that will result in improved retention.

The Poor Reader. Many adults, no matter how hard they try, find reading a difficult task. Not only do they read slowly, but they comprehend poorly as well. Recreational reading is as tiring as that necessary to business. All in all, any kind of reading is disagreeable for these unlucky individuals.

Recognizing their slow rate, many poor readers try to push themselves to greater speed. This often results in even poorer comprehension and they tend to regress to their usual laborious rate. They fail to achieve better comprehension when attempting more rapid reading because they have no concepts of appropriate methods. In a word, they don't know how to read rapidly.

In attempting to improve comprehension, poor readers again often experience disappointment. Despite repeated rereadings, or a line-by-line approach, they miss the major, significant ideas and remember only random details. This failure is also due to lack of training in reading techniques, to lack of skill in organizing ideas and seeing relationships. Chapters 3 to 7 are planned to provide training in various ways of reading that result in improved rate and comprehension.

The Competent Reader. Some will find no evidence of poor reading habits in the results of this first test. Both rate and comprehension score good or better according to our standards. These results imply that in a general reading situation, the individual performs with reasonable efficiency. Other reading skills are tested later in this chapter and will give additional information.

You may feel that, although your rate and comprehension are fairly adequate, you would like to improve them further. Within reasonable limits, this is quite possible. Increases in the speed of handling materials and better results in retention are often obtainable even for good readers. Studies of the reading habits and methods of college students and adults show that even the best readers do not employ all the various devices and reading techniques which are recommended. You will undoubtedly find suggestions of new and better ways to read in the remainder of this book, if you wish to improve your present status.

ARE YOU FLEXIBLE IN READING?

Before going on to direct efforts to improve your reading, we suggest that you take a second reading test to measure other important reading habits. You will learn a great deal about your knowledge and skill in various reading techniques from this test, and the information will permit much more intelligent use of the other sections of this book. Therefore, it is most desirable that you use this test now to evaluate your other reading abilities.

You may need as much as an hour of uninterrupted time to complete the test. In addition, you will need the assistance of an alarm clock or some person to help you time the First Reading, which must be completed in *exactly three minutes*. Remember to follow the directions carefully in order that your efforts will be comparable with the standards for the test results.

TEST OF READING FLEXIBILITY [2]

This is a test to discover your ability to read for different purposes. Three different reading situations are suggested for the same selection, "How to Forecast." Work through each of the following plans before going on to the next one.

FIRST READING

Suppose that you found this article "How to Forecast" while looking through a magazine and wished to gain a general idea about the kinds of information it contained. Allow yourself *only three* (3) minutes to look or read through the entire selection beginning on page 28. Then answer questions 1 through 10 without checking back to the selection. These questions deal with the general ideas or the main points the article presents. You will not be asked any very detailed questions after this brief reading. Remember, you have only *three minutes* to cover the *whole* article.

[2] By Paul C. Berg and George D. Spache, Reading Laboratory and Clinic, University of Florida, Gainesville, Florida. Copyright 1956 by Paul C. Berg and George D. Spache.

(*Do not read further on this page until you have completed the* FIRST READING.)

SECOND READING

Presume now that you have several specific questions about forecasting that you would like to have answered. As you turn again to the article, questions 11 to 20 come to your mind. Before you read the first of these questions, you will need to make an accurate record of the time. Write down the time you begin to answer question 11 and again when you finish with question 20. Write these times right above question 11. Now answer questions 11 to 20, finding the answers from the reading as quickly as you can. As soon as you have found all of the answers, again make a record of the time.

(*Do not read further on this page until you have completed the* SECOND READING.)

THIRD READING

Now read the entire selection as you would to answer detailed questions. As soon as you have completed the reading, answer questions 21 to 41 without referring back to the article. Write down the time you begin this reading and again when you finish. Do *not* include the time for answering the questions.

Questions on "How to Forecast"

FIRST READING

1. What is business forecasting?
    a. Recognizing secondary and general consequences and tracing the effects of a policy
    b. Planning today for tomorrow's business
    c. Putting quantitative values to projected economic consequences
    d. Tracing all pertinent economic consequences

2. What place has "instinct" or "over-all feel" as a guide to business forecasting?

    a. It has no legitimate place.
    b. It has a very real place, especially in the small business.
    c. It is especially useful in the large business.
    d. It is equally useful in both the small and large businesses.

3. Business forecasting at Canadian General Electric is done:

    a. through consultation with a firm of economists, and knowledge gained from meetings and various publications.
    b. entirely by management.
    c. in consultation with the company's legal and economic staff.
    d. independently by a firm of Canadian economists.

4. Which of these is basic to any long-term business forecast?

    a. Estimation of a future labor force
    b. Estimation of the future Gross National Product
    c. Estimation of future population
    d. Estimation of future basic conditions

5. What is a useful starting point in estimating the long-term demand for specific products?

    a. A long-term forecast of basic conditions
    b. A long-term forecast of future population
    c. A long-term forecast of Gross National Product
    d. A long-term forecast of households

6. Individual indicators in making business forecasts should be:

    a. correlated in a definite or formulated manner.
    b. brought together in whatever way judgment indicates.
    c. treated individually and not in a correlated fashion.
    d. chosen in a definite pattern relative to the business studied.

7. In following the micro approach, it is necessary to:

    a. work with the thing to be forecast as a whole unit.
    b. follow through separately with each predictor to its logical effect.
    c. start by making a short-term forecast.
    d. break the thing to be forecast into its smallest possible units.

8. What may be safely said about forecasts as a method of predicting things to come?
   a. A forecast throws light on future trends and conditions.
   b. Forecasts simply reflect conditions and trends up to the time the forecast was made.
   c. A forecast is a plan for future activity.
   d. A forecast, carefully made, can be an unerring prediction of things to come.

9. What is the macro approach to forecasting?
   a. Looking at local conditions in the light of national trends
   b. Looking at the thing to be forecast by means of its smallest possible units
   c. Using outside economists to make forecasts
   d. Using one predictor as a valid indicator

10. One may infer from this article that the author's attitude toward business forecasting is:
    a. somewhat skeptical of any real value in most of it.
    b. one of complete acceptance as a plan to future activities.
    c. that it is a necessary way of making an informed guess as a guide to probable activity.
    d. that its prime use is in its percentage accuracy.

SECOND READING

Begun_____

Ended_____

11. How many basic types of forecasting are dealt with in this article?
    a. Two
    b. Four
    c. Six
    d. Eight

12. What are the most important factors in predicting business trends?
    a. Industrial production and employment
    b. Personal income and ability to buy
    c. Confidence of the public and the strength of its demands
    d. Prices and availability

13. What has been called "The greatest single economic discovery of our age"?

    a. Computation of Gross National Product
    b. The relationship between output and total demand
    c. Computation of national and disposable income
    d. Wassily Leontief's work on input-output

14. What does national and disposable income indicate?

    a. The number of people economically occupied
    b. Bank debits, bank loans, and savings
    c. Level of public confidence
    d. National spending power

15. Who predicted a severe depression for 1954?

    a. Professor Woytinsky of Johns Hopkins
    b. Colin Clark, Australia
    c. H. R. Bowen, Williams College
    d. Professor Boulding

16. What is the trend of increase per year in Canadian wholesale prices?

    a. One per cent compounded
    b. One per cent
    c. Two per cent compounded
    d. Two per cent

17. How often are long-term forecasts made at Canadian General Electric?

    a. Every ten years
    b. Every five years
    c. Every two years
    d. Every year

18. How often are short-term forecasts made at Canadian General Electric?

    a. Yearly
    b. Quarterly
    c. Biyearly
    d. Every three years

19. What department of Canadian General Electric is responsible for forecasts of the basic business outlook?

    a. Economic Analysis Section
    b. Cost Control
    c. Production
    d. Sales

20. How many staff divisions does the Canadian General Electric Company have?

    a. Two
    b. Four
    c. Six
    d. Eight

THIRD READING

Begun_____

Ended_____

21. How great a period do long-term projections cover at Canadian General Electric?

    a. Four years
    b. Six years
    c. Eight years
    d. Ten years

22. Long-term forecasts may be used to determine:

    a. capital requirements.
    b. changes in company policy.
    c. the effect of proposed legislation.
    d. all of the above.

23. A careful forecaster will try to arrive at his final figures by approaching the problem:

    a. from a single line of approach.
    b. from at least two different directions.
    c. from at least three or four different directions.
    d. from one or more approaches according to his particular problem.

24. What may be said of the relationship between long- and short-term forecasting?
    a. Long-term forecasting is usually much more difficult than short-term.
    b. The variables used for both long- and short-term forecasting are approximately the same.
    c. A long-term forecast usually follows a short-term forecast.
    d. Short-term forecasting is usually much more difficult than long-term.

25. In the author's opinion, forecasting:
    a. is much overrated in difficulty.
    b. is improving as new and better information becomes available.
    c. really means planning for the future.
    d. is becoming more difficult as the size of businesses increases.

26. Product forecasts at Canadian General Electric are done by:
    a. the Marketing Research Department.
    b. the Economic Analysis Section.
    c. the product departments.
    d. the Department of Sales.

27. What may have the greatest influence on the validity of future predictions?
    a. Wassily Leontief's work on input-output
    b. Lead-lag indicators
    c. "Built-in" stabilizers, such as old age pensions and unemployment insurance
    d. Electronic calculators

28. In making a forecast, Canadian General Electric represents their over-all prediction by:
    a. precise and single figures.
    b. a maximum or minimum range.
    c. a narrow or minimum range.
    d. a wide or maximum range.

29. For how long a period are short-term forecasts made at Canadian General Electric?
    a. Four quarters ahead
    b. Three quarters ahead

    c. Two years ahead

    d. One quarter ahead

30. What is of primary importance to the small business in making forecasts?

    a. The use of outside economists

    b. An economic analysis section

    c. A marketing research department

    d. Good sources and a constant flow of statistical information

31. Indicators of business trends of the past and future are best:

    a. treated as separate bits of information.

    b. combined by statistical procedures into a single index.

    c. weighted mathematically and arranged in a series.

    d. combined in whatever way judgment indicates is wise.

32. What does the author see for the future of the art of forecasting?

    a. New indexes and electronic devices will create exact predictions.

    b. Forecasting is improving and is becoming a reasonably reliable basis for operation.

    c. The complexity of modern business creates so many variables that prediction is becoming impossible.

    d. Forecasting will hold a much lesser role than it previously has.

33. Of what value is Gross National Product as a business indicator?

    a. It provides evidence of spending power.

    b. It indicates demand and the public's confidence.

    c. It indicates confidence and ability to buy.

    d. It indicates the over-all level of national economy.

34. In making a forecast, of what use is knowledge about bank debits, bank loans, and savings?

    a. They indicate the demand for goods and the confidence of the public.

    b. They indicate manufacturing levels.

    c. They provide evidence of the over-all level of the economy.

    d. They indicate confidence and ability to buy.

35. What happens if the total demand for output of goods is greater than the actual output?

    a. There is a trend toward inflation.

    b. Unemployment is indicated.

    c. There is a trend toward "hard" money.

    d. There is an unusual amount of consumer credit being given.

36. The author uses the word "series" to refer to:

    a. a group of indicators combined into a formula.

    b. a fact developed for forecasting purposes.

    c. several related facts arranged and weighted mathematically.

    d. a number of cycle or trend indicators.

37. In the stock bonus offered by Canadian General Electric to new parents among its employees, how many employees finally collected?

    a. 13.

    b. 15.

    c. 72.

    d. 189.

38. In "The Case of the G.E. Babies," how did the statistician know that the estimate of babies born to the company's parents in a given period would be greater than the national average?

    a. Factory workers have more children than the national average figures.

    b. The employees were relatively young with no children or aged persons among them.

    c. He took account of the incentive offered by the company's stock.

    d. The company's parents are known to have a higher birth rate than those of other manufacturing concerns.

39. Why did the statistician for "The Case of the G.E. Babies" still underestimate the true number of births for October 15, 1953?

    a. Such intangibles as births cannot be forecast.

    b. The forecaster did not consider enough of the modifying variables, such as the personal incentive.

    c. There are more babies born in the autumn than at any other time of the year.

    d. Forecasters tend to under- rather than overestimate.

40. The author suggests that forecasting is intended to:

    a. achieve a high degree of accuracy in its forecasts.

    b. produce relatively exact and accurate estimates.

    c. result in a reasonable guess regarding the future.

    d. provide information to guide present decisions.

41. What are some of the implications of this article? (Choose as many answers as you need.)

    a. Accurate forecasting is still relatively impossible.

    b. Economic forecasting is an essential guide to business decisions and to planning productions.

    c. Forecasting is probably done best when it is the specific task of designated individuals in the management structure.

    d. Short-term forecasting is more feasible and practical for the small business than long-term.

    e. Forecasting for a small business need not result in a precise figure but a range of probable data.

    f. Forecasting is not actually a prediction of the future but rather a summary of current conditions and trends.

How to Forecast [3]

by J. N. Milne

Everyone wants to know the future or thinks he does. Whether rich man, poor man, tinker, tailor, soldier or sailor, whether buyer or seller of stocks, bonds, house or car, whether investing in more land, education, insurance or cutting commitments of consumer credit, all wonder what tomorrow, next year and the beyond have in store. But the wise do not consult the palmist at the fair, neither the crystal nor the star gazer. Days have changed since Cicero wrote "I shall always consider the best guesser the best prophet." Forecasting is the essential pre-requisite to planning and planning whether by individual, business or government can no longer be based on a feel-

[3] J. N. Milne, "How to Forecast," University of Western Ontario, *The Business Quarterly*, 20 (No. 2, Summer, 1955), pp. 73-81. Used by permission.

ing in the seat of one's pants. Here John N. Milne, head of Canadian General Electric Marketing Research, outlines the care which should precede a prophecy and how the individual and smallest business also have available the necessary information for an intelligent forecast.

Forecasting, the prophesying or estimating of future happenings or conditions, must be indulged in by all segments of society if they are to plan ahead. Those called upon to undertake economic forecasting prefer to call their work projections rather than prophecies, though the inclusion of the prophetic reference in the definition reminds us that the Oracles at Delphi and Dodona once prophesied for the Ancient Greeks in ways not unlike those used by witch-doctors more recently in more primitive areas.

While the words of a good modern-day forecaster are not accepted quite so literally, and while he must state the basic assumptions containing his forecast—the most he can lose if he is wrong too often is his job, and not, fortunately, his head.

Henry Hazlitt has called "Economics" the science of recognizing secondary consequences, of seeing general consequences, and of tracing the effects of a policy, not only on some special interest in the short run, but on the general interest in the long run. Economic, or business forecasting, as we practice it, puts numbers on these consequences as they are projected into the future.

RECENT HISTORY

Possibly because few, if any, minds can encompass all facts, and trace all pertinent consequences, the recent record of economic forecasting lists many failures and leaves much room for improvement. Professor H. R. Bowen of Williams College stated the case very neatly in Detroit recently, when he said "There are four types of forecast—those that are right for the wrong reasons, those that are wrong for the right reasons, those that are wrong for the wrong reasons, and those that are right for the right reasons."

Following the war, we were deluged with forecasts as to the future of our economy, and really only one strong voice, that of Professor Woytinsky of Johns Hopkins, disputed the idea that depression was inevitable. However, even he was wrong recently, when he predicted late in 1953 that '54 would exceed '53 by some five percent. By contrast, Colin Clark, the Australian, was the voice of doom a year ago when he predicted a recession so severe that, by the middle of 1954, no political measures would be able to contain it. As a parallel, even doctors can be wrong—but no one can deny that the good they do far outweighs their mistakes.

These facts are recited, not to disparage those who made the forecasts, but simply to ask, "Why forecast when the record shows such seeming odds against success?"

It is human nature to tackle difficult things and attempt improvements on the past, and the possibility, however remote, of being able to tell something about the future is always intriguing. Coming events do cast their shadows before—the problem is, simply, how well can we delineate those shadows?

The final answer, of course, lies in the inescapable fact that economic forecasting is necessary. Every business decision based upon an appraisal of future events is a forecast. And a manager has a better chance of being right if he makes use of the best techniques and the best practitioners than he has by guessing without their help.

Modern business recognizes these facts when it sets up special groups to perform the forecasting function, and reminds itself that the prime use of a forecast is as a frame, or setting for today's decisions, and not its percentage accuracy when the forecasted date arrives. Or, put another way, the estimate of tomorrow's economic flavour helps to determine a manager's "yes" or "no" answer today. A forecast is not a plan, any more than a road map is a plan for your automobile trip; both are merely guides to reasonably probable routes.

INSTINCT

Despite the immense amount of intensive work that has been done to make economic forecasting a science, there is no question that there is still a great deal of art involved. For, in the process of working with and examining the voluminous statistics now available, one tends to develop an unexplainable "over-all feel" for conditions. Probably this is the same intuitive force which enables businessmen to make seemingly off-the-cuff decisions—sometimes with amazing accuracy. However, the larger a business becomes, the more difficult it is to retain this feeling, and the more necessary it is to systematize the forecasting process.

COMPANY BACKGROUND

A brief outline of the way in which my company works will help my explanation. The Canadian General Electric Company is divided into four staff divisions, and six operating divisions which in turn are divided into operating departments. These departments are each headed by a manager, who, operating under general Company policies and assistance provided by the staff divisions, is responsible for all phases of his particular business from manufacturing to selling. The Economic Analysis Section is part of the Marketing Research Department and is a staff group. This section collects and co-ordinates basic economic information, makes studies of current economic conditions and trends, and is responsible for forecasts of the basic business outlook.

This section has many customers for its forecasts throughout the Company. Each of the seventeen operating departments, performing as a separate smaller company, must be apprised of the future general business climate in which it can expect to be operating, and in which it must produce and sell its particular products. Within the staff and operating departments are those interested in investment, man-power requirements, product development and sales forecasting for example; all of whom make use of short and long-term forecasts as aids in the establishment of their respective programmes.

OUTSIDE ASSISTANCE

Since anyone in this type of work is, for obvious reasons, always in danger of losing his objectivity, and since two heads are frequently better than one, we believe in making use of as much outside assistance as possible. For these reasons we retain a firm of Canadian economists, in consultation with whom our forecasts are prepared. And since the job is a two-way proposition, we provide them with all possible assistance and information.

Published literature and attendance at pertinent meetings provide us with authoritative and up-to-date thinking, and a speaking acquaintance with some of the continent's top-notch economic thinkers. To gain these ends we maintain membership in such associations as the Canadian Political Science, American Economic, American Statistical, and American Marketing Associations.

Finally, we subscribe to a number of periodicals such as the Financial Post, the Economist, the Wall Street Journal, university quarterlies, and many others. Additionally, we receive bushels of essential statistics from Ottawa, London, Washington and the United Nations—most of which are basic to economic analysis and forecasting.

LONG-TERM FORECASTING

While the number and types of forecasts can be infinite, we classify them, essentially, into two types—long and short-term.

Our long-term forecast, made once a year, is a ten-year projection of certain fundamental series such as population, labour force, employment, families, households, Gross National Product and its principal components, and the Index of Industrial Production.

In the making of this forecast, much emphasis is placed upon trends which must be watched to determine rates of growth and changes therein; and in this process all good statistical techniques are used.

Basic to any long-term forecast is a good estimate of future population—for, from population figures it is possible to estimate the labour force, and from it, Gross National Product. G.N.P. can also be built up by considering what may happen in the four main sectors of the economy—Government, Personal, Business and Foreign. In fact, all sound forecasters attempt to arrive at an end figure from at least two different directions, thus providing a cross-check on the reasonableness of their estimates.

Long-term forecasts of basic conditions are useful as a starting point in estimating the long-term demand for specific products, provided a logical relationship can be found to exist between unit sales of the product and one or more of the series developed in the forecast. For instance, having forecast the number of households, it is not too difficult to estimate the sales of an appliance such as a refrigerator. Good statistical techniques are used in this process—though judgment must also play an important role in the final distillation.

For example, one of our product departments manufactures a component of many electrical devices. These complete devices are used in homes, in industry and in business offices. The forecaster concerned has tied together, in a multiple correlation, the series giving number of households and the Industrial Production Index, along with past industry sales of his product. The historical relationship so determined is projected, from our forecasts of these two indicators, thus developing possible industry sales in the years to come. His next step is to decide, based upon our present and planned future facilities and products, our participation in the industry's sales. He thus ends up with a forecast, in units, of his product's sales for the next ten years.

If he wishes to translate his forecast into dollars, he has two choices: either he can multiply the units by today's prices and forecast in terms of current dollars, or he can assume constantly rising prices and increase each year's figures by a given amount. The historical trends, since Confederation, show an increase in wholesale prices of slightly better than one per cent per year compounded—not of course without some major declines en route.

Long-term forecasts are also used: to determine capital requirements; to help determine changes in general company policy; to help meet expected labour conditions and wage trends; to estimate the possible effects of new or proposed legislation; to determine possible economic changes in the industries from whom we sell or buy; and so on.

SHORT-TERM FORECASTING

Our short-term forecast is made quarterly for at least four quarters ahead. Here the emphasis shifts from trends to cycles and to immediately apparent changes in direction. This is a very difficult process, compared to long-term work, and involves detailed studies of the immediate prospects in particular industries, in investment intentions, in changes in inventory, in financing and credit facilities, in labour income, in consumer spending—just to mention a few considerations.

Those involved in production scheduling and sales budgeting for the immediate future must make constant decisions as to purchases of raw materials, size of labour force and optimum inventories; and in our quarterly forecasts we provide indicators useful for these purposes.

PRODUCT FORECASTING

The Marketing Research Department forecasts basic overall indicators, and is expert in the techniques of forecasting. However, we do not make product forecasts—these are the responsibility of those in the product departments. They start with the information we supply and use it to prepare long or short-term budgets for their products.

The main difference between long and short-term forecasts so far as products are concerned is that, usually once a year, area estimates can be obtained from the field. Districts will estimate, account by account, their probable sales, and may even get from larger customers figures on their anticipated purchases for the coming year. The department, based on our indicators, can make a quarterly forecast which is compared with the field estimates, and judgment must then be used to reconcile the two, if major differences exist.

FUTURE OF THE ART

Earlier I indicated how much in error many forecasters have been, and suggested that the overall record leaves much to be desired. Certainly there is a vast field for improvement and much more will be accomplished over time.

Nevertheless, it is a fact that forecasting techniques have improved in recent years and are becoming a reasonably reliable basis of operations—because the process of economic change is better understood—because government policy is more predictable—because data are better—and because greater use is being made of survey techniques.

Still further signs of improvement are in the offing—as for instance:

(a) The work of the National Bureau of Economic Research and others, on lead-lag indicators, which, while no touchstone, at least are useful tools to add to the forecaster's kit.

(b) Wassily Leontief's work on input-output, even though it may not throw too much light on forecasting, should prove useful in determining the effect on the whole economy of changes in its parts.

(c) Econometric studies and model building which encompass all economic activity.

(d) The increasing incidence of "built-in" stabilizers such as Family Allowances, Old Age Pensions, Unemployment Insurance which dampen the speed and effect of changes.

(e) Finally, electronic calculators, which may well have the major impact—for they make possible much more prompt reporting of statistics relating to the immediate past, and provide an opportunity to assess the future much more quickly and completely in a series of forecasts based upon varied assumptions. In fact they permit mathematical calculations impossible of completion heretofore.

DO-IT-YOURSELF IN THE SMALLER BUSINESS

What can a smaller business with somewhat more limited facilities do about forecasting? Of primary importance are good sources, and a constant flow of statistical information. The D.B.S. publications on the National Accounts, figures on the industry involved, and their monthly Statistical Review are indispensable. Concurrently, subscriptions to the Financial Post, Business Week and the Wall Street Journal give advice on day-to-day happenings, as also the financial pages of the daily papers. There are many other sources, but these will be indicated by the nature of your particular business.

The next step is to chart certain series in order to develop a feel for the way things are going. Many statistics, of course, are not available until some time after the events have occurred, and you must look for those which are as recent as possible.

For example, G.N.P. figures by quarters are not available for two or three months after the event. However, some statistics such as car-loadings, department store sales, bank clearings, motor vehicle productions and business failures are quite current and serve to provide some indication as to present trends.

It would be rather monotonous to list all the indicators that might, or should, be watched, but some of the more important are:

1. *Gross National Product*—which, while much out of date, does indicate the overall level of the economy.

2. *National and Disposable Income*—which, also late, provides evidence of spending power.

3. *Consumer Expenditures, Construction Contracts Awarded and Retail Sales*—which jointly give a general indication of the level of public confidence.

4. *Manufacturers', Wholesalers' and Retailers' Inventories*—which act as guides to confidence and availability.

5. *Bank Debits, Bank Loans and Savings*—which indicate confidence and ability to buy.

6. *Industrial Production and Employment*—indicators of demand and confidence.

7. *Orders Received*—indices for various manufacturing sectors, particularly those producing heavy capital goods—good indicators of manufacturing levels in the months to come.

There is no magical way of putting these all together, but rather you should attempt to absorb the important information into whatever net picture your best judgment indicates. These statistics will tell something about five main things: Demand, Ability to Buy, Confidence, Prices and Availability.

Confidence and demand are the main factors, for without them business cannot progress. You must decide whether people, in the mass, are confident or afraid of the future, and whether their demands are strong, medium or weak. Are prices right or too high, thus encouraging or discouraging buying? Is their confidence backed up by adequate buying power? Finally, will goods be available to meet their demands?

THE MICRO APPROACH

A good principle to follow is to break the thing to be forecasted into its smallest possible segments. For example, if you are trying to estimate industrial production, the first step is to separate durable and non-durable industries and then further separate them into their individual components such as iron and steel, textiles, food processing and so on. Then call upon your knowledge of conditions in these industries as gleaned from the daily press, magazines, or good contacts in those industries in an attempt to forecast the possibilities for each industry. While you can not possibly call the turn correctly for all of them, at least by giving consideration to each it is reasonable to expect that estimating errors will tend to average out, and that the overall total may not be too far astray. In our work we use precise and single figures, rather than a maximum or minimum range. This is done to ensure a common base for all projections as they reach top management in consolidated form. In forecasting for a small business the maximum-minimum approach may have far more merit.

THE MACRO APPROACH

A second method, which can be used as a check on the first, if time permits, involves the use of the national accounts. Economics tells us that the total demand for the output of goods and services is the sum of the demands created by households, business, government and foreign trade, and this total is the amount which the economy as a whole can absorb. If this demand is less than output, unemployment is indicated; if demand exceeds output, there is a tendency towards inflation.

Professor Boulding has called this relationship between output and total demand "the greatest single economic discovery of our age." This is a simple truism that is often overlooked in forecasting.

Speaking generally, the output of a nation depends principally on three things:

(a) The number of people who are economically occupied, which, of course, bears some relation to the total population.

(b) The energy of these people and their growing technological skills or their productivity per man hour; and

(c) The length of their work week.

If these three factors are isolated and analyzed, along with population growth, it is possible to develop gross national income figures for future years.

As a further check, the various components of the G.N.P. can be forecast separately.

CAUTION

Finally, it must be re-emphasized that no forecast can be an unerring prediction of things to come. In essence, it is no more than an informed opinion, though the better informed the opinion, the closer we can come to the mark. The Wall Street Journal recently said, with some justice, that—"No forecast should be regarded as throwing any light on the future, but only as reflecting conditions and visible trends up to the time the forecast was made."

As a closing comment "The Case of the G-E Babies" emphasizes what can happen. On January 14, 1953, G-E announced that it would award five shares of stock to any employee who had a baby on October 15th, 1953—the Company's 75th Anniversary. Application of the U.S. birth rate to G-E's 226,000 employees yielded a prediction of 15 births, and since the original number of investors was thirteen, the Company announced that they expected thirteen winners. A G-E statistician quickly pointed out that since the employees included no children, and few over 65, they were not comparable to the U.S. total. A new, more statistically correct, estimate predicted 72 births on the big day.

As it turned out, there were not 13, 15 or 72 babies born on October 15th, but 189.

Where did the estimate fail—well, among other things, no allowance was made for the incentive provided by the Company's stock. This oversight was rectified by the employees who enjoyed creating children and who, regardless of their then present status, wished to become capitalists.

They evidently knew a good thing—for in a generally declining market, G-E common rose, during the pregnant months, from \$59⅛ to \$78⅞, and during 1955 reached a relative value as high as \$167.

Answers on "How to Forecast"

First Reading	Second Reading	Third Reading	
1. c.	11. a.	21. d.	32. b.
2. b.	12. c.	22. d.	33. d.
3. a.	13. b.	23. b.	34. d.
4. c.	14. d.	24. d.	35. a.
5. a.	15. b.	25. c.	36. b.
6. b.	16. a.	26. c.	37. d.
7. d.	17. d.	27. d.	38. b.
8. b.	18. b.	28. a.	39. b.
9. a.	19. a.	29. a.	40. d.
10. c.	20. b.	30. d.	41. b., c., e., f.
		31. d.	

Number right_____   Number right_____   Number right_____
(Possible score 10) (Possible score 10) (Possible score 24)

STANDARDS

	First Score	Second Score	Third Score	TIME IN MINUTES Second	Third
Excellent	Above 5	Above 9	Above 16	Below 13.5	Below 14
Very Good	5	9	15-16	13.5-17.5	14-18
Good	4	7-8	13-14	18-21.5	18.5-23
Fair	3	6	10-12	27-28	23.5-29
Poor	Below 3	Below 6	Below 10	Above 28	Above 29

Before attempting to interpret your scores in the various parts of the Flexibility Test, let us explore your reading habits and attitudes. These habits and attitudes are the most important aspects of your reading. The extent to which they can be modified will, in the final analysis, determine the nature of your improvement in reading. You may read about and even practice new ways of reading but unless you can adopt these ways as new habits and believe in them, there will be little change in your reading. Unless you can alter some of your beliefs and attitudes toward the act of reading, you will be unable to live with the new habits and techniques taught here.

Therefore, it is essential to evaluate your present habits and attitudes before any discussion of the implications of your Flexibility Test scores. The Inventory below samples some of your fundamental attitudes and practices. Answer these questions as honestly as possible. Give the answers that really reflect your feelings rather than those you think the author would approve. The more you are willing to contrast your opinions with those of others, the sooner we can set about discussing and clarifying them.

INVENTORY OF READING HABITS AND ATTITUDES

Indicate whether you A—agree, D—disagree, or ?—are doubtful about each of these items.

A   D   ?   1. One may determine whether he is a flexible reader by comparing his rates of reading different materials.

A   D   ?   2. Fast readers generally have better comprehension than very slow readers.

A   D   ?   3. The basic characteristic of all efficient readers is reading with a purpose.

A   D   ?   4. Learning to read for ideas rather than reading words more quickly is the only sound way of increasing rate.

A   D   ?   5. The major difference between the effective and the ineffective reader is skill in various reading approaches.

A   D   ?   6. A good reader can read a group of three or four words in a fraction of a second.

A   D   ?   7. The most important way to increase reading efficiency substantially is to increase rate of reading.

A   D   ?   8. If the reader really tries, meanings of unknown words may often by found by careful reading of the context.

A   D   ?   9. Vocabulary improvement can be achieved only by cultivating an active interest in words and their characteristics.

A   D   ?   10. Most adults have a much greater reading vocabulary than what they use in speaking or writing.

A   D   ?   11. The efficient reader reads to remember all the details and main ideas in the material.

A   D   ?   12. Difficulties with concentration are usually due to lack of planning or lack of interest in the reading.

A   D   ?   13. Vocabulary increases almost as rapidly during adulthood as during childhood.

A   D   ?   14. The average person listens to another with only about 50 per cent effectiveness.

A   D   ?   15. If used effectively, listening is an easier and better way of acquiring information than reading.

A   D   ?   16. Reading improvement can only be achieved by conscientious practice of new methods and approaches.

A   D   ?   17. A shelf of general and special dictionaries and other aids to word study is essential to growth in vocabulary and word usage.

A   D   ?   18. The reading of facts presented in graphic, tabular, or other mathematical forms is difficult for many otherwise well-educated adults.

Indicate whether you follow these practices A—always, S—sometimes, N—never.

A   S   N   19. I try to make my business writing natural and personal but forceful.

A   S   N   20. When reading rapidly, I am able to read for ideas, skipping unimportant words.

A   S   N   21. Before reading any important material, I preview or look over its content thoroughly to decide how to read.

A   S   N   22. When trying to find a specific fact, I look over the material very rapidly rather than reading line by line.

A   S   N   23. I deliberately change my rate from one selection to another according to the way I think it best to read.

A   S   N   24. When reading materials of only moderate difficulty, I skim selectively rather than read line by line.

A   S   N   25. I read a wide variety of printed materials with equal ease and enjoyment.

A   S   N   26. I tend to say or think each word as I read in order to get good comprehension.

A   S   N   27. I try to get the meaning of an unknown word by pronouncing it to myself.

A   S   N   28. When reading persuasive or propaganda material, I am apt to react to the author's attitude before reading the entire selection.

A   S   N   29. I consciously analyze parts of a word to discover its meaning, if I do not recognize its meaning immediately.

A   S   N   30. Whenever I read, I read for some definite purpose and this purpose influences the way I read.

A   S   N   31. I pay little or no attention to new words other than to secure a temporarily satisfactory meaning.

A   S   N   32. I find it difficult to read statistical material intelligently and critically.

A   S   N   33. I tend to use my usual rate of reading when looking for a single fact, name, or number.

A   S   N   34. I try to think along with the writer to recognize his facts and evaluate his beliefs and attitudes.

A   S   N   35. I use the dictionary for much more than the meanings of words I need to know temporarily.

Answers to the Inventory

The first eighteen statements refer to attitudes and beliefs. The correct answers are:

1. A	7. D	13. D
2. A	8. A	14. A
3. A	9. A	15. A
4. A	10. A	16. A
5. A	11. D	17. A
6. A	12. A	18. A

The next group of statements refers to habits and practices. The correct answers are:

19. A	25. A	31. N
20. A	26. S or N	32. N
21. A	27. N	33. N
22. A	28. N	34. A
23. A	29. S	35. A
24. A	30. A	

Our statements are phrased in the form that they would be given by an ideally competent, flexible reader, which, of course, few of us are. The statements, with their correct modifications, represent the goals toward which we must all work if we wish to be truly efficient readers.

The following paragraphs contain our comments on the Inventory, point by point.

1. Using different rates under different reading circumstances is a primary characteristic of the flexible reader. Most other readers are seriously handicapped by lack of skill in making these adjustments. You may gauge your own flexibility by means of the discussion, later in this chapter, of your performances in the Flexibility Test. Chapters 3 to 6 are particularly devoted to teaching you the various techniques necessary to acquire flexibility.

2. Contrary to popular opinion, this statement is quite true except in very detailed material. In general, those who read more rapidly secure more comprehension than the slow readers. After you have tried reading for ideas in chapter 5, you will certainly recognize the value of performing reading at a rapid, thinking rate.

3. Because of his attention to purpose, the efficient reader makes many adjustments of rate and comprehension. Thus he achieves greater concentration and retention, and conserves time and energy. His reading is better organized because of the many techniques he uses to accomplish his various purposes. And finally, because of planning purpose he is able to apply information directly to his reading aims. A technique to aid in planning purpose, previewing, is presented in chapter 3.

4. Speed in reading is directly related to the reader's ability to recognize and relate to ideas he encounters in reading. Only as he learns to read for ideas, can the slow reader increase his rate of comprehension. This basic element of rate of reading is explained and practiced in chapter 5.

5. The reading techniques which make the difference between effective and ineffective reading are taught in chapters 3 to 6. They include previewing, skimming, scanning, and reading for ideas.

6. Reading is actually done by a series of stops or fixations as the eye sweeps across a line. At each fixation, the rapid reader sees at least several words. Studies with various mechanical training devices show that many persons can read as many as five or six words in a thousandth of a second. Such speeds are achieved when the reader learns to react to ideas rather than words, as illustrated in chapter 5.

7. The idea that reading is improved by simply increasing rate has been strongly oversold to the public, in our opinion. It is true that increase in rate is desirable but intelligence in knowing when to use various rates, how to read with different techniques which result in greater over-all speed, and how to relate rate to the reader's purposes and comprehension aims—are fundamental to permanent gain in rate. Our views are thoroughly discussed in chapters 3 to 6.

8. There are a number of ways of deriving meanings of new words from context, or the way they are used by the author. Several of these are illustrated and explained in chapter 9 as an aid to more intelligent reading.

9. A healthy attitude toward words is fundamental to continuous vocabulary growth. This attitude underlies successful use of the techniques for learning words outlined in chapter 9.

10. As discussed in chapter 11, most of us can recognize or read many more words than we ordinarily use in our speech or writing. To increase these smaller vocabularies, we must make definite attempts to transfer terms and words from our reading vocabulary.

11. Unless perfect comprehension is desired, the efficient reader never reads to remember all the main ideas and details. Rather, he reads selectively by previewing and skimming, as described in chapters 3 and 4, and then strives for the degree of comprehension appropriate to his purposes. Only the naïve student or the untrained adult attempts the questionable goal of perfect comprehension in everything he reads.

12. Occasional difficulties with concentration are common to all readers. But if this trouble persists or is manifest particularly in one type of reading, it is probably due to lack of interest or unresolved worries. Lack of specific purpose in reading or failure to plan reading to accomplish definite aims also results in concentration troubles. As explained in chapter 3, previewing material to organize the reading act results in better concentration and attention.

13. Vocabulary growth during adulthood is slow and relatively insignificant for most persons. Unless distinct efforts are made, such

as those suggested in chapters 9 and 11, speaking, writing, and reading vocabularies remain comparatively static.

14. A number of research studies indicate that listening is an ineffectual medium of securing ideas as it is used by most individuals. The average person listening to another hears and understands only about half of the speaker's ideas. Like other communication skills, listening can be markedly improved, as by the steps outlined in chapter 11.

15. Over a long period of time, we tend to remember more of what we have heard than what we have read. Perhaps this is one explanation for the longevity of rumors and superstition. Because of the greater ease of learning through listening, and the greater retention, this ability should certainly be exploited to its fullest potential. Suggestions for improving listening are given in chapter 11.

16. The most important element in any reading improvement program is the attitude of the learner. No book or instructor can really do anything to make you read better. We can only show you the ways in which your reading could be made more efficient. Any subsequent improvement depends entirely upon your efforts to practice and apply the reading techniques suggested here. Reading improvement is very much a "do-it-yourself" task, despite all the expert guidance we try to give.

17. One of the surest ways to continuous vocabulary growth is the frequent use of dictionaries and other aids to word usage that meet your particular needs. Access to these reference materials helps keep alive a curiosity about words that results in expansion of your word power. Chapter 9 offers a number of suggestions about the selection and use of these essential reference tools.

18. Many adults find the reading of mathematical materials a difficult and frustrating task. Lack of confidence in their ability to read intelligently and critically contributes to these feelings. Chapter 8 is planned to help you read statistical materials with greater understanding and critical insight.

19. Much of our business correspondence is characterized by an utterly impersonal tone and indirect, almost unreadable language.

Clarity, warmth, and readability are some of the qualities of letter writing illustrated in chapter 11.

20. Slow reading is often caused by attention to words rather than ideas, and accompanied by consequent lack of comprehension. The fact that fluent, good readers read relatively few words yet retain more is incomprehensible to the individual who believes that comprehension is achieved only by close attention to each word. Practice in reading for ideas is provided in chapter 5.

21. Efficient reading is planned, purposeful reading. Rate, comprehension, and the reading technique to be employed are carefully chosen to accomplish the reader's specific purposes. Previewing, a technique for rapid evaluation of reading materials to permit planning of purpose, is presented in chapter 3.

22. When trying to find specific details, individuals differ considerably in their time requirements. Some read almost line by line while others read no more than is necessary to locate and identify the fact desired. Scanning, a technique for finding facts rapidly with a minimum of reading, is stressed in chapter 6.

23. Change of pace in reading according to the purpose of the reading is one of the hallmarks of the flexible reader. An efficient reader may vary from a study rate of less than 200 words per minute to skimming at several thousand words per minute, as he wishes. This flexibility demands skill in the reading techniques of previewing, skimming, and reading for ideas presented in the early chapters of this book.

24. Skill in techniques that permit rapid, selective reading, such as skimming, is essential when the volume of reading matter is large. If used flexibly, skimming may function as the initial reading in difficult material, as the complete act of reading in familiar or light matter, or as a method of quick review. Chapter 4 emphasizes the values of this useful reading method.

25. It is difficult for the poor reader to realize the values as well as the pure joy of wide reading. Most poor readers read as little as possible even when they do not actively dislike and avoid reading. The major purpose of this book is to enable adults who are missing

these aspects of a fuller life to reach their intellectual and cultural potentialities through greater enjoyment of reading.

26. Vocalization, or saying each word audibly or inaudibly, is a major handicap to skillful, rapid reading. The vocalizer never really learns to read much faster than he can talk. Reading never becomes a true thinking process, an exchange of ideas between the writer and the reader. To profit from reading, and to accomplish it at the normal speed of thinking, you must learn to read for ideas, as suggested in chapter 5.

27. Some readers labor under the mistaken impression that unknown words met in reading are more readily recognized if they are pronounced aloud. This is true only for small children who are just learning to read. Their auditory or hearing vocabulary is larger than their reading knowledge. After the ages of eleven or twelve, however, the individual who reads with reasonable skill recognizes infinitely more words in reading than he could if he heard them spoken. Recognition of word meanings is much more effectively accomplished by some of the techniques outlined in chapter 9 than by oral pronunciation.

28. One of the more difficult skills needed for critical reading of propaganda and persuasive writing is the ability to withhold emotional reaction. If you react to the author's statements before carefully reading them, you have failed to recognize the facts that he has used, or the way in which he has presented or misrepresented these facts. You have failed to identify the faulty logic he has employed. As a result, objective rebuttal or destruction of his arguments is impossible. Chapter 7 will aid you in acquiring skill in evaluating persuasive material and in learning to recognize common devices used to influence the reader.

29. Analysis of the root or stem of a word, or of its prefix or suffix is often helpful in determining its meaning. A clearer understanding may be obtained by recognition of the meaning of the stem, or of the modifying influence of the affixes. However, this approach has limited values because of the great number of stems and affixes present in our language. Few readers know enough stems so thoroughly that analysis by this method is rapid and accurate. Most of

us will find other aids to word meanings such as the context, in the several ways described in chapter 9, helpful more often than analysis by roots and affixes.

30. Planned, purposeful reading is synonymous with intelligent, effective reading. Our purposes may vary from the profound to the trivial, but they should guide our manner of reading. This relating of purpose to method of reading is emphasized in the discussion of the values of each reading technique taught in this book.

31. Most of us are too lazy or uninterested to pay much attention to the new words we meet. For this reason, our vocabularies grow very slowly and we are constantly handicapped in trying to express ourselves. Only by active interest in words and use of the many suggestions for vocabulary improvement given in chapter 9, will our vocabularies continue to expand.

32. Are you, too, uncomfortable with charts, graphs, or tables? Do you stand in awe of these evidences of the statistician's skill? Or, would you like to be able to evaluate, to react critically to such materials? Chapter 8 will teach you some of the basic questions to ask when you read statistical data and will help you feel more secure in this reading situation.

33. The proper reading technique to be used when searching for a single fact, date, or number is certainly not line-by-line reading. This looking for facts can be done much more rapidly than the usual reading rate by use of the technique of scanning presented in chapter 6.

34. Reading is truly a thinking act, with the reader attempting to think along with the author and react to the ideas, not the words. Reading, as a thinking act, can only be accomplished by reading for ideas as taught in chapter 5. Once this ability has been achieved, the reader may progress to critical or evaluative reading, as practiced in chapter 7.

35. If used effectively, a dictionary should yield much more than the simple meanings of certain words. Correct pronunciation, the derivation of the word, its correct usage in various ways, as well as its spelling are all readily found in any good dictionary. This information about a word is essential to correct future use and hence

to your vocabulary growth. Further suggestions regarding dictionary use are given in chapter 11.

WHAT DO YOUR SCORES MEAN?

Now that we have evaluated your present reading habits and attitudes by means of the Inventory, let us go into the meaning of your scores in the Flexibility Test.

The First Reading provides the measure of what the reading specialist calls skimming, or the act of reading quite rapidly for main ideas. The questions were based on the facts presented in the various headings and the opening and closing sentences of each paragraph. If you are skillful in skimming, you would have shown it first, by being able to cover the whole selection in the three minutes allowed for the First Reading. Secondly, you would have answered five or more of the first ten questions correctly.

The ability to skim and cover material in an organized fashion with comprehension of the main ideas is one of the hallmarks of the flexible reader. Slow readers, poor readers, and even very fast readers are not skilled in this approach. While fast readers may complete the selection, their comprehension is often poor because of lack of a systematic coverage of the content. The usual methods of attempting to read straight through or reading randomly at very high speed will not work for this type of reading situation.

As we shall demonstrate later, the skill of skimming is essential to truly efficient reading. It is serviceable for securing a preview or overview of material you will later read more carefully. Sometimes it may be the complete act of reading, as in situations where you must decide whether something is worth reading. It can function as the first reading of memos, letters, announcements, directions, advertisements, and even technical reports. Skimming is a practical time-saver for a rapid survey of a great deal of the mass of reading matter that comes to the businessman's desk. Chapters 3 and 4 are particularly related to the ability to skim.

The Second Reading provides the measure of scanning, or finding facts or information rapidly. Since the answers to all the questions are contained in the article, the score or number of right answers to this part is not highly significant. Practically anyone who could read the questions could find the answers, if given enough time. The important performance here is the time required to find the answers. The average untrained adult takes about twenty minutes to find the ten answers, a rather slow performance. Some individuals need only five minutes, while a few take as long as forty-five. In other words, those without ability to scan rapidly take nine times as long as skilled readers to find a few specific facts in a short article. It is not surprising that so many business people complain about the volume of materials they are compelled to read, if they are as slow in organizing their facts as some who have taken this test.

Scanning is another indication of flexible, skillful reading. Unlike skimming, it is not an organized coverage of an entire selection. But it does involve some of the same kind of thinking that makes successful skimming possible. To find specific facts quickly, the reader must recognize the structure or organization of the material. He must be alert to the significance of major and minor headings, and deduce which facts are likely to be found under each heading. He must notice the presence of statistics, tables, graphs, or other illustrative material and quickly note their general meaning. If he has already skimmed the content, he may remember the general arrangement of information and use this to better advantage when scanning.

Scanning is useful in such materials as indexes, reference books, and detailed technical reports. It also functions in the collation of information in answer to a certain problem. Preparation of reports is also dependent upon the ability to scan to find relevant facts quickly. Like skimming, scanning is one of the attributes of the efficient reader. Further explanation and training in scanning is given in chapter 6 of this book. We believe it is one of the important reading techniques.

The Third Reading—complete and thorough—is the most common type of reading situation. The questions involve specific facts, as well as inferences and conclusions, to sample several types of comprehension. Many individuals can perform better in this task than in skimming and scanning. Slow readers, or even some poor readers can achieve reasonable comprehension if given the opportunity to read thoroughly. They sometimes conclude that their reading is acceptable because of the comprehension shown in the Third Reading or in the earlier General Reading Test. As we have tried to suggest, good comprehension while reading at extremely slow rates is not efficient reading. Nor do these individuals succeed in their attempts at skimming or scanning, which are equally as important. Being able to comprehend while reading at reasonably rapid rates is also a characteristic of the flexible, efficient reader.

You may make the same type of interpretation of your performances in the Third Reading as in the earlier general test. The same patterns of reading appear as the slow, the fast, the poor, and the competent reader. If you wish, you may make a comparison of your rate of reading in the Flexibility Test with your rate in the General Reading Test. Divide the number of minutes for the Third Reading into 2,800 to find your rate in words per minute.

If you are prone to be inflexible in your reading, you are likely to find the two rates of reading similar. Those who habitually read at a fairly constant rate are likely to find differences as small as 25-50 words per minute in these two performances. Actually "How to Forecast" compares in difficulty with materials used for study at the college level. "Morale and Productivity" is not much more complex than reading materials commonly found in junior high school. If your rates were similar, this is an indication of inflexibility. You are not accustomed to shifting gears according to the difficulty of the material, a common trait of the slow or inflexible reader. Reading "Morale and Productivity" even more slowly than "How to Forecast" is also indicative of faulty adjustment of the reader to his task.

By this point, we certainly hope you have secured some concepts of your reading abilities. You have evaluated your rate and comprehension in a general reading situation, and gained some idea of your status in these performances. You have attempted skimming, scanning, and thorough reading and appraised your flexibility. You are cognizant of your strengths and weaknesses and ready to secure the greatest returns for your investment of time and effort in using this book.

3

Previewing—A New Way to Read

What You Will Do
    Try previewing—a new approach to all your reading

What You Will Learn
    How to preview materials rapidly before actually reading
    them

Probably the major reading problem of the average business person of today is attempting to keep up with the great volume of reading material he tries to handle. Each day he struggles through several piles of memoranda, reports, directives, announcements, and forms. At least twice a day, he is presented with a fresh batch of correspondence—personal letters, business letters, advertisements, etc. On one corner of the desk is a group of trade and business magazines, awaiting his leisure. Near them is a pile of technical reports, reprints, manuscripts, and other unfinished matter. In his briefcase there are more departmental reports, a recent book, a copy of this week's edition of a news magazine, and several other odds and ends —all only partly or hurriedly read. Does this picture seem familiar?

This accumulation of unread materials is due largely to inadequate or inappropriate reading techniques. Many harried business people have only one approach to reading, a slow, careful perusal, as we have suggested before. They fail to recognize that different materials vary in importance or in the intensity of the attention they demand. Such individuals read in a habit-bound fashion, without relating the manner of reading to the value of the matter being read.

In this chapter, we will explain and demonstrate a new approach that can be used in almost all reading situations. It may be called previewing. It is a form of prereading or surveying material before actually reading it thoroughly. Previewing will enable you to cover large amounts of material in a relatively brief time, to secure the main ideas or an intelligent understanding of the entire piece with minimum effort. Most important of all, previewing aids you to make the decision whether more careful reading or any further reading at all is necessary. A great deal of the materials you attempt to read are of lesser significance. One rapid but complete preview is often sufficient to enable you to take whatever action is needed to dispose of them.

HOW TO PREVIEW

Most prose is written in a rather common structural pattern. Paragraphs are introduced by topic sentences that declare the main thought of the unit. Then the body of the paragraph, which illustrates or enlarges upon the main idea, follows. Finally, a summary or concluding sentence sums up the point, or points up inferences or conclusions to be drawn. Of course, not all paragraphs fall neatly into this pattern. Sometimes an idea may require two or three paragraphs for adequate treatment. In this case, successive paragraphs may be loosely joined by a transitional sentence that carries the reader forward. Each of a series of paragraphs dealing with a single idea does

(Continued on next page.)

Corporate Gifts: Investment in the Future [1]

by David Graham

Corporations contribute over $400 million annually to private philanthropy—a respectable donation, but it's not enough.

Private philanthropy receives over $4.5 billion each year, over 90 per cent of which comes from individuals. About half goes to religious agencies supported almost entirely by individuals, and another big percentage goes to causes with "heart appeal." Outside these areas, however,

[1] Adapted from *Commerce*, Vol. 52, No. 7, p. 15. Used by permission.

not necessarily open with a clear statement and close with a summary or conclusion.

But this writing pattern is very common and lends itself to the act of previewing or surveying rapidly. If we add the reading of the various headings to the topic and summary sentences, we can cover material quite thoroughly but quickly. Some reading specialists also recommend a complete reading of the first two or three as well as the closing paragraphs. This is probably desirable when the material is relatively unfamiliar or highly technical, but is not essential for the understanding of many types of reading matter.

Below, two versions of a short article are offered side by side. On one side is the complete article of about 800 words. On the other page, only the headings, topic and summary sentences are reproduced. The shorter version includes only those sentences you would read if you were previewing the selection.

Read the complete article first, in your usual fashion. Then read the previewing version. You will find that you understand almost as many ideas when you preview, as when you read completely. All the major ideas can be found in the preview version, and comprehension is as complete after previewing as after careful reading.

Since the article is about 800 words in length, you will have covered it at the reading rate of 400-800 words. This rate is very probably much faster than you normally use. But your comprehension after previewing will be adequate. Previewing is a technique that permits a systematic coverage of the facts of a selection with a considerable saving in time.

Corporate Gifts: Investment in the Future [2]

Corporations contribute over $400 million annually to private philanthropy—a respectable donation, but it's not enough.

Private philanthropy receives over $4.5 billion each year, over 90 per cent of which comes from individuals.

[2] *Ibid.*

corporate giving has in recent years become a very significant factor— especially for a large number of essential agencies that are in no position to undertake a mass appeal. For many agencies, corporate help represents the major portion of gift income and is essential to survival.

Legal concepts governing corporate giving have changed in recent years. Many states now have laws specifically legalizing certain kinds of corporate philanthropy. The Federal Government, since 1935, has lent encouragement by permitting business income tax deductions for charity. Moreover, court decisions in recent years have tended to broaden the base for giving.

Private giving diminishing: While the corporation has been growing in importance and capacity to give, one very important source of giving in the past is tending to dry up. Today the size of income taxes and death duties has sharply reduced the number of large individual donors. Big private fortunes are diminishing in number, and even men who have wealth must hang on to a larger part of their liquid assets in order to be ready for estate taxes. The era of the great individual philanthropists is for the most part past. It remains for corporations to share the responsibility of seeing to it that our social welfare needs are met.

Tax exemptions favor corporate giving: While present tax rates are high, their terms along with other provisions in the revenue laws have tended to make corporate giving more attractive. Corporations are permitted to deduct up to 5 per cent of net income before federal income taxes for contributions to charitable causes. Some corporations have organized tax-exempt foundations for the purpose of effecting a more centralized control of charitable contributions. This permits corporations to contribute greater amounts in good years to build up the foundation's capital, thus assuring the continuity of contributions in bad years as well as good ones. However, corporate giving averages considerably under the 5 per cent permissible deduction. At present, corporations on the average are estimated to be giving approximately 0.9 per cent of net income before federal income taxes.

Smaller companies most generous: The smaller companies, those with assets of less than $1 million, have proved relatively more generous, giving an average of about 1.13 per cent of their net income before federal income taxes. Harry A. Bullis, chairman of General Mills Corp., is authority for the statement that if the large and medium-size companies did as well, the result would be to double the amount of corporate giving! Why should corporations give more? The fact that they are in a better position to give is, of course, only part of the answer. The basic reason is that more is needed.

For many agencies, corporate help represents the major portion of gift income and is essential to survival.

Legal concepts governing corporate giving have changed in recent years.

Moreover, court decisions in recent years have tended to broaden the base for giving.

Private giving diminishing: While the corporation has been growing in importance and capacity to give, one very important source of giving in the past is tending to dry up.

It remains for corporations to share the responsibility of seeing to it that our social welfare needs are met.

Tax exemptions favor corporate giving: While present tax rates are high, their terms along with other provisions in the revenue laws have tended to make corporate giving more attractive.

At present, corporations on the average are estimated to be giving approximately 0.9 per cent of net income before federal income taxes.

Smaller companies most generous: The smaller companies, those with assets of less than $1 million, have proved relatively more generous, giving an average of about 1.13 per cent of their net income before federal income taxes.

The basic reason is that more is needed.

College and welfare agencies in critical financial need: Our private institutions of higher learning—especially the liberal arts colleges—are in a critical financial situation. It is estimated that they will require from $250 million to $300 million in business contributions annually—or practically as much as corporations are now giving to all causes. Welfare agencies also represent an area of increased need. For much as any of our cities may be doing through agencies supported by Community Chests or related funds, there isn't one that couldn't do more. It is a paradox that in a period of unprecedented growth and prosperity cities find welfare needs greater than they have ever been. The truth is that prosperity tends to blind us to problems of its making. Economic growth has conferred a greater capacity to satisfy our wants, but is has also imposed greater needs. At the same time, inflation has sent wages and prices soaring so that the dollars we contribute buy less and endowment income that we used to count on so heavily doesn't stretch as far.

The institutions and causes that serve as the objects of our philanthropy represent, in a very real sense, our social capital, our investment in a better, more meaningful life. The challenge we face is to increase this social capital so that it is commensurate with our enlarged needs.

PREVIEWING VS. COMPLETE READING

What are some of the basic ideas you would gain from a thorough, line-by-line reading of this article? At least these nine:

1. Private philanthropy receives most of its support from individuals, rather than corporations.

2. For a few agencies, corporate gifts represent a significant part of their gift income.

3. Corporate giving has been furthered by state and federal tax exemptions and other provisions in income law.

4. Private giving, on the other hand, is tending to diminish.

5. Deductions for corporate charitable contributions are allowable up to 5 per cent of net income before federal taxes.

6. However, corporate gifts average less than 1 per cent of net income.

7. Smaller companies are somewhat more generous than the large ones.

College and welfare agencies in critical financial need: Our private institutions of higher learning—especially the liberal arts colleges—are in a critical financial situation.

At the same time, inflation has sent wages and prices soaring so that the dollars we contribute buy less and endowment income that we used to count on so heavily doesn't stretch as far.

The institutions and causes that serve as the objects of our philanthropy represent, in a very real sense, our social capital, our investment in a better, more meaningful life. The challenge we face is to increase this social capital so that it is commensurate with our enlarged needs.

---

8. College and welfare agencies need more corporate philanthropy, particularly because of the decreasing value of their endowment dollars.

9. These recipients of corporate philanthropy should be strongly supported since they represent our social capital, our investment in a better future.

If you look over the second version of the article, or preview it, you will find that practically all these main ideas are present. Only the detail of the per cent of net income before federal taxes which is allowable for charitable contributions (idea number 5) is missing.

This article is particularly adaptable to previewing. Its style is quite factual and straightforward. The paragraphs tend to follow the outline of main ideas presented in topic sentences, followed by details, and finally by concluding or summarizing statements. The headings are quite succinct and provide good clues to the major idea of the succeeding paragraph. This type of organization is quite common in business and management publications and lends itself to the method of previewing or surveying before actual reading.

OTHER FACTS ABOUT PREVIEWING

There is one caution to be observed in using previewing. Avoid the tendency to preview too rapidly. Speed is achieved in previewing by the selective, organized approach in which only the most important portions are read—not by very rapid reading. Comprehension is achieved only by careful reading of the selected portions.

Remember that the purpose of previewing is to enable you to make a quick review of the major facts in a selection. You are not trying to read completely. Rather, you are trying to decide whether this material justifies more careful reading, or what it is all about.

Some slow readers may feel guilty about previewing. It just isn't reading as they know it. It's too superficial and too quick to be "good reading." These are the assumptions of the naïve, inexperienced, or untrained reader. The best readers, who cover large amounts of material with good comprehension, must use some form of previewing to accomplish their goals. Previewing is a recognized, accepted technique recommended by all leading authorities on reading improvement. It is not just an artificial type of reading resulting in superficial understanding. It is an integral part of the good reader's skills. Previewing is essential to wide, comprehending reading.

Try previewing in the article that follows. In this trial, read *only* the headings and the opening sentence of each paragraph. The questions you will answer are based on the ideas presented in these portions of the article. Some questions will demand inferences and conclusions you may have drawn from this previewing. But if you read thoughtfully, rather than rapidly, you will have no difficulty in answering such questions.

Bonds That Behave Like Stocks [3]

Add together the effects of the 1955 bull market in stocks, and the record corporate needs for money, and you find this as one result: More convertible debentures will probably be sold this year than in any previous year in history.

Both big companies and little are in the swim, with convertible

[3] Adapted from *Business Week,* October 1, 1955. Used by permission.

issues ranging in size all the way up to the $637-million issue now being floated by American Telephone and Telegraph Co. (which has already sold over $3-billion of convertibles in the postwar period). Mother Bell's offer of these debentures to stockholders is not only the biggest convertible issue ever, but it's the largest single offering of corporate securities in history.

Strange Creature—The stock market boom is an essential part of this picture. Convertibles are inextricably tied to the stock market because they can be swapped for common stock.

The convertible is a strange sort of Wall Street creature; it is a debenture—that is, a bond that is not secured by any specific asset, but only by the earning capacity of the issuer. Yet most people who buy them—and companies that float them—put more emphasis on the convertible as a chance to share a company's future earnings on an equity basis than on the fixed-income aspects.

Companies usually float convertibles because they regard this as a good way to issue new common without diluting the shareholder's equity at the time of issue. Investors and traders regard convertibles as a call—or option to buy—the stock of the issuer at a stated price at some future date. "And," points out one Streeter, "this option pays interest while you hold it."

The prices of convertibles generally move in sympathy with the price of the common stock into which they can be converted, thus making for much wider fluctuations than in the prices of straight non-convertible debentures.

At the market opening this week, for example, when bonds were holding firm, convertibles in general were off—taking their cue from the violent drop in the stock market.

Facing Both Ways—Some investment advisers tell clients to forget the sometimes confusing dual nature of convertibles, and regard them either as a bond or a stock. But other advisers say, "If you wouldn't buy both the bonds and the stock of a company, don't buy their convertible debentures."

The dualism shows up most strongly when a would-be purchaser of convertibles goes to his banker to borrow money against them. If the borrower regards the debentures as common stock under a rather inconvenient disguise, he may get a pleasant surprise. With a few exceptions, the banker doesn't stick to stock margin requirements in making the loan, but will lend on the convertibles just as though they were regular debentures.

Big and Little—While current interest is focused on the huge AT&T offering, there is plenty of activity in a number of issues floated earlier this year: Bethlehem Steel, with $191-million of convertibles; General Dynamics, one of the year's early favorites; and Southern California Edison, which had a price rise from par to 117¾ in just a few months. There may be another king-sized issue still to come—if Radio Corp. of America decides on a public offering this fall, it will be a convertible issue of around $100-million.

Small, little-known companies, such as Bogue Electric Mfg. Co., have also had good luck with convertible issues this year.

Attractions—A big one is that the corporation usually can get more capital through a convertible issue than through a non-convertible or a common offering. The buyer is paying something for the conversion privilege, and what it represents—a call on future earnings.

Convertibles also give a company these advantages:

While the bonds are outstanding—that is, prior to conversion—the interest paid on them is tax deductible; dividend payments on a regular common issue come out of after-tax profits.

Most convertible issues are subordinated debt—the company is still free to float secured debt issues, or even other debentures.

A convertible issue won't depress the price of the outstanding common as a regular common offering would. Stockholders are often so relieved to know that a new issue of common isn't forthcoming that the price of the common is actually bid up.

A convertible offering allows the company to expand its equity base without immediate dilution of outstanding stock holdings. That's because the bonds are usually converted over a period of perhaps 10 years or more. (Occasionally, if the price of the common stock rises very fast, all of a convertible issue may get converted within a couple of years: That happened in the Fruehauf Trailer issue of 1952.)

Investor Gains—With the stock market strong, and conversion prices set a few points above market price at time of offering, convertibles issued so far this year have almost all showed good gains. Bethlehem convertibles were offered at par, sold last week around 127. The AT&T issue, also offered at par, was selling about 128. American Potash and Chemical, offered at 102, was at 117 bid; and Continental Baking at 117 compared to its 102 offering price. In each of these cases, the strong showing of the debentures is directly attributable to the strength of the company's common stock.

Because the whole point of a convertible issue is to get it converted, the issuer generally will sweeten it up a bit, not only with conversion prices set near the market price, but with anti-dilution features also. The latter make allowance for any future issuance of common or more convertibles, by trimming back the conversion price of the convertible in proportion to the amount of new common issued.

Margins—Probably the major factor in the sustained strength of the convertible bond market, aside from the stock boom, is the fact that most banks will lend to an individual up to 80% of the purchase price of a convertible. (To buy the company's stock outright would take 70% of the buyer's own money under present margin requirements.)

This means that a speculator or investor in a company's stock can buy that stock via a convertible debenture—if the company has some outstanding—on as little as a 20% margin. To the banker, the debentures are debentures, though the borrower sees them as practically common stock.

But there's a point where the banker may regard the debenture as stock, too. One banker points out that when a convertible issue rises much above 105, it acts very much like a stock, and reacts more sensitively than ever to the price of the common. At these higher levels, the bank may lend somewhat less than it would if the convertible sold nearer par.

Rates—Quality of issue is another factor in determining how much a bank will lend and convertibles as a rule don't get a top rating from the rating services, because their price fluctuates too widely. Most banks will lend only 65% to 70%—sometimes even less—on lower grade convertibles with narrow trading markets, compared to 80% on high grade convertibles, such as AT&T, with very broad trading markets.

Tightening in the money market is not being felt as keenly in the loans on convertibles as in other loans. One banker points out, however, that "a year ago we were actively looking to lend on convertibles, and now we are simply servicing our old customers." This bank gets around 3⅝% to 4% on loans on top-grade convertibles.

Not All Hay—Despite the handsome record rung up this year, convertibles have a few disadvantages, too. For one thing, their close alliance with the stock market can work against the investor as well as in his favor. You only have to look at the General Dynamics issue, one of the year's most spectacular.

The bonds, $40-million worth, were offered at 102½, convertible into General Dynamics common—a top bull market favorite at that time—at $75 per share, just $2 more than the market price. The whole convertible issue sold in a few hours on the first day of offering, and the price spiraled to 116. Most of the money going into the bonds was borrowed, according to Streeters close to the offering.

But now General Dynamics has faded slightly from market favor, and its stock last week was off about 15 points from the price on the day of the convertible offering. The convertibles had dropped to 105⅛, not much above the offering price. The stock hasn't been close to the conversion price of $75 since the offering.

Squeeze—Many convertibles have sinking funds, set up to retire a fixed amount of bonds each year at the call price. Whether it has a sinking fund or not, almost every convertible issue is callable at the option of the company, usually at slightly above the offering price. An investor can get squeezed by the call price if he isn't on his toes.

Late in August, for example, Phillips Petroleum called the remainder of its outstanding convertible issue, due in 1983. The price on the bonds had risen to 113⅞, well above the call price of 103⅜.

When the company called the bonds, holders had four choices:

Convert the bonds to common at the conversion price of $65 per share. (The common then sold for $73.75 a share.)

Sell their debentures at the market price.

Surrender debentures for redemption for a total of $104.60 per $100 principal amount of debentures—still some $9 below their market price.

Sell the bonds, via an agent, to an investment group, which would pay $104.83 per $100 principal amount of bonds.

Phillips' action in calling the bonds caused a flurry of selling in the debentures, and the price fell 5⅞ in one day. The price of the stock reacted, too, selling off $1.50, though within a week the prices of both had recovered. Net result of calling the bonds is to force conversion one way or another, for bondholders stand to lose their market gains if they wait until the company redeems the bonds.

Sliding Scale—Another feature that often takes some of the edge off the possibility of future capital gains on convertible debentures is a sliding scale conversion price. The outstanding Sinclair Oil debentures, for instance, have a conversion price of $44 per share until 1963; then the price goes to $48 a share, rising again to $52 per share in 1968.

Questions on "Bonds That Behave Like Stocks"

1. Why do many companies float convertible bonds rather than issue more stock?

    a. The convertible pays interest only after it is converted to common stock.

    b. Convertibles do not "water down" the value of present stocks.

    c. The fixed income aspects of the convertible are more attractive to buyers.

    d. They prefer that the buyer invest in future earnings of the company.

2. The convertible is technically a debenture in that:

    a. it is secured both by potential earnings and by specific assets.

    b. it is secured by equity in the company's fixed income.

    c. it is an unsecured promissory note.

    d. it is secured by potential earnings of the issuer, and not by any specific asset.

3. The fluctuations in the prices of convertibles:

    a. are rather minor and do not in general move in sympathy with the price of common stock.

    b. are much greater than in the prices of nonconvertible debentures.

    c. rise and fall in exact relationship with nonconvertible debentures.

    d. show the same trends of movement as nonconvertibles, but not nearly as great.

4. The first sentence of paragraph 9 states that "The dualism [of convertibles to regular debentures] shows up most strongly when a would-be purchaser of convertibles goes to his banker to borrow money against them." This apparently indicates that:

    a. the amount of loan allowed is quite different between the convertible and regular debenture.

    b. the bank cannot loan against the security of a convertible.

    c. the amount loaned on the security of a convertible will be much lower than that loaned on a regular debenture.

    d. the banker will lend against a convertible as quickly as against a regular debenture.

5. Before a convertible has been converted to common issue, the interest or dividend rate paid on them by the company:

    a. is tax deductible.
    b. must come out of after-tax profits.
    c. is greater than after conversion.
    d. is less than after conversion.

6. The effect of most convertible issues on the freedom to float other debentures or secured debt issues:

    a. is to depress the value of other issues to the value of the convertible issue.
    b. does not necessarily depress the value of other types of secured debt issues.
    c. is to stop sales on other issues while the convertibles are on the market.
    d. tends to increase the amount of other debentures or secured debt issues sold.

7. Convertible bond issues seem to be popular with:

    a. large corporations.
    b. small corporations.
    c. both large and small corporations.
    d. the buyer rather than the issuing corporation.

8. Convertibles offered during the year that this article was written showed:

    a. good gains in price levels.
    b. relatively fixed price levels.
    c. a slight dip in price levels.
    d. a rather large drop in price levels, particularly those issued by the smaller companies.

9. About how much will most banks loan against the purchase price of a high quality convertible?

    a. Up to 80 per cent
    b. Only up to 50 per cent
    c. Only up to 25 per cent
    d. Banks do not loan against convertibles.

10. Why is it that convertibles usually do not get a top quality rating from the rating services?

   a. Their security backing is not as sound as is other debentures and stocks.

   b. They are nontransferable.

   c. Their prices remain too static.

   d. Their prices fluctuate too widely.

11. What effect has tightening in the money market had upon loans secured by convertibles?

   a. The effect has been felt most keenly on convertible loans.

   b. There has been little difference relative to the type of secured loan.

   c. The effect has not been as great as in other secured loans.

   d. There has been no effect on loans secured by convertibles.

12. When an investor holds his convertibles until they are retired by option of the company, the investor:

   a. will probably make more in the transaction than if he had converted earlier.

   b. is likely to make an additional profit out of the conversion above the market price.

   c. stands a fairly good chance of losing if he waits for the call price.

   d. may still elect to hold them as convertibles.

13. The sliding scale operating when convertibles are offered for conversion:

   a. works in favor of the investor who waits as long as possible before conversion.

   b. does not influence probable future capital gains of the investor.

   c. is not related to the time element of conversion.

   d. works against possible future capital gains.

    Key: 1. b 2. d 3. b 4. d 5. a 6. b 7. c 8. a 9. a 10. d 11. c 12. c 13. d.

Were you able to preview successfully? Score your comprehension by the answer key that is printed just above. If you answered about 70 per cent of the questions correctly, your comprehension was adequate. This article was somewhat more difficult to preview than the earlier articles. Its style is less compact; many two- or three-sentence paragraphs are not tightly integrated. In several places, a series of facts is enumerated rather than grouped into a cohesive paragraph. However, previewing is still a practical, time-saving approach to gaining an overview of the main ideas.

The structural looseness of the article plus the rapidity of previewing combine to give the feeling of only superficial comprehension. Yet the major characteristics, the advantages and disadvantages of convertibles, are all contained in the opening sentences. All these main ideas as well as a number of details are covered in the act of previewing. Thus even in materials that are informally or somewhat loosely written previewing provides a reasonable degree of comprehension.

Of course, some of you, particularly the engineers, are not satisfied with average comprehension. You feel you must retain all the facts. But this kind of perfectionistic reading is exactly what prevents you from doing more reading and from reading efficiently. Certainly an article such as "Bonds that Behave Like Stocks" does not demand or justify the time and concentration necessary for complete comprehension. You were probably not studying this article while on the way to your broker's office to invest your entire capital in convertible bonds, were you?

If you are dissatisfied with your degree of comprehension, you may certainly read the article again as completely as you wish. But previewing is intended to prevent your reading so laboriously when the material is not highly significant. Previewing is intended to function as a time-saving device. Used intelligently, it will help you to give the degree of attention and concentration really appropriate to each piece of reading matter.

Try the complete act of previewing on this second article. Read the headings, topic and summary sentences carefully and thoughtfully. Be ready to answer inferential as well as factual questions. The article is based on the report of a team of American experts who studied management practices in a number of European countries.

American Opinions of European Industry [4]

The members of the American Teams, who were carefully selected by the National Management Council as American specially qualified industrial leaders, brought to Europe a wide experience at all levels in industry. They represented the best of progressive American management concepts and looked upon the problems of their European colleagues with the utmost sympathy and understanding. In making their reports, they fully recognized the difficulties confronting European industry as a result of the numerous dislocations of the overall European economy, as well as the national economies, which resulted from the recent war and the subsequent disruption of East-West trade in Europe.

Before setting forth these suggestions of the American team members it should be emphasized that in their statements, both written and oral, the American team members made clear that in technology there is no difference between Europe and the United States. In fact, they saw many instances where European industry was actually in advance technically over that of the United States. One prominent American team member repeatedly stated that he had never seen a bad management practice in Europe that he had not seen in the United States and equally that he had never seen a good management practice in the United States that he had not seen in Europe. The fundamental difference between European and American management is that good management practices are followed by a greater percentage of American than of European industrial enterprises.

Despite European opinion to the contrary, the American seminar teams discovered that the basic management problems in industry are approximately the same in all European countries. These problems can be solved by the European industrialists themselves if management will adopt the principles and take action along the lines suggested below.

I. TOP MANAGEMENT ATTITUDES

The industrial management seminar programme afforded an opportunity for over forty of America's professional industrial managers to observe, at first hand, conditions in nine intensely industrialised countries of Europe. Together, these Americans visited hundreds of industrial

[4] Adapted from *Problems of Business Management,* published 1954 by the Organization for European Economic Co-operation (3, Rue André-Pascal, Paris-16e), pp. 13-17. Used by permission.

enterprises and sat round the table with over 2,000 leaders of European industry.

On the basis of their observations and experiences during the programme, the Americans were unanimous in stating that the most important single problem confronting industry in Europe is how to change the attitudes of its top managers. In this connection, they pointed out that American high productivity and production stems firstly from the favourable attitudes of top management and, secondly, as the result thereof, from the favourable attitudes of American labour. On the score of attitudes the American teams believe that European top management must acquire a sense of realistic optimism, enthusiasm and confidence—in itself, in its subordinates, and in the future of its enterprises. In their opinion, they found too many instances in Europe where top managers:

(a) resisted constructive change;

(b) failed to realise that their primary function is to plan for the future;

(c) concerned themselves too much with the day-by-day operations of the enterprise;

(d) failed to delegate responsibility to their subordinates, or

(e) failed to give these subordinates adequate authority to carry out such responsibilities as were delegated.

The Americans feel that the industrial enterprise should be dedicated to the service of the community and the nation, of its customers, of its labour force, and of its shareholders or investors. American top managers who follow this service-concept usually make more profits for the enterprise than those who do not.

II. SUBORDINATE MANAGEMENT

The American team members were quick to see that European enterprises, on the whole, are not utilising to their own advantage the well-established and proven methods and techniques for the effective selection, training and placement of subordinate managers. During the sessions, there was considerable discussion over the place of the foreman in the enterprise. The Americans emphasized the fact that in the United States foremen are part of management, not of labour, and that in the selection of foremen, more consideration is given to their leadership qualifications than to their skills as workmen. Foremen should be trained to serve as the effective link between management and labour. There is a need, the Americans were aware, in Europe for providing able subordinate managers with opportunity for advancement—from the bottom to the very top ranks of industrial management. It is felt that only through the planned training of subordinate managers combined with the possibility of promotion can there develop in Europe the concept that industrial management is a profession. In this lies the answer to the question, which should be one of the major preoccupations of progressive top management, "Who will be the managers of the enterprise twenty years from now?"

III. HUMAN RELATIONS`

European top management should also pay greater attention to human factors by basing its policies on the proper use of manpower and upon respect for the dignity of the worker. Since high productivity is an attitude first of management and second of labour, the Americans believe that European managers should take pains to explain to their workers the reasons behind the policies and decisions of the enterprise. It is suggested that top managers should recognise also the direct relationship between high productivity in the enterprise and sound human relations policies and methods. There should be within European industry freer channels of communication, upward as well as downward, between management and labour, and between top and subordinate management.

The teams thought that the general European practice of either nation-wide or industry-wide setting of wage levels, working conditions, production incentives, and terms of employment—instead of by agreement between management and labour at the individual plant level—goes far to prevent workers from acquiring a sense of participation in the enterprise. By a "sense of participation," the American reporters did not mean participation in the profits or the direction of the enterprise, but that management and labour can be an interdependent team working together for the benefit of the enterprise.

IV. STATISTICS AND MANAGERIAL CONTROLS

Many European enterprises, the Americans discovered, do not prepare adequate and reliable statistics for use in the control of the various operations of the enterprise. For example, European top management has not generally employed surveys, questionnaires and other studies to develop statistics for making plans in connection with production, the financial needs of the enterprise, more effective marketing and distribution, etc. The employment of adequate and reliable statistics can result in the better use of working capital of the enterprise through improved production and purchasing schedules, inventory control, budget control, cost control and low-cost handling of materials in the production processes. Their American colleagues felt that European managers should intensify their study of cost figures which may be reduced by closer adherence to the delivery dates promised to customers, and to quality and specification standards.

The American participants in the seminars urged their European friends to consider the beneficial effects of the lower cost cycle upon their enterprises. Lower costs make for lower prices, expanded and deepened markets, and greater total profits. These benefits can be employed to:

(a) pay labour higher wages to increase its purchasing power;

(b) offer the customer lower prices, greater product value and better service; and

(c) provide the enterprise with greater capital for reinvestment to assure its continued healthy existence, its growth and development.

V. MARKETS AND MARKETING

Throughout the seminar programme and in every country, the European participants constantly complained that their country forms too small a market to permit adaptation of advanced marketing ideas and practices. Tied directly to this complaint was a similar one of ever-shrinking international markets for the products of European industry.

An American answer to these statements is greater preoccupation with the lower-cost cycle mentioned above, which can result in the deepening of present markets and in the development of new ones—both at home and abroad. Related to this idea is the recognition that local workers often are, or can be made into potential customers.

There is a need for European enterprises to improve the selection and training of sales personnel. Too frequently, the teams found the sales department to be the "poor cousin" of the enterprise—if it existed at all. European companies often hire the best engineers available for their production departments, but pay scant attention to the qualifications and training of their sales personnel.

Sales, with too many European enterprises, means simply the taking of purchase orders for products already produced, rather than the planned and aggressive development of markets. The Americans urged the greater use of market research and surveys, not only in marketing and distribution operations, but also in connection with new product development, re-design of existing products and in planning production schedules. Careful analysis of sales statistics can often result in the elimination of products which form too small a percentage of total sales volume to warrant continued production. This elimination permits greater concentration (in both production and marketing) on those products which make up the bulk of sales volume, in lowering their costs and in increasing the amount of working capital available.

VI. EXCHANGE OF MANAGEMENT INFORMATION

The American participants in the seminars frequently had difficulty in convincing their European colleague that there are, in fact, no management secrets, and that "the closed door (of the enterprise) keeps out more ideas than it keeps in." They urged a greater exchange in Europe of management "know-how" and experience through the extension of management activities such as meetings, conferences and seminars with fellow-members of the same industry, or the same branch of management activity, as well as with members of other industries. The team reports reveal the need for publishing, in the national language, more management literature, such as books, manuals and magazines, to enable both top and subordinate managers to keep abreast of progress and developments in their own and other countries.

VII. EDUCATION FOR MANAGEMENT

The high degree of technical skill and knowledge of European managers was quickly noted by the American participants in the seminars who understand that European universities and technical schools provide technical education at a level at least equal, if not superior, to that of any other part of the world. The Americans, however, were astounded at the general lack of university courses in industrial management.

They pointed out that many American universities have faculties of industrial engineering, management engineering or business administration. Beginning only about forty years ago, American universities each year now add ever-increasing numbers of youthful graduates to the lower ranks of professional managers in United States industry. The Americans stress the need for European industry and universities to study ways and means of attaining closer co-operation to the mutual advantage of both.

The team members remarked that education for management does not stop with graduation from the university or technical school. The ever-increasing complexity of modern industry obliges the progressive manager to continue his formal education even after he has embarked upon his career. This need can be met in Europe by providing more evening and weekend courses in the universities and technical schools which could co-operate more closely with industry and management associations or committees.

Questions on "American Opinions of European Industry"

1. What was found to be the fundamental difference between European and American management?
   a. Technical know-how by American management is much more advanced.
   b. There is a greater following of good practices by European management.
   c. There is a greater following of good practices by American management.
   d. Technical know-how by European management is much more advanced.

2. The American management team agreed that the most important problem facing European industry is:
   a. how to change the attitudes of its top managers.
   b. how to overcome dislocations caused by the war and disrupted East-West trade.
   c. the difficulty in maintaining adequate sources of supply for raw materials.
   d. the difficulty in getting and maintaining continuous markets.

3. One finding of the American team contrary to the consensus of European opinion was that:
   a. management problems were approximately the same throughout Europe.
   b. a closer adherence to management policies was maintained by American management.
   c. European managers were not properly selected.
   d. European managers concerned themselves too largely with day-to-day operations.

4. What, according to the American team, should be a major concern of European top management?

   a. Selecting and training managers for the future
   b. Rebuilding to a pre-war level
   c. Providing subordinate managers with opportunity for advancement
   d. Greater attention to the particular facets of their companies' operations

5. A factor which is not stressed as contributing to poor relations between European labor and management is:

   a. the extremely low wage scales.
   b. nation-wide or industry-wide setting of wage levels.
   c. little or no communication between the two.
   d. improper use of manpower.

6. In answer to European management's complaint that their markets were too small for the adoption of advanced marketing practices, the American team suggested, as a basis for market expansion:

   a. tighter cost and managerial controls.
   b. more statistical controls.
   c. greater attention to the low-cost cycle and improved selection and training of salesmen.
   d. improved selection and training of salesmen and higher wages to workers.

7. A large proportion of European industrial selling deals mainly with:

   a. planning and developing markets.
   b. simply taking purchase orders.
   c. analysis of sales statistics and planning production schedules.
   d. new product development and redesigning existing products.

8. The American team reported that managerial training in Europe emphasized:

   a. technical skills and knowledge.
   b. industrial and business management.
   c. industrial and management engineering.
   d. business administration along with technical skills.

9. Some of the concepts of industry apparently lacking in the thinking of European management are:

   a. aggressive development of markets.
   b. the profit motive.
   c. the service motive.
   d. mass production at low unit cost.
   e. protection of management secrets.

   Key: 1. c   2. a   3. a   4. a   5. a   6. c   7. b   8. a
   9. a, c.

How successful were you in previewing this time? Did you answer about 70 per cent of the questions correctly? By this time, you ought to be getting the feel of previewing: the habit of thinking your way through, of mentally summarizing the ideas presented in each paragraph.

This article deals with a topic more commonly familiar to management personnel than the preceding one. It provides a contrast of ideas generally accepted by American management with the European viewpoints. Because of the familiar content, the article is particularly suited to previewing. But this familiarity is present in a great deal of the reading matter offered to the average businessman. Detailed, intensive reading in this type of material is certainly not necessary, or even desirable. The average reader is not concerned with the fine details of such an article. He does not attempt to memorize the differences between American and European philosophies of management. If he reads it at all, it is because of general interest rather than in an effort of seeking specific information. Previewing is sufficient to secure the general ideas the average reader desires. How much of the materials you read could be attacked this way? Try previewing for the next few days and see for yourself how you can dispose of certain types of reading quickly and adequately by this approach.

Now, a final trial at previewing. This time you are to pretend that you are about to attend a conference on automation. You will be expected to participate actively in discussing the possibilities of automation in your business. You have been given the article below to prepare you for the conference. This time you will probably want to do more than just preview. You will want to read thoroughly as well. Preview the article, and answer the twelve questions based on this approach. Then read the article completely, and answer the remainder of the questions. Time yourself for the second reading, omitting the time needed for the questions.

Automation [5]

The word had a rather unspectacular birth in the automotive industry. In the summer of 1948, Ford Motor Co. was setting up some new production lines for a model changeover. Before the high-priced presses and automatic machine tools were bolted in place, company brass gave a lot of serious thought to mechanical means of loading and unloading the parts that would pass between these mechanical marvels. Stepped-up production was essential if Ford was to catch up with Chevrolet. Delmar S. Harder, now a vice-president, summed up Ford's goal with the phrase "What we need is more automation."

Unwittingly perhaps, Harder coined the word that a lot of people were waiting for. "Automation" was immediately snapped up by economists, industrialists, and labor leaders and redefined to suit their own needs. In the seven years that followed, the meaning that Harder originally ascribed to the term—"handling parts between successive production operations"—was lost in the shuffle.

It's at this point that emotion gets into the act. A situation creates a word. A word did not create a situation. The intuitive feeling that most of us have about being lifted up bodily by a spurting technology seems to be at the heart of the matter.

Probably the first man to take notice of our new technology in a philosophical sense was Dr. Norbert Wiener, one-time child prodigy, MIT professor, and world-renowned mathematician. Wiener re-invented the word "cybernetics" to describe the new science on which automation rests. But his theory, too, was popularized and made unrecognizable.

Automation is well on its way to becoming what the Baltimore Sun has already called "the Cliché of the Year." Practically everybody has taken a point of view. Here are just a few of the major factions.

Engineers and designers are generally optimistic, unafraid of the future. They see automation as a quantum jump—a qualitative as well as quantitative spurt in productivity. In mechanization, they have reached a point where the speed of the machine operator is the only limit on the speed of production. By removing the operator, the only limit on speed becomes the machine.

[5] Adapted from *Business Week,* October 1, 1955. Used by permission.

Labor leaders have seized on the word as a new slogan. It has caught on to the extent that each new machine that rolls through the plant gates today is subject to much closer scrutiny by the workers than it was 20 years ago. Still, the labor unions have not really pounced on the science-fiction horrors of automation. Most of their efforts have gone into maneuvers to insure a painless transition when and if more highly automatic equipment does arrive. UAW-CIO tried to use the word as a wedge in obtaining a guaranteed annual wage. But when the chips were down, it had very little to do with the final outcome.

The crystal ball set—economists, sociologists, and free-lance writers—are split right down the middle. The more publicity-conscious prophets have let their imaginations run wild to produce ghastly science fiction, underscoring the horrors of lost jobs and predicting machine control of people. Other forecasters blithely skip over any short-term snags to concentrate on a vision of an age of plenty far in the future. Either way, they tend to scare people.

Management is on the fence. It recognizes the need for greater productivity, what with increasing population, scarcity of raw materials, sharpened competition. At the same time most executives refuse to be quoted on the subject except in highly legalistic terms. They're afraid of possible labor repercussions. When management does speak out, it's usually to pour oil on already troubled waters.

I. WHAT IS AUTOMATION?

Three attributes appear in the descriptions with surprising frequency. By themselves, there's nothing particularly startling about any of them. But there may be something in the synergistic effect of the three working simultaneously:

Workers are employed more and more outside the production process. They are maintenance men, they sell and distribute finished products, they think up new things for the machines to make, they administer. Few wield tools or operate machines; these rarely, if ever, touch the product itself.

Product flow is controlled by "feedback" devices. That is, a system of machines and controls has been devised that is capable of adjusting its own operation in the direction needed to obtain a desired result rather than simply following a preset cycle of operations.

Built-in adjustments in machines go back at least to James Watt's flyball governor. They are an important part of automatic elevators, wartime gun control mechanisms, navigational controls on aircraft and missiles.

The product has been designed specifically for automatic production. It may serve the same general purpose as one that Grandma used, although it may lack certain esthetic values. But because it has been designed especially for automatic production, it can be made more quickly and more cheaply per unit. It probably has fewer but more complicated parts. Emphasis is on efficiency.

Keeping in mind the features of mechanical production utilizing feedback to turn out specially designed products, it's fairly simple to identify four areas in which automation is active today:

Continuous process.   This is the oldest and perhaps most common variety of automation. It's also one of the most advanced, because liquids are a lot easier than solids to adjust by feedback controls. It achieves its greatest efficiency with round-the-clock operations. The future will probably witness a continuing trend toward fluidizing more solid products to cash in on the efficiencies of continuous flow. Pulverized coal in steam plants is probably the granddaddy of the move, but a lot of work is being done today with sand in foundries, continuous casting.

Multiple tool.   This is sometimes referred to as "Detroit Automation" because it is best exemplified by the block-long machine systems that are operating in the auto plants. On a somewhat less spectacular scale, the same sort of thing is happening all through the metalworking and packaging industries. In this area, however, it is often difficult to determine where automation begins and mechanization ends, if there is any difference at all. When a system of machines performs hundreds of steps without human intervention, it's usually called automation. When it performs one or just a few, it's called mechanization. The dividing line is not clear.

Numerical control.   While one segment of the machine tool industry has been headed toward high-production systems, largely at the behest of auto makers, a smaller one has been concentrating on flexibility, with the aircraft industry as a potential customer.

The flexibility group concentrates on a single machine that produces a wide variety of products. The machine is hooked up to an electronic computer, and instructions are fed into the computer by means of punchcards or magnetic tape. The "input" contains numerical instructions ordering the work piece or the tool to move a thousandth of an inch in a specific direction.

Data processing.   Just as a few machine tools have become accessories of computers in the factory, so some office machines have been absorbed by other giant calculators called data-processing machines.

These electronic giants, which may cost upwards of $1-million, are fed information tape or punchcards. The information is stored in electronic devices, where it can be recalled in fractions of a second. When other directions are fed into the giant brain, it can perform a variety of accounting tasks. But the full implications of these machines' ability to "remember" are just beginning to catch on. It's possible to feed huge quantities of raw data into these machines—more than any human mind could hold—and then direct the machines to tap this undigested stockpile of data and come up with specific answers.

II. A NEW INDUSTRY

The industry that has sprung up to produce the machines, controls, and brains of automation, is not a clearly defined one like automaking or motion pictures or mining. It's more an across-the-board term like mass production. In fact, it's difficult to call automation an industry at all. It's an assemblage of perhaps 1,000 companies, with roots in at least a dozen older industries.

Companies that advertise their products as automation usually fall into one of three groups:

Machine builders. This is the largest and most heterogeneous group. At the top of the list are about 250 machine tool builders. Most of them, certainly all the big names, are becoming more and more control-conscious. Benefitting from their activities are the companies that supply fixtures and accessories, and the power transmission group (belts, conveyors, bearings). The large industrial machinery companies (presses, transfer machines, rolling mills, etc.) and speciality machinery makers (cigarette, mining, packaging, steam generating, etc.) are involved, though the bulk of their business is in older forms of mechanization.

Control makers. There are only a handful of companies of any size in the strictly instrument end of the business, but they have done much of the research groundwork on automation. They make the great variety of sensing and activating devices that are feedback's outward evidence.

Despite the selectness of this group of companies, the Instrument Show in recent years has been luring 500 exhibitors or so—evidence that the fringes overshadow the nucleus. Control also must include the wires and components. This brings in all the giants of the electrical and electronic industries.

Brain specialists. Smallest—in number but not in size—and most easily identifiable participants in automation are the makers of electronic computers and data-processing machines. The big names of the business machines industry are all deeply involved, and getting more so. There's some evidence that at least one of the biggest will derive 50% of its gross sales from automation this year.

III. A SECOND INDUSTRIAL REVOLUTION

When you try to compare the rather nebulous concept of a Second Industrial Revolution (as automation is frequently called) with a concept of the First Industrial Revolution, you encounter enormous difficulties in trying to determine where one ends and the other begins. They are closely tied, but if any projections are to be made, it's necessary to look at motivations. Three will do as a starter:

Mechanization.   Historically, the economic force behind mechanization has been the high cost or scarcity of labor. In the early days of the First Industrial Revolution, machines were avowedly designed to replace manual labor—to do the same jobs as human beings but to operate more quickly, more uniformly, and more cheaply. Management's approach at the time was rather cold-blooded. Displaced workers had to go back to the farm or starve. With the rise of organized labor, such action is no longer possible. Workers are stockholders, customers, people.

Supermechanization.   Expensive labor is a factor but not the dominant one when mechanization becomes big business. When a company is selling hundreds of thousands or millions of identical products, the problem is how to handle the great bulk of materials involved. Then you have to mechanize the mechanization itself. Otherwise the job would be too big for one man and maybe even for a labor force the size of those that built the Pyramids. For example, men simply could not handle the red-hot ingots weighing many tons in a contemporary steel mill. They couldn't handle the radioactive materials in an atomic plant. They couldn't pick all the crops at the peak of harvest on a 100,000-acre farm. They couldn't keep track of sales, accounting, and inventory of a big retail chain.

Innovation.   As a factor in our expanding technology of the last 150 years, the invention of new products and processes has been just as important as mechanization. This trend has created far more jobs than mechanization eliminated. One observer has estimated that at least 40-million of the 65-million jobs today are dependent on this type of progress. He builds his case on the fact that only a few hundred years ago, Indians led a very marginal existence in this country where mechanization and innovation have exploited countless resources.

In automation today the factors of mechanization, supermechanization, and innovation are all at play. But another factor that's putting the squeeze on workers is unique in our history. That is the labor supply. We are living in a decade during which high birth rates and low death rates have pushed our population to record levels. This comes at the same time that the size of the labor force is being held down by low birth rates of the depression years, by high standards of living that allow youngsters to remain in school longer, and by more liberal retirement policies.

IV. MORE JOBS OR LESS?

Of course, when you get right down to it, the fundamental question is this: What is automation going to do to the worker? Is it going to create jobs or is it going to eliminate them? Is it going to downgrade workers or is it going to upgrade them? And exactly when is all this supposed to take place? What is the timetable?

There's no real answer and no real basis for one,

There will be "pockets of unemployment"—to use the NAM's phrase—and there will be individual hardships. It's always difficult for a family to tear up its roots in one community and move on to another where there is work. But the roots today are not so strong as they once were. The automobile has increased our mobility tremendously—and World War II showed that we could be mobile even without the automobile.

It's almost as certain that the biggest reduction in jobs in the next few years will occur in offices rather than in factories. In the last few years, only a handful of data-processing machines have found their way into offices. Most of them have gone to engineering labs. But in the next two years, orders already on the books at Sperry Rand and International Business Machines indicate that at least 10 times as many will become available.

Another factor that will soften the blow of displacement—on the records, at least—is the perversity of human nature. Some people never get the word, and they go on for generations making money even though efficiency experts have pronounced them dead and buried. The garment industry is the most blatant example. In an age of mechanization, it still puts a premium on handwork. Handcrafts are also imperishable.

When noncompetitive industries do mechanize, the old craftsman is seldom fired. More likely he is put at the same pay on a downgraded job. The old specialty disappears with his retirement or transfer. As with the girl in the accounting office, the worker displaced is the one not hired.

The challenge for automation thus is to find employment for the people who will not be hired in dying industries. Ultimately, it's in industries not yet born that the job future lies. But it's impossible to tell exactly what new frontiers science will crack to produce these jobs.

Up to now, there have been no mass layoffs. In fact, it's probable that the postwar growth of the electronics industry alone has more than offset any displacement in employment over-all. Added to this are two large and dynamic new industries—atomic energy and guided missiles —that are entirely dependent on automatic controls. The fast-growing chemical and plastics industries, and even the long-established telephone business, are searching frantically for more workers despite gains they have made in automation.

In management circles, the consensus of opinion holds that the future will take care of itself as the past has done. Experience in electronics, guided missiles, and atomic energy supports the view that the trend will be toward greater worker specialization and technical training. In these industries, too, productivity rates are climbing much faster than employment rates.

The labor-prompted Congressional investigations may interrupt the trend. The unions are demanding guarantees of employer-financed retraining programs and severance pay for all workers who are displaced by automation. If this demand gets the blessing of Congress and of public opinion, management might have to do a lot of careful planning and cost accounting before it bought new labor-saving equipment.

Still, it's hard to refrain from straight-line projections of the historic upgrading of labor. A century ago, a laborer contributed nothing but his brawn to lay the rails across the country or to dig a ditch; today his grandson or great-grandson operates a machine in mass production or a highly specialized function. Today's worker is more skilled, better educated, better paid than his ancestor.

With automation, there will be more "dress up" jobs, more shift work, more leisure if the trend toward shorter work weeks continues, higher pay if productivity continues to climb.

There'll be a continued demand for tremendous numbers of highly skilled men, to program computers as well as to build and maintain them. Even in the most completely automatized factory, we'll still need engineers, electronics experts, electricians, mechanics, pipe fitters, tool makers.

We'll need more salesmen to dispose of the added output. Most of all, we'll need managers and creators who can take advantage of the promised efficiencies of automation.

Under these conditions, our educational system faces an unprecedented challenge. With change all around us, it is no longer enough to train tomorrow's workers for today's jobs. The jobs may very well have vanished by the time the trainees get out of school. Yet we don't know precisely what the new jobs will be.

In this uncertain technological future, the odds are against a man with a narrow pinpointed training. The best, most flexible schooling a youngster can have is a good grounding in fundamentals, particularly mathematics and sciences. Vocationally, that gives him room to take advantage of the specialized jobs that develop. In a world of increasing leisure, too, the humanities are important, teaching people to get more out of life and to be better citizens.

Clearly, inadequate preparation could be just as big a contributor to future unemployment as the new machines could be.

Questions on "Automation"

AFTER PREVIEW

1. In what industry did the word *automation* originate?

   a. Aircraft
   b. Automotive
   c. Business machines
   d. Armament

2. What was originally meant by the term *automation?*

   a. A system of machines and controls capable of adjusting operation to a desired result
   b. Production adjusted by the input of numerical instructions on punched cards or tape
   c. Mechanical handling of parts between successive production operations
   d. Storing of information in electronic devices, where it may be recalled almost instantly

3. Who has (have) apparently accepted the idea of automation the most optimistically?

a. Labor leaders
b. Economists and sociologists
c. Management
d. Engineers and designers

4. Which statement best indicates the use of workers in the automation process?

   a. They sell and distribute finished products.
   b. They work as maintenance men.
   c. Their work takes place outside the production process.
   d. They are employed mostly as designers and engineers.

5. The products of automation and the products from conventional machines:

   a. usually serve different purposes.
   b. are usually designed the same with comparable cost per unit.
   c. may have the same purpose but are designed differently.
   d. usually have the same purpose and design.

6. The oldest and most common variety of automation is:

   a. multiple tool.
   b. continuous process.
   c. numerical control.
   d. data processing.

7. Automation, as a new industry, may be classified into three general areas. Which one of the following is *not* a type of company producing automation products?

   a. Machine builders
   b. Control makers
   c. Brain specialists
   d. Innovators

8. What has been the historical force behind mechanization?

   a. Increased demand for goods and services
   b. High cost and scarcity of labor
   c. Union demands for shorter working hours
   d. Innovation and invention

9. In the gradual trend toward automation, which of the following has *not* played a leading part?

    a. Mechanization
    b. Supermechanization
    c. Innovation
    d. Labor supply
    e. Attitude of labor unions

10. What is automation going to do to the employment of the worker?

    a. More jobs will be created.
    b. There will be fewer people employed.
    c. There will be the same number employed, but with a shorter work-week.
    d. There is no present basis for a reliable answer.

11. The biggest reduction in jobs in the next few years will occur in:

    a. factories.
    b. maintenance and like service occupations.
    c. offices.
    d. supervisory positions.

12. The best educational preparation a person can make for tomorrow's technology is:

    a. a broad liberal arts background including mathematics and science.
    b. training in business administration.
    c. on-the-job-training in the theory and practice of automation.
    d. specialized training in electronics and automation.

AFTER COMPLETE READING

13. About how old is the term *automation?*

    a. About two years
    b. About ten years
    c. About forty years
    d. About seventy-five years

14. The article states that "each new machine that rolls through the plant gates today is subject to much closer scrutiny by the

workers than it was 20 years ago" (seventh paragraph). Why do you suppose this is true?

a. There is a certain amount of fear by the worker that machines for automation will sometime replace him.

b. Machines used in today's processes work at such fine tolerances that careful inspection of incoming machines is necessary before they may be used.

c. The size and complexity of today's machines are much more interesting to inspect than the relatively simple machines of 20 years ago.

d. The statement refers to machines leaving, rather than entering the plant. Thus it refers to the manufacturer's inspection before the machine is released for distribution.

15. The labor unions, in their attitude toward automation, have:

a. tried to play up the job dislocations that it will create.

b. used it as a successful wedge in gaining a guaranteed annual wage.

c. tried to insure a painless transition from mechanization to automation.

d. played up the science-fiction horrors of being finally overpowered by a spurting technology.

16. Management's attitude toward automation has been one of:

a. unqualified vocal support.

b. relative silence with an attempt to placate labor.

c. skepticism toward the final dislocations caused by automation.

d. wholehearted acceptance.

17. The devices which control product flow are called:

a. feedback.

b. continuous flow.

c. multiple tool.

d. numerical control.

18. What is the outstanding characteristic of multiple tool, or "Detroit Automation"?

a. Block-long machine systems

b. Numerical control systems

    c. Continuous process

    d. Feedback device control

19. The largest group of industries producing equipment for automation is the·

    a. control makers.

    b. machine builders.

    c. instrument makers.

    d. brain specialists.

20. What group of companies is most commonly identified with automation?

    a. Machine builders

    b. Control makers

    c. Instrument makers

    d. Brain specialists

21. Why has supermechanization or automation become necessary?

    a. Industrial jobs have become too big for human labor.

    b. Expensive labor would in turn make product too expensive.

    c. There are too few workers available to turn out goods and services.

    d. The job of training workers for the complex tasks of modern technology has become too difficult.

22. What factor has tended to create more jobs than mechanization has been able to eliminate?

    a. Population growth

    b. Abundant resources

    c. Innovation

    d. Supermechanization

23. What machine will very likely replace many office-workers?

    a. Calculator

    b. Multiple tool

    c. Numerical control

    d. Data processing

24. How are the outmoded craftsman and the office-worker being displaced?

a. Workers in these areas are being laid off.

b. The worker displaced is the one not hired to fill disappearing positions.

c. He is downgraded both in job level and pay.

d. In most instances he is retrained to fill the job which replaced his.

25. The present relationship between productivity rates and employment rates indicates that:

    a. employment is climbing much faster than productivity.
    b. productivity is climbing much faster than employment.
    c. they are both climbing at about the same rate.
    d. although productivity is climbing, employment is slightly on the downgrade.

26. Certain labor-prompted Congressional investigations may have the outcome of:

    a. curtailing the rate at which it is economically practical to buy new automation equipment.
    b. speeding up the rate of installation of new automation equipment.
    c. producing laws to prohibit too rapid change-over to automation.
    d. producing legislation making it impossible to lay off workers displaced by automation.

Key: 1. b   2. c   3. d   4. c   5. c   6. b   7. d   8. b   9. e
10. d   11. c   12. a   13. b   14. a   15. c   16. b
17. a   18. a   19. b   20. d   21. a   22. c   23. d
24. b   25. b   26. a.

FUTURE VALUES OF PREVIEWING

If you are securing the greatest values from previewing, you are likely to find that both your rate and comprehension were better in this selection. Previewing should result in sharpening your comprehension, and increasing the rate with which you can assimilate ideas when reading completely. Thus previewing the selection should result in somewhat greater speed when reading completely, as well as better total comprehension.

In this article you followed a different pattern than when merely previewing. Some materials you are called upon to read may require both previewing and reading completely. But they probably aren't as numerous as you think, particularly if you are inclined to be a slow, cautious reader. Now, honestly, isn't it true that much of what you must read is repetitious and basically familiar? Then why waste time reading it slowly? Use previewing for all it's worth. Remember that the values of previewing are threefold: to preread before actually reading completely; to help you decide how much further reading is necessary; and to cover materials of lesser importance thoroughly but rapidly.

The practice in previewing that we have given you in these three articles should have prepared you to use this reading technique effectively. You have used it to cover simple, familiar materials for general ideas. You have used it as a preliminary step to more careful reading. Make these applications in your own reading—to save time, to read more planfully, to read more competently.

If you are interested in the topics of the articles used in this chapter, here are a number of similar books and articles.

"Can the United States export its methods?" *Business Week,* November 14, 1953, p. 116.

Challenge of Automation. New York: Public Affairs Press, 1955.

"Company gifts: bars go down," *U.S. News and World Report,* Vol. 35, November 13, 1953, pp. 104-107.

Compton, W., "Corporation support," *Annals American Academy,* Vol. 301, September, 1955, pp. 140-147.

"Consumer market is growing in Western Europe, but it's still a long way from what the U.S. has," *Business Week,* February 26, 1955, pp. 130-132.

Diebold, John, *Automation.* New York: Van Nostrand, 1955.

Diebold, John, "What is automation?" *Colliers,* Vol. 137, March 16, 1956, pp. 38-40.

Engstrom, E. W., "Automation, significance for our industry and commerce," *Commercial and Financial Chronicle,* Vol. 182, December 22, 1955, pp. 2758-2759.

"Europe has yen for goods made in U.S.A.," *Business Week*, December 24, 1955, p. 50.

Kellogg, E. C., "Europe's boom means dollars for U.S.," *Iron Age*, Vol. 175, May 26, 1955, pp. 51-53.

Miller, Stanley R., "Recent trends in corporate financing: increased use of convertible and subordinated issues," *Commercial and Financial Chronicle*, Vol. 176, November 20, 1952, pp. 40-41.

"Our corporations become patrons of the liberal arts," *Saturday Evening Post*, Vol. 227, March 5, 1955, p. 10.

Powers, M. L., "Glamour world of industry," *World Oil*, Vol. 142, January, 1956, p. 56.

Richards, J. R., "Questions concerning corporation giving to education," *School and Society*, Vol. 77, June 13, 1953, pp. 375-377.

Shultz, George P. and Baldwin, George B., *Automation: A New Dimension to Old Problems*. New York: Public Affairs Press, 1955.

Solow, Herbert, "Automation: news behind the noise," *Fortune*, Vol. 53, April, 1956, pp. 159-166.

Soule, George H., *Time for Living*. New York: Viking Press, 1955.

Whyte, W. H., Jr., "What are the foundations up to?" *Fortune*, Vol. 52, October, 1955, pp. 110-113.

Whyte, W. H., Jr., "Where the foundations fall down," *Fortune*, Vol. 52, November, 1955, pp. 140-141.

4

Skimming—A Way of Reading Rapidly

What You Will Do
    Try skimming—a systematic, rapid reading technique

What You Will Learn
    How to read certain materials rapidly but thoroughly

In the last chapter, you were introduced to previewing, a method of prereading materials before actually reading them. This previewing technique can be broadened slightly so that it may be the entire act of reading in some materials.

HOW TO SKIM

Skimming is, as the name suggests, a process of allowing your eyes to travel over a page very quickly, stopping only here and there to gain an idea. There are many different ways of skimming such as reading random sentences that seem to stand out, or reading only the center third of each line. But we believe that a better-organized approach is best for most readers.

The reading of headings, topic and summary sentences can be broadened to include watching for cue words within the paragraph. These are words or phrases such as *first, second, for instance, some, others, finally, therefore.* Many authors use such cues to introduce the facts supporting the main ideas of the paragraph. Therefore, combining the technique of previewing with attention to cue words forms skimming—a new way of reading rapidly but completely.

This type of reading is useful for securing more than just the general ideas you gain from previewing. It is suitable for materials of moderate difficulty in which you are interested in some details. Remember we are not yet trying to do complete, thorough reading of technical or difficult matter. This is a rapid reading technique— quick, but reasonably thorough. Skimming, done in this fashion, is simply previewing in a somewhat more thorough manner. It is a rapid and systematic coverage of material too difficult or too important to be disposed of merely by previewing.

There is one caution to be observed in this way of reading. In skimming, speed is achieved by reading only selected portions of the entire selection. Speed is not achieved by reading these portions very rapidly. In other words, the sentences actually read are read carefully and thoughtfully. Skimming results in saving reading time because it provides a systematic, but brief coverage of the facts. Skimming does not actually require very rapid reading.

Try skimming the following article, "Poor Management Tempts Employe Thefts." If you think it will help you to get a better understanding of the material, read the first paragraph all the way through before you begin skimming. Read the remainder of the article by headings, topic and summary sentences. After reading the opening and closing sentences of a paragraph, look through rapidly for cue words that may point up important details—if you feel you need any more facts to support the main idea. Then, read the last paragraph all the way through to secure a general, summarizing idea.

Poor Management Tempts Employe Thefts [1]

by Joseph P. Blank

Every businessman stands a good chance of being robbed. It won't happen at the point of a gun. While in process, the theft is painless and secret. It's being committed by an employe. In all likelihood he's being assisted in the crime by the boss's innocent collusion.

Thefts by employes have steadily risen in volume and cost during the past ten years and now rank with fire as the chief cause of business

[1] Joseph P. Blank, "Poor Management Tempts Employe Thefts," *Nation's Business,* 43:84-85 (July, 1955). Used by permission of the Chamber of Commerce of the United States and the author.

loss. The take, according to conservative estimates, is $2,000,000 every working day; or more than $500,000,000 this year.

The crimes strike every kind of business, from the two-man hardware store to the automotive corporation with 40,000 employes. About $30,000,000 of the loss is covered by insurance. The remainder is pure blood out of the heart of a business.

The crime is insidious and shocking because the thief frequently is a long-employed man or woman of unquestioned integrity. No common denominator can be found in the thefts. These criminals cut through all economic, social, national, religious and racial brackets, and include every business title from chairman of the board down to charwoman. Aside from the employe thiefs in retail, wholesale and manufacturing establishments, the roster includes the treasurer of an aid society who stole $2,119; the auditor of an athletic club, $5,897; secretary of a fraternal order, $13,302; treasurer of a labor union, $25,000; chief clerk of a hospital, $15,000; treasurer of a university, $44,000. Even the insurance companies, which are hypersensitive about internal thefts and try hard to forestall them, have been clubbed hundreds of times for as much as $180,000 by suddenly unscrupulous claim adjusters and executives.

Most embezzlements don't hit the big figures. They're under $10,000 like the $2,596 lifted by a bookkeeper who never seemed to have enough money in his pocket. He solved this problem by forging checks, then destroying them after cancellation by the bank.

No business is immune from thefts. Offices suffer losses in pencils, typewriter ribbons, books and stamps. When this pilferage becomes flagrant, it can hurt. One manufacturer figured an "excess consumption" of $12,000 in office supplies for a single year.

Retail concerns are especially vulnerable. The clerk in a good market slips a pound of bacon into his coat pocket. The girl at the cosmetic counter of a drug store drops a lipstick into her purse. In one instance a detective agency was called in to find the person who took $16,000 from a department store safe. Using a lie detector the investigator questioned everyone who worked near the safe. Although the thief escaped detection on the first go-around, 36 out of 52 people admitted thefts of ties, socks, lingerie, costume jewelry and other articles.

While petty pilferage does nibble at profits, it's the big, business-crippling theft that worries management, the insurance companies and the district attorneys. The experts know several basic facts about these crimes. The crooks usually are men and women with no past criminal records. Sometimes they are driven to crime by neurotic compulsion, like misguided resentment against the boss or achieving self-esteem by proving they can outsmart the company. Generally, they steal out of a desperate need for money. The need, according to insurance men who review 30,000 claims a year, is first provoked by gambling—horses, poker, a get-rich-quick stock deal. Other reasons include "another woman," keeping up with the Joneses, extraordinary family expense like big medical bills, bad associates and inadequate income.

Without exception, investigators agree that the employer's slipshod way of protecting his business lends a helping hand to the criminal. Robert M. Bernstein, executive vice-president of Wilmark Service System, a firm that sets up methods to prevent losses at point of sales, estimates that 77 per cent of theft opportunities can be closed by active enforcement of normal business regulations.

Here are some general safeguards, based on recommendations by insurance companies, private detection agencies, the U.S. Department of Commerce and such experts as the late J. K. Lasser:

Know the business history of key people, especially those who handle money. Applications of new employes should be investigated before they are given access to cash or checks.

Always investigate the job of any person who refuses a vacation. It's wise, too, to find out specifically why an employe needs to arrive early or stay late on the job.

Establish the iron-clad rule that a numbered sales receipt must accompany every purchase. Station the cash register in the open where it can easily be seen by customers and employes. Keep the cash register change fund as low as practicable. The customer should witness the entire transaction; taking the package should be the last step in the sale. If money seems mysteriously short at the end-of-day tally, a clerk may be turning cash over to a confederate, i.e., giving the "customer" change for $5.00 when only $1.00 was presented. In taverns, restaurants or drug stores, a waiter or waitress may get into the habit of undercharging in the hope of receiving a big tip in return.

Divide labor involving money. A non-sales person should balance cash against sales slips or cash register tape. Bank statements should be reconciled by a person not connected with cash or the handling of checks. The person who opens mail should not post the accounts.

Checks should be numbered. Requisitions and purchase orders should support bills. Payment should be made only on proof that goods were received.

People who handle cash should not prepare the payroll. The job of signing payroll checks should be delegated to a person who had no hand in the preparation of the payroll. Occasionally check the payroll against the actual number of working employes.

Withdrawals from petty cash should be based on signed slips bearing the amount of money written out (no numerals) in ink. Petty cash should be checked at unannounced intervals.

Stock room clerks should not take inventory.

If possible, do not announce in advance the arrival of auditors.

And finally, the experts advise, every proprietor or member of management should take a good objective look at his business. Have haste, laziness and attempted efficiency corrupted sound methods and left open needlessly tempting avenues for theft? It's foolhardy to bank on the fact that no known inside pilferage or embezzlement has yet struck the business. It can always happen tomorrow.

Questions on "Poor Management Tempts Employe Thefts"

1. The incidence and cost of employe theft:
   a. have risen in the past ten years.
   b. have maintained a fairly constant figure from year to year.
   c. have dropped slightly in the past ten years.
   d. have shown a marked decrease because of better management practices.

2. What are some of the surprising facts about employe theft?
   a. Most thefts are small and perpetrated by trusted employes.
   b. Large businesses are particularly susceptible to small thefts.
   c. Thefts by employes are one of the minor types of business loss.
   d. No type of business seems free from employe thefts.

3. What kind of business is most susceptible to employe thefts?
   a. Banks
   b. Offices
   c. Wholesale and manufacturing establishments
   d. Retail establishments

4. The kind of theft that is the greatest worry to management is the:
   a. small steady nibbling at profits.
   b. theft of money rather than goods or merchandise.
   c. theft of merchandise rather than money.
   d. large theft that seriously disrupts the finances of the company.

5. What seems to be one of the main causes for the great amount of thefts by employes?

   a. Inefficient and careless hiring methods
   b. Inadequate investigation of employes before hiring
   c. The constantly rising cost of living
   d. Inadequate supervision of sales and the handling of money

6. What are some of the effective safeguards that management can employ to reduce employe thefts? (Choose as many as you need.)

   a. Carefully separate the jobs involving the handling of money.
   b. Insist upon a numbering system for checks and sales receipts.
   c. Employ outside auditors at regularly recurring intervals.
   d. Maintain close personal supervision over all employes handling money or stock.
   e. Occasionally review your methods of handling money and stock to eliminate opportunities for theft.

   Key: 1. a   2. a, d   3. d   4. d   5. d   6: a, b, e.

Were you able to secure a fair degree of comprehension of the article on employe thefts? Nine answers were called for in the six questions. If you answered six to eight correctly your comprehension was adequate. If you avoided the tendency to read too rapidly, you would have been able to comprehend the main ideas of this selection by skimming.

You noticed, of course, that the number of questions based on the article was small and that the questions were general rather than detailed. However, this choice of questions was appropriate to the kind of reading you were doing. Skimming cannot be expected to yield a great many details or very complete comprehension. It is a type of reading suited to materials that are not important or difficult enough to require very careful reading. For example, skimming is particularly useful in reading announcements, advertisements, memos, general directives, "How's Business" articles, news magazines, trade journals, and the like. Skimming is most useful when complete, detailed comprehension is not necessary.

Have you realized how much time skimming can save you? Compare the time required to skim the next article, and the time you would have spent if you had read in your usual fashion. The editorial "Is 'Big Labor' Good or Bad?" is approximately 900 words in length.

Measure accurately the time you need to skim it. Divide this figure into 900 to find your rate of reading when skimming.

Is 'Big Labor' Good or Bad? [2]

Benefits of the Merger May Outweigh Potential Dangers

Not everybody thinks it is a good thing to have labor united in one big organization. For instance, hot-tempered Mike Quill tried in vain to keep his transport workers out of the newly merged A.F.L.-C.I.O., charging that it gave license to "raiding, racketeering and racial discrimination." Yet one might use the same words as reasons to applaud the merger. The new charter creates a no-raiding agreement which should lessen jurisdictional disputes, a terrible plague to industry and labor. It gives the central federation greater powers than the old A. F. of L. possessed to investigate and punish racketeering. And while certain unions still discriminate against Negroes, both President George Meany and his chief deputy Walter Reuther are determined to wipe this out. All of these are gains for labor and for all of us.

There may be some potential dangers in a united labor movement, too. Some fear that Big Labor will one day form its own party and attempt to capture government. Others fear a union "monopoly" of the work force, still others that a combine of Big Labor and Big Business will rook the public. Well, let's look at these so-called dangers.

Politics. All past experience indicates that no one can control a labor vote (witness the recent defeat in Ohio of labor's supplemental unemployment pay plan). In the future as in the past, labor is likely to exert tremendous influence through the Democratic party, but it does not yet, nor is it likely to, control that party. No practical politician believes that labor will, or can, start its own party. Americans do not like to regard themselves as frozen into any particular class.

Monopoly. Despite labor's 20-year growth from 3.5 million members to 17 million, unions have not been able to organize more than one third of U. S. wage and salary workers. Their number grows as the work force grows, but the union percentage of the total has even slipped a bit, indicating a plateau has been reached. A major reason is that the remaining unorganized two thirds of the work force is either in small plants, which are difficult to organize, or else belongs to the white-collar category which does not identify itself with labor. Some unions undoubtedly will expand, in expanding industries like chemicals, but others also will be declining. The prospect of any union monopoly on the work force, therefore, seems slight.

Combination. The postwar decade has seen a continuous spiral of wage boosts followed by price boosts, but the demonstrated ability of Big Labor and Big Business to hold friction to a minimum has brought about an atmosphere of cooperation which keeps productivity rising. Economists question whether unions, for all their gains (as in pensions, health benefits, minimum wage, etc.), exercise any genuine control of real wages. Those are determined by an industry's state of health. If an industry is depressed, so is its take-home pay, regardless of the wage rates. And if take-home is boosted in a declining industry, the number employed diminishes. So far, the higher-wage, higher-price structure has had a sound basis in rising real wages based on higher productivity, culminating, in 1955, in the most prosperous year in our history.

In sum, we see no solid reasons to be afraid of U. S. labor. It seems likely that, whatever political adventures labor may undertake in coming years, its greatest gains will continue to be made in the economic area where its continued cooperation with management keeps productivity rising.

The big thing that both labor and management need to learn is that while each goes on using out-worn, emotion-charged symbols ("exploiter," "Marxist," etc.) the real character of their differences has changed altogether, just as the shape of the whole economy has changed in 20 years. About the only "class" issue in 1954's congressional session was whether workers should have a $100 tax cut or stockholders a $50 dividend credit—hardly a fearful class struggle. There is no class struggle in America in spite of Adlai Stevenson's back-handed "let's you and him fight" attempt to discover one in his speech to the new federation.

The fact is that labor and management are far closer together than either seems to realize. It is symptomatic that the new organization's charter strikes out all references to the class struggle that were in the old A. F. of L. preamble. It is significant also that at last week's N.A.M. convention guest George Meany and host Charles Sligh, N.A.M. chairman, lost their tempers in an argument which revolved mainly around emotional symbols. Actually, Sligh has never had a strike in his four plants, and Meany has never led one anywhere. Before they lost their tempers, Meany had, however, pointed out the important truths—that both sides believe in the profit system and management's right to manage, and that both oppose government control and world Communism. For all this agreement on major objectives, it is a healthy thing for management and labor to continue to be watchdogs, one of the other. But both have a greater obligation: to keep productivity and real wages rising and business profitable and expanding.

Questions on "Is 'Big Labor' Good or Bad?"

1. The real differences existing between labor and management:
   a. continue to remain relatively the same.
   b. are becoming more and more a class struggle.
   c. have changed altogether in the last twenty years.
   d. are not nearly as important as they were twenty years ago.

2. The epithets or "name calling" habits of management and labor:
   a. are much the same as they have always been.
   b. have disappeared with the changing shape of our economy.
   c. are much less in evidence than they were twenty years ago.
   d. continue much the same because the basic differences remain relatively the same.

3. In the last twenty years, unions have been able to:
   a. organize a majority of the workers.
   b. unionize a greater percentage of the work force than previously.
   c. organize only about a third of the workers.
   d. gain a greater control of the political voice of the worker.

4. The writer of this editorial believes that the merger of the labor federations will:
   a. create a monopoly in labor.
   b. produce a greater control of the labor vote.
   c. force a continued spiraling of wages, thus creating inflation.
   d. have little effect on our present way of life.

5. In your opinion, which of the following wrote this article?
   a. A Democrat
   b. A Republican
   c. A pro-union writer
   d. An antiunion writer

Key: 1. c   2. a   3. c   4. d   5. b.

WHERE DO WE GO FROM HERE?

If you compared your rate when skimming with your usual rate, you probably discovered that skimming permits you to cover materials four or five times as fast. It is true that the skimming rate is not an actual measure of the words per minute you read in that type of reading. In skimming, you did not read all the words, as you often do when reading completely. But the comparison of the time required for skimming with your other methods is valid. You will cut your reading time by much more than half if you use skimming when it is appropriate.

Of course, the practice of skimming in these two articles may not have been sufficient for you to become adept at this way of reading. Changes in reading habits and in pace of reading come slowly to some individuals. But by this time, you certainly have an understanding of how to skim. Having learned how to preview, skimming is simply the next logical step in rapid reading.

The next step is one only you can take. There is nothing we can do to implement further your application of skimming in the materials you must read. Keep using this technique as frequently as you can. Use previewing to help sort your reading materials according to their significance and difficulty. Then follow through with skimming in those requiring some attention to details.

Your skill in comprehending materials read in this fashion will grow with use of the technique. If you can overcome your former habit of slow, cautious reading, you will continue to improve in skimming. Your comprehension and rate both when skimming and in other reading situations will increase.

If you enjoyed reading these particular articles, here are several others on the same topics.

Elmore, L. K., "Stopping not-yet-started embezzlement," *Banking,* Vol. 46, June, 1954, p. 78.

Fitch, R. E., "Organized labor's new leviathan," *Christian Century,* Vol. 72, August 31, 1955, pp. 995-996; November 9, 1955, pp. 1299-1301; November 30, 1955, p. 1403.

Knebel, F. and Mollenhoff, C., "Can big labor clean house?" *Look,* Vol. 20, March 6, 1956, pp. 30-32; April 17, 1956, p. 19.

Lens, Sidney, "Will merged labor set new goals?" *Harvard Business Review,* Vol. 34, March-April, 1956, pp. 57-63.

"Lie-detector tests on workers," *Business Week,* April 28, 1951, p. 24.

"Plant pilferage: on the rise," *Business Week,* December 4, 1954, p. 128.

Sligh, Charles R., Jr., "What industry expects from organized labor," *Commercial and Financial Chronicle,* Vol. 133, January 20, 1956, p. 5502.

Thayer, F. and Bower, J. B., "How papers can prevent cash and inventory pilferage," *Editor and Publisher,* Vol. 89, February 25, 1956, p. 11.

"United States eyes Sweden's labor pattern," *Business Week,* February 25, 1956, p. 126.

5

Reading for Ideas—The Art of Reading Rapidly

What You Will Do
 Try reading for ideas—a basic approach to rapid reading

What You Will Learn
 How rapid reading is really accomplished

In preceding chapters, we have dealt with various reading techniques such as previewing and skimming. In general, these tend to result in quicker, better-organized reading. However, the rapid reading of continuous text was not actually involved. These techniques illustrated various efficient ways of reading, rather than rapid reading itself, as it is generally understood.

The techniques of skimming and previewing are not adaptable to all reading situations. They do not lend themselves, for example, to the reading of short stories, novels, essays, and other types of general reading. But there is a method of reading these kinds of material with greater speed and better retention. This approach we call reading for ideas.

WHAT DOES READING FOR IDEAS MEAN?

The only real difference between the adult who both reads slowly and comprehends poorly and the good reader is the extent to which each succeeds in getting ideas from printed matter. As we

101

have said before, the poor reader tends to read almost word by word. His rate is often below 200 words per minute in fairly simple material. He reads almost as though he were saying (or thinking) each word to himself. In fact, he reads not much faster than he could say each word.

These word readers can think and talk as fast as the next person in conversational situations. Often their vocabularies are just as broad and fluent as those of other people. But because of habit, or caution, or merely lack of training, they seem unable to function as quickly and as fluently in reading as in other types of communication.

It is true that there are some individuals who think slowly, or struggle with words. There are a few who sweat blood when they try to explain something or dictate a letter. But the number of these is extremely small, and such nonverbal individuals do not account for very many of the mass of slow readers among adults today. Our suggestions are not addressed to this severely handicapped few but to the average slow reader who shows difficulty only in reading rapidly.

Following the example of Phillip B. Shaw in his *Effective Reading and Learning,* we might illustrate word-by-word reading by asking you to read this sentence in reverse. Start at the right and read to the left.

.later ideas and first words recognizing of matter a not is Reading

Of course, you can read the sentence and you do gradually comprehend its meaning. But how slow the process is. Moreover, you probably had to repeat the sentence mentally before its meaning became obvious. You probably read slower than you could have said the sentence and much slower than you could have thought it out. This is the way the slow reader operates—recognizing one word after another, often rephrasing the thought mentally before comprehending. Why is it necessary to think a moment about the meaning of the sentence, after reading? Because the word-by-word process is unnatural, so much slower than common speech rates, or the speed of normal thinking. For this type of reader, the act of reading is obviously not a thinking process. He does not think along with the writer—or read for ideas.

HOW TO READ FOR IDEAS

We have tried to clarify in some detail the concept of reading for ideas. A clear understanding of this concept is most important if you—a slow reader—wish to change your reading pattern. Any permanent change in your speed of reading must be accompanied by a clear-cut knowledge of what it is you are trying to overcome and what it is you are trying to accomplish. You must break this habit of recognizing words and substitute a continuous thinking process— reading for ideas.

We have prepared a number of selections that will help you to break away from word-by-word reading. These selections are adapted by deleting as many of the less important words as possible. To maintain as natural a reading situation as possible, blank spaces are present where the omitted words normally would occur. This type of arrangement does not disturb the natural arrangement of thoughts, or sentences, or the length of line.

We have used this type of material for several years with college students and adults. With the average slow reader, the spaced material quickly gives a feel for rapid reading. It results in a recognition that reading all the words is not essential to reading—and that reading is really a matter of thinking along with the writer. It results in improved comprehension as well as increased speed.

This reading situation is somewhat artificial and we cannot supply as many articles arranged in this fashion as you may need. However, the device works excellently in demonstrating to very slow readers what we mean by reading as a thinking process—or reading for ideas. In using such material in a reading clinic, we have found that three or four pieces are usually sufficient to get the feel of fluent reading. Even extremely slow, word-by-word readers tell us that after several trials they understand and are able to read for ideas rather than words. Of course, an abrupt change in their reading habits does not occur immediately. Some take several weeks of practice in reading in this thinking manner before very great changes in rate in general material appear. But once having achieved the sense of reading a stream of ideas, slow readers show gradual but definite increase in their rate.

This feeling for reading ideas rather than words is essential in overcoming slow reading. Our device of phrasing words aids in this development, particularly when rate of reading is under 200 words per minute. Those who usually read faster than this are probably omitting some words and phrasing some ideas. If you usually read simple literary materials such as a novel faster than 250 words per minute, you probably do not need very much of this type of training. The evidence on which these conclusions are based is quite obvious. The word-by-word reader tends to say or think each word as he reads. For this reason, he does not read any faster than he normally talks. For most persons, the average rate of speech is about 150-225 words per minute. Those who read faster than this must be phrasing

(Continued on next page.)

Brainstorming

Group Ideation—A Super-Productive Process

Can you use new ideas in your business? Do you have problems which need a fresh, creative attack? If so, you will be interested in "Brainstorming," a group approach to creative solutions of management's problems.

The discovery of the values of brainstorming are attributed to Alex F. Osborn of the Batten, Barton, Durstine and Osborn advertising firm. Several years ago Mr. Osborn began using groups of employees to brainstorm such problems as new product names and sales slogans. The practice has been picked up by such companies as the New York Telephone Co. to find answers to their acute problem of personnel recruiting, and the Carborundum Co. which brainstormed the problem of better use of certain equipment not employed to capacity.

Certain ground rules have been evolved through Mr. Osborn's experiences with sessions arranged for various business firms and at several university training centers. Those who are to brainstorm an idea are usually seated around a table. The group is composed of perhaps a dozen persons of equal or comparable rank. The members may be entirely drawn from lower levels or those usually active in policy-making discussions.

A leader proposes a rather specific idea or problem to be explored. Criticism of ideas offered must be entirely withheld. Stress is placed upon getting the group in a positive mood. The members are encouraged to offer whatever ideas come to their minds that bear upon the solution of the problem. "Free-wheeling" thinking is welcomed. The wilder the ideas, or grouping words into ideas, and omitting some words since they read faster than their own speech rate. Those whose reading rate is as slow as their speech rate are probably reading word by word. For these slow readers, learning to read for ideas is essential, if they are to improve rate in continuous reading.

The article "Brainstorming" is, in its entirety, approximately 800 words in length. The second version, on the facing page, has been adapted by deleting 350 words or 44 per cent of the article. Read the complete article first in your usual fashion. Time yourself for this reading. Then read the second version. Time yourself for this reading.

---

you use new ideas in   business?   have problems
which need   fresh, creative attack? If so,   interested in
"Brainstorming,"   group approach   creative solutions   management's problems.

discovery   brainstorming   Alex
F. Osborn   Batten, Barton, Durstine and Osborn advertising firm.
began using groups   employees
brainstorm   new product names   sales slogans.
practice   picked up   such companies   New York Telephone Co.   find answers   acute problem   personnel recruiting, and   Carborundum Co. which brainstormed   problem   better
use   equipment not employed   capacity.
ground rules   evolved   Mr. Osborn's experiences   sessions arranged   various business firms   several
university   centers. Those   brainstorm   idea
seated around a table.   group   composed   perhaps   dozen
persons   equal   rank.   members   entirely
drawn   lower levels or those   active   policy-making

leader proposes   rather specific   problem   be explored.
Criticism of ideas   withheld. Stress
getting   group   positive mood.   members   encouraged
offer whatever ideas come to   minds   bear upon   solution
"Free-wheeling" thinking   welcomed.   wilder

the better. It is easier to tame down than to think up. Quantity of ideas is most desirable under the belief that the greater the number of ideas, the more likelihood of good ones.

The ideas which come out of such a session may be organized or implemented in several ways. In some companies, the discussions are transcribed *in toto* and then turned over to a policymaking staff charged with final solution. In other firms, the group is supposed to keep thinking about the problem for 24 hours. The leader assumes the responsibility of calling each member of the brainstorming session for other ideas that have occurred meanwhile. The assumption here is that by letting an idea simmer in the back of the mind a while, creative solutions may suddenly appear. Still another method of handling the ideas gained from brainstorming is to have the creative panel reconsider their ideas judgmentally. They may attempt to organize and implement their own creative gropings in a subsequent planning session.

The rationale of these ground rules has been carefully established by repeated experiments and evaluations of sessions. These studies have shown that free associations are much more numerous in group activity than when working alone. Group sessions outproduce solitary attempts at creative thinking by the same persons by a wide margin. In fact, in the same amount of time, the average person can think up twice as many ideas when working with a group than when working alone.

The intrusion of judgment tends to inhibit the flow of ideas. Even implicit judgment such as is present when members of the group vary widely in rank or prestige has a negative effect upon productivity of the session. When ideation is unhampered by self-criticism or the judgments of others, the average person can produce at least 10 times as many ideas.

Just how productive are brainstorming sessions? Some have found that about six per cent of the ideas from a session were highly practical. Others, such as Edward F. Dorset, president of Christmas Club, are much more optimistic. He estimates that 90 per cent of his salesman's ideas can be used.

The ideas evolved in brainstorming sessions are often simple and apparently quite obvious. They are not always radical or esoteric solutions to the problem proposed. But one of the main values of the session is the fact that it does produce practical ideas that otherwise never would have been offered to management. Brainstorming brings to bear a great mass of possible solutions on any important problem chosen for thought.

Even those who are inclined to be critical of brainstorming admit that it may have tremendous values for situations other than their own. Several of the more progressive firms of management consultants such as John R. Martin Associates of New York, and Edward Glaser and

the better.   easier   tame down than   think up. Quantity
most desirable   greater   number   ideas, the
more   good ones.

ideas   of   session   organized
several ways.   some companies,   discussions   transcribed *in toto*   turned over   policymaking staff
final solution.   other firms,   keep thinking about
problem   24 hours.   leader   calling
each member   brainstorming session for other ideas   occurred meanwhile.   assumption   letting   idea simmer
back of   mind   solutions   suddenly appear.
another method   handling   ideas gained   brainstorming
have   creative panel reconsider   judgmentally.
attempt   organize   implement   creative gropings in   subsequent planning session.

rationale   ground rules   established by
experiments   evaluations of sessions.   studies
shown   free associations   more numerous   group activity
than   working alone. Group sessions outproduce solitary attempts
creative thinking   same persons   wide margin.
same amount   time, the average person   think   twice as many
ideas   working with   group than   alone.
intrusion of judgment   inhibit   flow   ideas. Even
judgment   present when   group vary
widely   rank   prestige   negative effect upon productivity
When ideation   unhampered   self-criticism or   judgments
of others,   average person   produce   10 times   ideas.
how productive   brainstorming   ? Some   found
about six per cent   ideas   highly practical.
Others, such as Edward F. Dorset, president   Christmas Club,
more optimistic.   estimates   90 per cent   salesman's ideas
be used.
ideas evolved   brainstorming   often simple   apparently   obvious.   not always radical   esoteric solutions
to   problem   one   main values   is
fact   produce practical ideas   otherwise never
offered to management. Brainstorming brings   great mass
possible solutions   any   problem chosen
Even those   critical of brainstorming admit
tremendous values   situations other than
own. Several   more progressive firms   management consultants
as John R. Martin Associates   New York,   Edward Glaser and

Associates of Pasadena are playing an active part in bringing brainstorming to the notice of their clients. The psychological training of these particular consultants has enabled them to adapt the basic principles of this group creative approach to varying situations. They have helped various firms to overcome the problems of suppressing criticism, of releasing the inhibitions of younger officers so that they may operate more creatively, and the integration of brainstorming procedures with planned programs of problem analysis now used by many businesses.

LEARNING TO READ FOR IDEAS

Did you read the phrased version more rapidly than the original? Were you able to think along with the author? Did you realize that all the ideas were present despite the omission of many words? Now do you see what we mean by reading for ideas? This is the way the rapid, comprehending reader performs. If he misses a point, he may reread a few words or a sentence a bit more slowly, as perhaps you did in trying the second article. But then he moves rapidly along from one phrase to the next, from one idea to the next.

If your habits of reading are not too set or your reading pattern too rigid, you achieved a feel for rapid reading in trying this single article. If you didn't get this feeling from the one article, you probably will after trying the others. You will realize that it isn't necessary to read every word, any more than you think out every word in a sentence before you say it. Reading is a flowing of ideas, a meeting of minds of the author and reader, just like conversation. Some slow readers are a bit disturbed by the fragmentary arrangement, a word here, a phrase there. But this is the way we think, not word by word as some of us read. This also is the way we converse. We talk out our ideas, not in exact, complete sentences but in fragments, in spurts. If we are in harmony with our listener, sometimes it isn't even necessary to express a complete idea. He senses our meaning before we are finished because he thinks along with or even ahead of us. This same kind of harmony of thinking must accompany the act of reading. If it doesn't, as in word-by-word reading, the reader loses his place, or must reread for ideas, or achieves little real comprehension.

Some of you may be upset by a feeling that you are not achiev-

Associates   Pasadena   playing   active part   bringing brainstorming to   clients.   psychological training   these
   consultants   enabled them   adapt   basic principles
group creative approach   varying situations.   helped various
firms   overcome   problems of suppressing criticism,   releasing
inhibitions   younger officers
and   integration   brainstorming   with planned programs
   problem analysis   used   many businesses.

---

ing any comprehension in this kind of reading. You will discover that this is not true, for you will show reasonable retention in the questions appended to subsequent articles. This feeling of insecurity, of being unsure of understanding, is a common experience in the change-over to rapid reading. It soon disappears. There are several probable reasons for this feeling. If you have been a slow reader, you are now reading faster than you are accustomed to. You are forcing yourself to assimilate ideas faster than previously, and this is a disturbing experience. Part of this feeling of insecurity is also due to the fact that you may have read slowly because of cautiousness. Reading faster is dangerous to comprehension, you feel subconsciously. You may be assured, however, that these feelings are mistaken. First of all, if you are of at least average intelligence and are a slow reader, you can probably read or assimilate ideas faster than you are now doing it. You can learn to read for ideas and consequently read faster because you can think faster than you are now reading. In other words, reading for ideas merely helps you to read at a speed closer to your actual capacity, your speed of thinking.

Secondly, in fairly simple, continuous material faster reading is accompanied by better comprehension. Because you read and assimilate ideas rather than words, you understand and retain more. You will comprehend better at a reading speed that is in keeping with your ability to absorb ideas than you would at a word-by-word rate. There are limits, of course, to this fact. Rapid reading of highly detailed or technical materials is not conducive to a high degree of comprehension. Unless such material is quite familiar, the ideas are too numerous or too complex to be assimilated rapidly. Therefore, your rate must be adjusted to the difficulty you experience in reading each piece or type of reading matter. But in reading simple, general materials you will secure better comprehension if you read fairly rapidly in an effort to absorb ideas.

Some of you, particularly the lawyers, mathematicians, accountants, and engineers, are disturbed by the absence of some words. The need for the careful, detailed reading common to these occupations often results in a rather rigid habit of slow reading. But even the slow reading ingrained by vocational demands can be overcome, at least in those situations where very careful reading is not essential. With a determined effort, most slow readers can achieve greater speed in general reading matter.

Try the next three articles arranged for reading for ideas. Keep moving along; don't try to guess the words that are omitted. Keep thinking along. Try not to reread even when a sentence does not seem to make sense.

Time your reading of each article. Expect your speed to be greater than that achieved in the reading tests you took earlier. Don't be concerned about your comprehension. If it doesn't reach 70 per cent at first, it will later.

What I See for 1956 and Beyond [1]

by Roger Ward Babson

Eighty years young and one of America's foremost economists, Roger Ward Babson has been described as a Yankee genius who confesses having "made more money out of statistics than anyone else in the United States." He pioneered the field of investment guidance, accurately predicted the 1929 stock-market crash, and became a millionaire several times over.

Even as the young but ambitious son of a prosperous merchant in Gloucester, Mass., he preferred peddling vegetables to playing. When tuberculosis struck Babson as a young man, he moved his budding business into a frame lean-to, kept all the windows open, and worked in a woolen coverall, striking the typewriter keys with rubber mallets.

With his wife, the indomitable Yankee went on to found Babson's Reports and the non-profit Babson Institute in Wellesley, Mass. These organizations preach their founders' view that prosperity inevitably gives way to depression, that patience is the key in both

[1] Roger Ward Babson, "What I See for 1956 and Beyond," *Family Weekly*, January 1, 1956, pp. 4-5. Adapted. Used by permission.

financial and family affairs, and that there is no substitute for thrift. Indeed, one of Babson's books is entitled "Twenty Ways to Save Money."

The accompanying article presents Babson's outlook on America's economic situation; but he maintains extraordinary interests in other subjects, too. For example, he founded the Gravity Research Foundation at New Boston, N. H., in the belief that gravity can be overcome and its power harnessed in public utilities.

Not only America,   world,   brink   glorious new era.
    believe   entering   third   great   Renaissance   comparable
        15th Century,   brought about by printing, and
18th Century,   harnessing   steam and   industrial revolution.

    Now   entering third great industrial revolution.   based
on   harnessing   atomic energy,   development   labor unions,
    aviation.   years ahead may make   last century look like
    Dark Ages!
    This   long-range outlook.   for   years immediately ahead,
    believe   Isaac Newton's law of action and reaction,   law by
which I have been making economic analyses   forecasts   more than
half century.

    means   America   normal line   growth   any artifi-
cial prosperity,   inflation   otherwise, must sometime be compen-
sated for. I see no economic crash on   horizon today,   , as
did   1929.

    forecasting   stock market,   mistake   attempt   pick
winners.   future course   different industries   foretold   reasonable accuracy, but   difficult   determine   advance
which companies   that industry   most successful.   wise,
    ,   diversify funds over   broad list   good stocks.

FORESEES A BALANCED BUDGET

    believe defense spending   remain stable   Federal budget
    balance this year.   incomes   savings   increase due to
higher wages, greater consumer spending,   higher exports.
    price level   continue much as   is;   ,   dollar may
    get cheaper. "Good times" should continue   we avoid World War
III,   I believe   war is coming—if not   five years, then
    in 25 or 50.

During World War II, comparatively few babies   born
United States.   not normal number   teen-agers purchasing
goods at present. Over   next five years,   , this situation should
change   real bulge in   purchasing power   1960.

It seems   both Republicans   Democrats   determined
keep business humming   until after   November election.
     do this   promising large expenditures   new roads, urban
development,   removal   more controls.

In addition, many   inventions, processes,   products   come
on   market this year. Other   surprises   American consumer   on drawing boards   in test tubes.   ,   we will
have   economic collapse some day,   cannot see it   present
time.

     ,   next depression   not   brought on by stock-market
speculation.   come as   results of   building collapse cou-
pled   exorbitant demands by union   . Still, I do not object
labor troubles—   sign   growth.   ,   not want to
live in   country   did not have some labor troubles.

IS BUILDING BOOM AT ITS HEIGHT?

     present boom   building   small homes may be at   height.
Too many families   buying   houses   only   few hundred dollars down,   promised payments over   long period. When unemployment increases—   it will some day—houses bought on   shoestring
     come back onto   market.   young people   go   live
with   parents,   vice versa.

     ,   business will go along   as   is   next few
months. After   election—whichever party   successful—business might   decline   could suffer   real depression
two   three years.   those who   patient   keep out of debt
come through depression.

Although   statistician, I   learned   world   ruled
not by figures but   feelings.   greatest things   simplest
things,   most powerful things   most tender.   greatest
force   love   the   real security   hard work, self-denial,
courage.

     , nothings warps   judgment as   worry   fear for
future. Faith, hope,   serenity provide   ground   which
progress   security develop.

     progress   security   this country depend on   children
of   middle class.   wish   parents   spend more time

money   training   children   less   trying   to   accumulate
    inheritance for them. Children   not need   inherit money so
much   have   attention   parents while   young.
    character standard   more important than   gold standard.
    success   economic systems   dependent upon   righteous
leaders   righteous people.   ,   national character—
, whether   spiritually   materially minded.
    days to come, America will need more   spiritual crea-
tive power   causes men   pull the cart instead of ride   —
to work, think,   build instead   depending on interest, pensions,
    government aid.

1. Advances in aviation will see further development of jet planes and even research into rocket flight.

2. This nuclear power plant is not a fantastic dream but is scheduled to be built and operating by 1960.

3. Abundant harvests indicate a prosperity that will continue into the new year and many years to come.

4. Atomic energy will find many new uses in the nation's laboratories, industrial plants, and hospitals.

5. New inventions will roll off the drawing boards, and into production to delight the U.S. consumer.

6. Defense spending is likely to remain at its present levels; there is no danger of a big war in 1956.

7. Production will continue to set a new record; no major depression is foreseen for the immediate future.

Questions on "What I See for 1956 and Beyond"

1. According to Babson, what will cause the next economic depression?
   a. Stock market speculation
   b. Unbalanced federal budget and excessive federal expenditures
   c. Building boom collapse and exorbitant union demands
   d. A bankrupting war

2. When does Babson think another major depression will come?
   a. He does not foresee one.
   b. One will come in the relatively near future.

    c. Certainly one will come, but not in the foreseeable future.

    d. One may not be expected to come for a great many years.

3. Why does Babson think that the housing boom will not continue in an upward spiral?

    a. The boom has already created enough housing for potential buyers.

    b. Too easy initial financing will cause many homes to come back onto the market during any economic slump.

    c. Young men are coming more and more to bring their brides to their parent's homes.

    d. The price of homes is rising too high for the average earner.

4. What does Babson feel is the strongest basis for the future economic stability of the nation?

    a. An emotionally stable and morally trained and educated middle class

    b. A stabilized economy grounded in sound economic principles

    c. A society from which friction between management and labor will have disappeared

    d. The technological processes of our inventive genius

5. Which type of stock-buying would seem best, according to Babson?

    a. Investment in a particular company

    b. Investment in a particular industry

    c. Investment over a broad listing of stocks

    d. Buying outright rather than on margin

6. On what basis does Babson make his assumption of an eventual depression?

    a. Deviation from normal line economic growth must be compensated for.

    b. Growth in population guarantees a growth in production of goods and services.

    c. Innovation and invention will produce long-range high productivity.

    d. Harmony between labor and management guarantees a long-range economic stability.

7. Regarding World War III, Babson predicts that it:

    a. will not come in our generation.

    b. is coming but he does not predict when.

    c. will come in a relatively short time.

    d. most certainly will not come for another hundred years.

Key: 1. c   2. c   3. b   4. a   5. c   6. a   7. b.

The article you have just read was 1000 words in length as abridged. If you divide your reading time into 1000 you will find your rate in words per minute. This figure may be compared with your speed in the earlier selections. Increase in rate is one of the primary indications that you are securing a feel for reading for ideas. Of course, your rate in each successive trial in this spaced material will not necessarily be higher than the last. You may not show constant increase if one of the selections proves rather difficult for you. Progress in learning a new habit does not always show constant increment. You are more likely to experience regressions in your rate growth from time to time, although the over-all picture will be one of gradual gain.

Comprehension may vary similarly from one article to the next. Such factors as the number of questions to be answered, the familiarity of the content, as well as the ease with which you are learning to read more rapidly influence your comprehension. Don't be concerned if your per cent of comprehension varies. As you become more adept in reading for ideas, it will eventually settle down to a reasonable figure. As a general guide, it may be suggested that if your comprehension falls much below 70 per cent, you were probably reading too fast for this particular material. On the other hand, if comprehension is well above 70 per cent, you probably could have read somewhat more rapidly.

Read the next article, trying to get the feeling of reading for ideas. Remember to keep moving along from one idea to the next. Do not try to supply the words that are omitted. Gather your ideas from the words and phrases present. Keep trying for the feeling of thinking along with the writer. Record the time it takes you to read the article.

Advertising [2]

Advertising   miracle worker of   age.   big factor
building business.   major role   development
nation, promoting   high standard   living   making possible mass production   ,   lower prices.   stabilized employment   creating   all-year-round   demand   products, such
canned soup,   which once   highly seasonal.   adver-
tising   small   business   large   industry   very   different
things.   important   bear in mind what advertising can do, how
used effectively   limits   expected of it.

Everyone who sells   commodity   service advertises   —
even those   small businesses who never buy space   newspapers,
time on   radio or circulars   through   mail or   placed
doorstep.   "non-advertiser" gets   advertising through
talk   satisfied customers   friends, through   favorable contacts
others,   appearance   of business,   unselfish service
community   other things   cause people   like him
deal with him.

several basic factors   businessman, particularly   "small" businessman,   bear in mind about advertising:

Advertising   more than   effective ad writing   clever
sales talk.

advertising   best   some types business   not   right
others.

Money   wasted   advertising by failing   have   information   potential customers,   lack   experience   judgment,
spending   high   proportion   gross income and   other
ways.

finally,   purpose   advertising   to sell   help sell. Advertising which doesn't   , directly   indirectly,   be avoided.

retailer,   must wait   customers   come to
store, needs advertising more than   wholesaler   manufacturer
who sometimes   depend   on salesman.   not   fooled
by   "If   man makes   best mousetrap,   world   beat
path to   door." It won't.   world   go   door   hears
about   one   conveniently located   buy   second-best
mousetrap.

---

[2] "Advertising," *Your Business,* Albany: Department of Commerce, State
of New York, 1950, pp. 85-94. Adapted. Used by permission.

HONESTY IN ADVERTISING

retailer's advertising,   designed   to get,
to keep customers. False "sucker-bait" advertising   avoided. It is
expensive. A customer   discovers   "taken in" becomes
enemy. Better   one customer   come back than ten   come
once   advise others   stay away.

CUSTOMER CONTROL

businessman should never cease   "survey"   study
customers. Neighborhoods   . Customers' habits change. If
customer   drifted away,   try at once   learn why. Perhaps
misunderstanding   can rectify.   he or   employee
given offense,   correct before other customers   lost. If
beginning   get customers   adjoining neighborhood beyond
what   logical area,   find out why,   use reason in
advertising   same area. What attracts one   sell
customer's neighbors.   name for   practice of studying customers   "customer control";   customers can be controlled.

MAIL ADVERTISING

Mail advertising   rifle, not shotgun shooting.   various
ways   used effectively,   specific thing to   interest
specific people. Among   ways   mail advertising   en-
closures   go with   bill (don't send bills alone; make   stamp do
full job), telling regular customers   sales ahead   time (they appreciate   chance   make   choices before everyone hears of   sale),
announcing   new service or product (sometimes   manufacturer
distributors   help pay   ), sending circulars   self-mailing
folders   bulk mailing rates.

Advocates   mail advertising   call it "direct mail advertising"   point out   ,   , it   takes   message direct to
prospect.   does if list   carefully studied   chosen.   garage,   limit   list to   automobile owners,   limited area.   might limit   list   owners   certain makes
best equipped to serve, or for   service   not too much competition. Suppose,   ,   no dealers in town for certain cars   ,
presumably, inadequate service.   garage   makes   bid to owners   strong appeal in showing itself   prepared to do
job   their cars.

When   anyone   respond   to   appeal,
"mass"   medium   one   use.   newspaper, radio   bill-
boards   mass media.

USING NEWSPAPER SPACE

        use   newspaper,   store   located   convenient
    people   entire area covered by   newspaper's circulation
have   a   product   service   with appeal   .   , while a
downtown store   use newspaper advertising,   small store
    draws customers   few blocks around   cannot   with-
out paying too much for   benefit   receiving.   downtown
store,   department store,   finds,   ,   newspaper
ads   cheapest   most effective medium. Sometimes small neighborhood weeklies   good results   neighborhood stores.
retail stores,   food dealers, Thursday   Friday evenings   considered   best   days   Friday   Saturday   shopping days.
Real estate dealers   Sunday papers, Sunday   day people
    look   property   houses   daylight.

CAR CARDS

        effective way   reaching   customers   potential customers
    your   market   area—neighborhood   section   city—without
paying   more   than can benefit   use cards in   buses
    street cars.   retailer   buy   display in   lines
serving   own neighborhood—or   market area, if   extends
beyond   single neighborhood.   transportation lines   ,   ,
laid out   serve   people   various sections   town   city,
    buying only   lines serving his area   possible   retailer
confine   advertising   to   own customers   potential customers.

DOOR TO DOOR METHODS

Handbills, business cards, circulars   "throw aways"   effective,   announcements   openings or sales.   ,
should be used smartly   pitfalls   avoided. Responsible distributors   used   avoid placing them   litter premises
    irritate possible customers.   unlawful   put circulars
home mail boxes. Some communities   ordinances forbidding
distribution handbills.

RADIO ADVERTISING

Radio, like   newspaper,   mass medium. Of   homes, 95 per cent   one   more receivers,   set-in-use   average 18 per cent   daytime   28 per cent   evening. Competition   listeners   intense,   radio advertiser's problem   reach   audience   wants.   requires careful selection   type   content   program   announcements, placement best available time   ,   frequent   continued   repetition. Sponsors   buy complete programs or   spot announcements. Obviously,   program   more expensive   , repeated at regular weekly   daily time,   build   faithful audience.   , spot announcements,   comparatively inexpensive   attract attention by   insertion between programs   catch   "carry-over"audience   one program   another,   audience tuning receivers listen   program which follows.

Catching   holding   attention   audience requires careful program planning;   requires placing   program announcement at   desirable time   reach   audience.   , during   day   women   children do most of   listening,   night time audience   fairly equally divided   men   women.   gear   time   material to   classes   customers you serve.

Frequency   repetition   essential   successful radio advertising.   minimum   13 weeks   recommended   radio campaign, even spot announcements. Usually in that time   only begun attract attention.   , once attention   caught, radio highly effective   selling   a minimum cost per listener.

Questions on "Advertising"

1. Select several essentials of successful advertising for the small businessman.

   a. Honest rather than "sucker-bait" ads
   b. Constant study of customers
   c. Cleverly written sales copy
   d. Wide mail advertising
   e. Adequate use of mass media

2. Choose several of the media of particular value to the small retail shop or plant.

a. Selected mail advertising
b. City newspapers
c. Car cards
d. Radio and television
e. Small neighborhood weeklies

3. What are some of the common mistakes in the advertising program of the small businessman? (Choose as many as you need.)

a. Spending an insufficient amount of money
b. Failure to pinpoint advertising on potential customers
c. Inadequate customer control
d. Inappropriate use of such media as newspapers, radio
e. Faith in quality of product rather than aggressive advertising

Key: 1. a, b, e   2. a, c, e   3. b, c, d.

This article as abridged was 1400 words in length. Determine your rate by dividing the reading time into this figure. If, by this time, you are feeling more secure in reading for ideas, try this more rapid reading in materials of your own choice. Select relatively simple materials from popular magazines and general literary sources. Time each effort, and record your rate. Don't be too concerned about comprehension. You are not trying to read for fine details but merely for general impressions. Check yourself if you desire by attempting to summarize the main ideas of each selection.

Obviously, we cannot supply an unlimited supply of articles arranged to promote reading for ideas. If you are to learn to read fluently in recreational and nontechnical materials, constant effort on your part will be necessary. Learning to read more rapidly is not acquired in a few attempts. The flexibility necessary to using different rates of reading does not suddenly appear.

Keep trying to read for ideas in your own reading materials. Let your thinking flow along with that of the author. Remember you are trying to understand his ideas, not read the words he uses to express these ideas. Keep in mind that reading is a thinking process, not a matter of word recognition.

Read the last selection arranged to promote reading for ideas. As we have abridged it, it is 3100 words in length.

Executive's Wife [3]

by Martin Scott

Nowadays more and more firms, considering a man for a job, first conduct a subtle "wife inspection" to find out everything from how much she drinks to whether she overdresses or leaves dirty dishes in the sink.

A few years ago   , strapless dress cost   bright young man important promotion.   man—   Ted Durant—   in line   job   traffic manager,   on a level   company's top brass. His bosses wanted him to have   job.

Then came   company picnic. Durant's wife,   , wore   strapless dress.   not   revealing dress, but not   conservative as   bosses' wives   wearing. There was talk. Later on   more talk.   , Durant was bypassed,   traffic manager's post went to another man.

AN INCIDENT CAN BE MAGNIFIED

vice-president tried to explain it to Durant. He said: "   some outfits, such   incident   never happen.   here, where we're small, and   company prestige means   much in   community,   incident   magnified out of   proportion.   executives' wives get   talking.   decide one wife   'fast,'   lacks good taste,   does not make   public impression   ought   . , wives begin working on   husbands. Next   husbands , listening."

facts   this story   files   New York consulting firm   specializes   locating executives   large   corporations. points up a truth   is becoming   self-evident: man's wife   important part in a man's progress in   job.   concept applies not only to certain kinds   companies. applies to many types   organizations   widely scattered sections . Ted Durant's case   no means exceptional.   is true wife   bigger factor   small company   small community,   people   together socially more often than   worked

[3] Martin Scott, "Executive's Wife," *Cosmopolitan,* Vol. 139, No. 3 (September, 1955), pp. 46-49. Adapted. Reprinted by permission of Cosmopolitan Magazine.

in   metropolitan area. But even   some large firms in   biggest
cities,   man   approved   if   wife   approved.

A BRACELET SPOILED HIS CHANCE

wife   factor   in nearly every case   says
Benjamin Webster,   Ashton Dunn Associates, executive-locaters
wide variety   concerns.

"Many   companies for which we   find executives," Webster continues, "   insist upon meeting   wives of candidates
."

Webster and other executive recruiters   tell tale after tale in which
conduct   appearance of   wife   kept   husband from
job   which he   eminently suited.

,   ,   case   Jack Bristol,   considered for
production job   large chemical company. Bristol's wife   ,
, "an exotic creature."   poised   perfect manners,
she did have   penchant for wearing large quantities junk jewelry.
made   mistake   wearing   especially   gaudy   bracelet
night she and   husband went to meet prospective employer and wife.

employer's wife   picture of graciousness.   appeared
delighted   have   Bristols in   home.   , near   end
evening, she leaned toward Mrs. Bristol and inquired sweetly, "My dear,
wherever did you get that odd bracelet?"

Webster, who was present, later said, "I knew   Bristol wasn't
going to get   job. Just on   basis of   jewelry,   employer's
wife   formed   opinion."

Webster's hunch   confirmed.   chemical company
executive called   Webster

. He said Bristol was   nice enough fellow, but   wasn't
sure   he would work out.

In another instance,   highly successful electronics engineer
being considered for $50,000-a-year job   invited, with   wife,
for tea   home   company president.   politics   introduced.   engineer's wife expressed   views, quietly enough, but
more firmly than   occasion demanded.

distinct chill descended   .   several awkward
pauses until   engineer and   wife departed.   following week
engineer learned   services no longer sought   .

sometimes   happened   even   man   rare skills
abilities   queered by   wife. Peggy Zimmerman, who works for

another New York executive-recruiting firm,   spent
three months   search   man   take charge   ceramics
research laboratory   . Mrs. Zimmerman began with   list
two thousand prospects   narrowed it   to five.

man who looked like   best bet lived in Ohio. Preliminary
interviews indicated   ideally suited for   job. Moreover, he was
interested   ,   looking forward to making   change.

representative   went to call upon   man's wife in
her home. "   place   dirty," Mrs. Zimmerman says, "   day-old
dishes in   sink.   thirteen-year-old daughter used too much make-up,
and   mother didn't seem bothered by it.   ,   wife sat gossip-
ing about   neighbors."

,   .   husband did not get   job.

picture has   brighter side,   .   not uncommon
wives   help   husbands   getting jobs. Mrs. Zimmerman—
, most people in   executive-recruiting business—   recall
many times   husband   failed if   wife   not made good
impression on   boss-to-be.

SHE CAN "SELL" HER HUSBAND

,   young mathematician   up for post   com-
mand   computing laboratory   drug-manufacturing   firm. While
meeting   future employer   pleasant   articulate enough, but
personality   far from scintillating.   answered   questions
asked   said little else. His wife,   ,   vivacious
friendly. Without being   forward,   managed   communicate
to   employer that   husband   special   man   all sorts
latent abilities.
,   husband   given   opportunity.
Later   employer said to Mrs. Zimmerman, "   glad to get
Bowman on   team,   thank you for finding him   .
! Isn't that wife of his something!"

AN IMPRESSION OF WORTH

Personnel directors   corporations   executive recruiters,
, generally   agreed that   wife need not be as active in
interview, or afterward when   husband has   job, as   mathematician's   .   equally effective   passive role.
giving   impression   "worth and stability,"   assist in large measure. In 1951–52 William H. Whyte, Jr., and   editors of Fortune

survey   wives   material   chapter in Whyte's book, *Is Anybody Listening?* (Simon and Schuster, New York, 1952). found   corporation wife though   herself   "stabilizer"— "   keeper of   retreat,   rests   rejuvenates   man for next day's battles."

,   Mrs. Dorothy Carnegie, wife   "how-to-win-friends" man, holds   wife   active as possible. Mrs. Carnegie conceives   wife   dynamo in   home,   sparking   husband   newer   greater   triumphs, urging   onward— ,   , giving him   little rest.   written   book   illustrate   thesis, *How to Help Your Husband Get Ahead* (The Greystone Press, New York, 1953),   contains ten sets   rules   wife   apply   make herself   asset to   husband. Mrs. Carnegie's book   selling steadily since publication,   indicate   wives   becoming   conscious of   power   in their position.

          oddest thing about   emergence of   wife is   attitude of   companies that   literally led   out of   home   into factory; few companies   willing to admit   situation   exists. Some   say   exist to   degree, but   reluctantly, as   bald man admits   hair   getting   little thin on top.

          degrees vary according to   company.   personnel executive   International Business Machines Corporation   , "Yes, we like to meet a man's wife before we make up our minds about him."

, H. Frederick Willkie, when   director   Seagram's Distillery,   choose   young executives in part by   stability of   homes.

J. J. Evans, Jr.,   personnel director   Armstrong Cork Company,   not   policy   interviewing wives   young men approach   company   , but   said   "   skillful assistance" of   wife could make   difference between   man's succeeding or failing, once   hired. Evans   mention more than one instance   presence   wife during   crucial interview helped   hire husband.

SHE IS CAREFULLY SIZED UP

Alex Wertis, personnel manager   U. S. Steel Export,   never interviews   wife   with   husband. "But," he adds, "   requires five   six years   man   developed   consider sending him overseas,   during that time   size up   wife   carefully   ."   pamphlet   "So You Want an Assignment Overseas," Wertis listed requisites   success   looks for in young men.   with

"Adaptability," "Resourcefulness," "Personality," "Patience," "Languages,"   ,   section headed "Domestic Compatibility."
says, in part: "wife   anxious   overseas life as   husband. All . . . requisites apply to her as   him.   wife
unhappy . . .   make   husband unhappy.   wife   happy is
boon.   make friends easily.   willing, capable
charming hostess.   real interest in   life of   country in
which   living."

In   recent past, several corporations, while pretending no interest
in   man's home life,   placed such emphasis upon   wife
private investigating agency   look into   background   character. Not long ago   investigator   downtown New York detective
agency traveled   to Buffalo, New York, to check   on
spouse of   man   being considered   job   synthetic rubber plant in   South.   investigator had   list   questions about
wife   rubber company personnel director wanted answered.
included   :

What is her family background?

Where did she go to school?

Was she ever active in any radical political movements?

What are her politics?

Describe the interior of her house and tell what kind of a housekeeper
she is.

What do her neighbors think of her?

What do her close friends think of her?

Is she courteous to tradesmen?

Have she and her husband ever been heard to quarrel?

Does she take an active part in the community activities, such as
Community Chest, Girl Scouts, etc.?

If not, how does she spend her leisure time?

Is she considered an asset to her husband?

Sometimes even this   overcautious inquiry   not satisfy
employer.   some situations,   ,   wives   asked to
take psychological tests before being admitted   company "family"!

As yet   hard to tell what,   ,   new role of   wife
means in terms of   society.   may be one more symptom   of
widespread desire   conformity which,   , has gripped   large
segment of   population.   Benjamin Webster, who, while admitting

that he must inspect   wife before attempting to place   husband
,   deplores   necessity for doing it.
"   wife inspection seems   taking   character   individual flavor out of people," Webster says. "We inspect   wife
make sure she   fit in nicely in   world as   defined by
husband's job. This world often   narrowly restricted one,   ul-
traconventional rules that reduce   people   uniform parts of
machinery   difficult   individualist   exist happily."

IS IT A HEALTHY SIGN?

optimistic view holds   emphasis on   wife is   ac-
knowledgement,   , of   real   position and   worth.
wife's recognition of herself as   vital force in   husband's working
life   sense of participation,   feel   like   partner
less like   second-class citizen. Wife inspection, according to this view,
harbinger of   more wholesome relationship between   sexes.
,   unquestionably here to stay. Wife inspection
now so firmly entrenched in   unwritten policies   most companies
that   possible to formulate series   rules   propositions   , if
practiced by   company wife,   make her   important asset to
husband. Some of   postulates,   practiced with tact and dis-
cretion,   make   possible   aid   her husband's advancement.
, the rules   not miraculous. None   infallible key to
success.   simply follow   dictates of good taste   common
sense,   can   serve as   check-list for   conscientious woman.
Both when being interviewed, and after she has been accepted into
the "family," a wife ought to:

1. Dress simply   neatly, avoiding "trick" clothes or jewelry or
accessories—apparel that might not be acceptable in most situations and
localities.   sparing in   make-up.

2. Answer all questions politely and fully,   not in exaggerated
detail. Volunteer only   information   pertinent,   ask only
questions   need answering immediately. ("   ask about
diaper service after   moved into   new community!")

3. Keep   strong opinions—   politics, current events, art, music
literature,   housekeeping   child-raising—to herself.
plenty of time   self-expression after   found out   husband's boss and   wife   social set stand.

4. Avoid discussing   personal interests at great length. (
wife might be   able   enthusiastic mother,   ,   interview
is seldom   place to introduce bright sayings   charming anecdotes
about   little ones.)

5. Communicate   sincere interest in   husband's career and
desire to see him get ahead.

6. Show interest in   community in which she and   husband
be living. If   community   same—that is, if   husband
      promoted to   better job in   company—   wife ought to
indicate   interest in taking a more active part in community activities.
("Wives   public   relations experts in   city," brush manufacturer says. "We like   wives   work in   fund-raising drives
      serve on civic committees.")

7. Show   willingness   adapt   new conditions.

GROWTH IS ESSENTIAL

8. Indicate, without breaking   first three rules,   she has
"grown" with   husband   become   considerable person herself.
("Too often," says Benjamin Webster, "while   husband   out
growing   expanding in   personality,   wife   at home,
      ,   remains   same little girl   when   got married.
wife ought   attempt   grow apace with   husband.")

9. Avoid apologies.   applies mainly when   wife   husband   interviewed at home,   . ("A smart woman never
apologizes for anything," Webster says, "Once   took   couple
partners   law firm ·to   home   young fellow   scouting
partnership material.   late in   afternoon,   husband,
partners, and I arrived without   alerting   wife. She served
cocktails   got   some hors d'oeuvres. Everything   fine until
she said   one of   men I'd brought, 'If I'd known   having
party,   would have had   hair done.' Nobody had noticed   hair
. By apologizing,   called attention to it.")

10. Show   she likes people   put them at ease without making a fuss   .

11. Demonstrate   realization that   husband's work sometimes
      come first. ("In many cases, wives aren't willing   sacrifice," says
Webster. "   ought sometimes   show   understanding   hus-

band's problems in   job,   willingness   submit to   requirements of   job.")

12. Avoid excessive drinking.

13. Stay out of   office, but   friendly on telephone with
husband's secretary   female assistants.

14. Avoid   "shoptalk"   passing   company gossip.

15.   final rule   most important of all. Many,   jobs
promotions   lost because wives   too eager   impress,   put
on   act of some kind,   pretended   social position   did
not possess. Personnel directors, executive recruiters,   all people connected   wife inspection say   most dangerous thing a woman
do   attempt   be something she isn't.

    final rule   so important   many   others be violated,
provided it is observed.   very simple.   : *Relax   be yourself.*

Questions on "Executive's Wife"

1. In what kind of environment is the behavior of the executive's
   wife most important?

   a. In the small company and small community.
   b. In the large company in a small community.
   c. In the large company in a metropolitan area.
   d. The size of the company and community doesn't make any
      difference.

2. One is led to believe that the wife who is admitted to the interview session:

   a. should usually take an active part.
   b. should try to create an impression of quiet belief in her hus-
      band.
   c. should make it a point to brag about her husband.
   d. should, in most instances, take the dominant role.

3. Benjamin Webster, executive-locator for a variety of concerns,
   says that he deplores the trend toward inspection. Why does he
   say this?

   a. He feels that it robs the wife of her individuality.
   b. It makes his job all the more difficult.

   c. It eliminates many otherwise eligible young men.

   d. It makes husbands critical and demanding of their wives.

4. What is one positive value of wife inspection?

   a. It emphasizes the value of conformity of the wife to the husband.

   b. It emphasizes the help that the wife can be to her husband.

   c. It emphasizes the responsibility of the wife to her husband.

   d. It emphasizes the value of compatibility between a wife and husband.

5. What is the most important rule for a wife to remember when she is admitted to an interview along with her husband?

   a. Demonstrate an understanding of the importance of her husband's job

   b. Be herself

   c. Demonstrate that she has grown to be a considerable person herself

   d. Demonstrate her poise and ability in a group situation

6. What are some of the general characteristics of the wife that influence the attitude of her husband's employer?

   a. Dress, efficiency as mother and housekeeper

   b. Adaptability, compatibility with husband

   c. Looks, education

   d. Knowledge of business conditions through personal experience

Key: 1. a   2. b   3. a   4. d   5. b   6. a, b.

HOW TO CONTINUE READING FOR IDEAS

This is the last of the articles we have prepared for your practice in reading for ideas. The rest is up to you. If you will continue to try to read in this fashion, in appropriately simple materials, you will undoubtedly increase your rate in general materials.

As you have already realized, the difference between reading for ideas and word-by-word reading is more than simply the rate achieved. Reading is basically a thinking process with author and reader following parallel lines of thought. In our reading for ideas, we have tried to help you achieve the same degree of fluency you have in speaking and listening. If you can succeed in securing this habit, there is no reason why you cannot read as fast as you think, and much faster than you can speak. Theoretically, you can learn to read as fast as you can form associations between the author's concepts and your own experiences. Since you can probably now think at the rate of 500-600 words a minute, you will eventually be able to read uncomplicated continuous material at this rate. Furthermore, if you employ previewing and skimming intelligently, you can achieve even much greater rates.

These potential reading speeds are limited only by your reading background and experiences and your speed of association. In time, you can expect to be able to read at rates varying from a hundred words a minute or less to those in the thousands, depending upon the familiarity and simplicity of the material being read and the particular reading techniques you employ. Our records show individuals who have achieved skimming rates as high as 8000-10,000 words per minute with 80 to 100 per cent comprehension. What you will achieve is dependent largely upon the amount of effort you make and the development of skill in utilizing reading techniques and rates discriminatively. Most significant of all, you will enjoy reading more and begin to find the time for the reading you would like to do for recreational and cultural purposes.

Here are about a dozen articles and books that deal with the topics of the articles used in this chapter. You may find them interesting reading.

Arnold, T., "Depression: not in your lifetime," *Collier's,* Vol. 131, April 25, 1953, p. 24.

Cherne, L., "Your life ten years from today," *Vital Speeches,* Vol 22, February 1, 1956, pp. 252-254.

Hirsch, Julius, editor, *New Horizons in Business.* New York: Harper, 1956.

Lapp, C. L., "Key to success, your wife," *Life Insurance Courant,* Vol. 60, December 1955, p. 33.

Miller, H. H., "Ambassadors of good will or ill, government wives abroad," *New York Times Magazine,* February 19, 1956, p. 26.

Milner, R. E. D., "Before I hire your husband I want to meet you," *Good Housekeeping,* Vol. 142, January 1955, pp. 52-53.

National Bureau of Economic Research, *Short-term Economic Forecasting*. Princeton University Press, 1955.

Rappard, W. E., *The Secret of American Prosperity*. New York: Greenberg, 1955.

Suits, C. G., "Heed that hunch," *American,* December 1945, p. 45.

Whiting, C. S., "To make admen more creative, idea clinics, classes in brainstorming," *Printers Ink,* Vol. 253, December 9, 1955, pp. 23-25.

"World in twenty-five years: how the U.S. economy will reach around it," *Business Week,* October 31, 1953, pp. 96-102; November 28, 1953, p. 8.

6

Scanning—Reading to Find Specific Facts

What You Will Do
   Try scanning—another rapid reading technique

What You Will Learn
   How to collect facts and answer specific questions

This chapter will introduce you to a fourth rapid reading technique—scanning. Scanning means looking very rapidly over a paragraph or larger piece of reading matter to find the answer to a question you have in mind. There are many reading situations in which this technique is useful. For example, you may wish to find a name, date, statistic, or other single fact. Or you may want to find a phrase or general idea whose wording is not exactly known to you. Scanning is functional in the preparation and collation of materials and information, in finding figures and facts to support a generalization, and in exploring possible sources of various facts and data.

Scanning is the proper reading technique in the use of such sources as a telephone book, an almanac, a business directory, and a dictionary. Consultation of these does not involve reading in the usual sense of the term. Other uses for scanning are in looking for a single fact or statistic in a series of charts or tables, or in an annual report, or in collating a group of facts for a detailed report.

HOW TO SCAN

Scanning does not involve the act of reading, as we usually think of it in a line-by-line sense. Instead, you let your eyes run rapidly over several lines of print at a time, looking for the number, word, or phrase you are seeking. A clear concept of exactly what it is you are looking for is essential. You must be alert to recognize the word or fact when it appears. The rest of the page will seem to be meaningless symbols or forms while the words you seek will appear to stand out boldly when you approach them. Unlike the case in common reading, you will not attempt to understand all the words you scan, but will be interested only in the single fact you are searching for. If done properly, there is hardly a limit to the number of words you can cover in a minute. Your reading "rate" while scanning will, of course, be much greater than any you could use in reading continuous material.

If the material is familiar or brief, scanning for a certain fact is feasible as the initial approach to a body of reading matter. If, however, the material is lengthy or complicated, you will need to do some preliminary previewing or skimming to pinpoint your search. Utilize previewing or skimming to get a quick overview of the organization of the material. Narrow your search by these quick reading techniques to logical portions of the material, rather than search at random.

PRACTICING SCANNING

We have adapted several articles so that you may try scanning in them. Questions are inserted which can be answered by scanning the next portion of the article. In making these efforts at scanning, follow this procedure: First, read the opening paragraph if it is before the question. Second, read the question and probable answers. Third, scan the paragraphs that follow. Let your eyes move rapidly over the sentences until you come to the sentence or phrase that gives you the answer. When you think you have found the right answer, read this sentence only. Once you have found an answer, read no further in the paragraphs. Finally, mark your answer to the question by checking the possible answer you choose. In each section, be certain what you are looking for before attempting to scan. Sometimes the answer will be phrased exactly like one of the given answers. Other times, the correct answer will have the same idea expressed in different words.

What Makes People Absent? [1]

Question 1. Who or what, in the opinions of most executives, is to blame for absenteeism?

    a. The worker
    b. The company
    c. The foreman
    d. Personal problems

Absence rates have been suggested by some authorities as a measure of the effectiveness of an organization and the worth of its human relations policies. However, more often, and especially in recent years, since the concept of accident-proneness has taken hold, employee absence has tended to seem more and more like a function of the individual worker, rather than of his company or foreman. Studies that show most absences occurring among unstable people, or those with psychosomatic ailments, have led many executives to think of absences as solely a weakness of the individual worker. All too often, the executive has said to himself: "It's absenteeism. These people are absence-prone. What can management do but make sure it doesn't hire that kind? Or, if it hires them, get rid of them as rapidly as circumstances permit?"

Question 2. How many factors has research shown to be important in absenteeism among white-collar workers?

    a. Seven
    b. Eight
    c. Fifteen
    d. One

To redress that attitude, the executive who wants to know what the facts are—rather than looking for something to blame the facts upon—may well take a long, careful look at a new publication growing out of

[1] Adapted from *Modern Industry*, June 15, 1953. Used by permission.

the Human Relations Program of the Survey Research Center at the University of Michigan. It's entitled *Absences and Employee Attitudes in an Electric Power Company.* The study is based on absence records, plus attitude surveys, among white-collar and blue-collar (salaried and hourly paid) employees of Detroit Edison Co. The study was completed as a part of a research contract between the Detroit Edison Co. and the U. of M. The Center finds that eight factors in the relationship of white-collar employees to their supervisors, middle management, and the company as whole, have a close relationship to how often the men are absent from work. For blue-collar workers, it finds seven such relationships.

> **Question 3.** What factors are equally as important as the worker's personal problems in causing absenteeism?
>
> a. Personal factors
> b. Feelings about salaries
> c. Feelings about bosses and company
> d. Liking for work

The Center points out, as everyone in management knows, that a great many personal factors affect attendance. It makes clear that the study is not intended to deny these factors. It does demonstrate, however, that taking a random collection of workers at Detroit Edison, their feelings about their bosses and their company also had much to do with how steadily they came to work in the six-month period under study. "Management has generally assumed that absence rates are related only to the type of person an employee is," say Floyd Mann and Howard Baumgartel, who headed the study. "Responsible employees come to work regularly. Employees who do not, are believed to be irresponsible."

> **Question 4.** What may the number of group meetings called by a supervisor indicate?
>
> a. Concern with high absence rates
> b. Feelings of rapport between supervisor and workers
> c. Easy relations between supervisor and workers
> d. Extent of sharing in decision-making

Supervisors who create an atmosphere which makes for free and easy discussion of job problems have fewer absences in their work groups than supervisors who do not. Sixty-nine per cent of men in work groups having an absence rate of once in six months felt very free to talk over job problems with their supervisor. Only 29% in the group with the highest absence rate felt very free to talk about such matters with the supervisor. Furthermore, Detroit Edison supervisors who were rated high by their bosses were the ones whose work groups found it easy to talk about the job with them. These findings were backed up by similar findings in a tractor plant. There, the workers with highest productivity ratings had the easiest relations with their supervisors.

The foremen who hold group meetings keep down absence rates. The more the group and the foreman talk things over together, the fewer the absences. The University of Michigan considers the frequency with which a foreman holds group meetings is a rough measure of the extent to which he involves his men in solving problems. Group decisions, it says, give each person a feeling of responsibility for the success of the decisions. Management inventory showed that foremen who talk things over with employees are also those who rate high in management's eyes.

> **Question 5.** Which phrase summarizes the basis of low-absence rates in this paragraph?
>
> a. Group solidarity
> b. Acceptance by the group
> c. Foreman-employee discussion sessions
> d. Attain their goals

People like to be part of groups which they think can attain their goals. Of the groups whose absences averaged one or less in six months, 62% of the men said, "Our crew is better than others at sticking together." The higher the absence rates, the fewer the men who had this feeling of group solidarity. Among the groups where absences averaged four or more in a half year, only 29% expressed this shoulder-to-shoulder sentiment. In three different studies, the Survey Research Center has found this feeling of group solidarity significantly greater among high-production employees than among low. Supervisors who can generate such a feeling would appear to have a better chance of keeping more of their work crews at work more of the time.

The survey found some correlation between absence rates and the blue-collar workers' attitudes towards the group they work with. Men's answers to different questions were classified under three headings; the individual's feeling that he's part of his crew and accepted as such; his belief that all the fellows in his group have "lots of team spirit"; and his conviction that "our crew is better than others at doing things." Everyone is a social being, and wants to feel he's accepted by his group and is included in all its activities, says Research Center.

Question 6. What other factor contributes to regular work attendance among white-collar workers?

     a. Pay and job satisfaction
     b. Promotion policies
     c. Using best skills and liking the work
     d. Responsibility on the job

Job satisfaction—and attendance—don't rely solely upon the pay envelope. Four times as many low-absence blue-collar Detroit Edison employees said they had a good chance to use their best skills on the job, as were found among the frequently absent groups. Similarly, more men in groups with low rates said they usually had a feeling of having accomplished something at the end of a day's work. Among white-collar workers, satisfaction with a man's responsibility on the job seemed to play a similar role. This finding bears importantly on skill utilization and promotion policies.

Work attendance is related to how much a person likes the sort of work he is doing, the University of Michigan shows statistically from its Detroit Edison study of blue-collar workers. When the work a person does holds an intrinsic interest for him, he is enthusiastic about his job, receives greater satisfaction from his daily work life—and is much more apt to have a good attendance record.

A conviction that fellow crew members had plenty of "team spirit" was about 20% more prevalent among low-absence workers than among those frequently absent. Supervisors who can build a real team feeling will usually find the men pulling together. They will benefit from the resulting improved morale, it is pointed out. Backing up the utility study was a finding in the tractor-manufacturing company that more high- than low-production workers feel they are really a part of their work group—not just lone wolves. Foremen of high-production sections said their men helped each other more.

Key: 1. a   2. b   3. c   4. d   5. b   6. d.

Were you able to scan effectively? What seemed to happen when you searched for each fact? Did it seem to stand out, while the rest of the page was blurred? For many people, this sensation of the answer appearing to stand out from the page is quite marked. For others, particularly those who tend to read more of the text, the contrast is not as great.

Did you have to read more of the text to find some answers? The amount of actual reading needed for scanning varies according to the form in which the answer is found. When the answer is a simple word, phrase, or statistic, little actual reading is necessary to find it. The fact seems to pop out from its context. But when the answer is a complex idea involving a paraphrasing or interpretation of the words of the text, more reading is demanded. Since the exact form of the answer is not known, it does not seem to stand out from the rest.

The number of right answers you were able to find is not highly significant in this kind of reading. Given enough time, practically anyone could find the answers, since they are all contained in the text. The speed of your scanning is the critical element in evaluating your success. Each scanning should be completed in five to thirty seconds, including the time needed for careful reading of the questions. The range of time is due to such factors as the length of the material to be scanned, where the answer occurs, and how much interpretation of the words of the text is necessary to match the given answer. Thus the complete article should have required about two to four minutes, if you are scanning rapidly and effectively.

Now try scanning in this second article. First, read the introductory paragraph. Then read each question and its probable answers carefully. Third, scan each paragraph following the question. Read rapidly, looking only for the answer. As before, mark the answer you choose.

How to Create New Ideas [2]

by Jack W. Taylor

Man has always been curious about the faculty of creative intellect that has raised him above the animals. And this, in turn, has given rise to considerable research on the subject. In an effort to gather and integrate the facts of the matter, the author has investigated a great deal of the research on creative intelligence, and attempts here to present his findings

[2] Jack W. Taylor, "How To Create New Ideas," *Supervision,* August, 1954. Reprinted by permission from *Supervision* Magazine, copyright 1954.

in a form that can be used, not merely to understand the subject, but—more importantly—to develop creative ability.

Question 1. What is the basis of creative ability?

      a. It is an innate faculty.

      b. It can be learned.

      c. It is a trial and error process.

The notion persists popularly that creative ability is some strange, mysterious, almost magical faculty possessed exclusively by the blessed, chosen few. "Either you have it, or you don't."

Don't you believe it!

The ability to create can be learned. The origination of ideas is just as definite a process as the production of material things. In this production, the mind follows an operating procedure that can be learned and controlled. And, just as with any other skill, its effective use is largely a matter of practice.

Question 2. How difficult is it to master the art of creative thinking?

      a. It is an easily obtained process.

      b. It takes greater mental effort than almost any other task.

      c. It requires only a small amount of effort.

There is a definite formula that you can master and apply to this process. Before you examine the formula, however, here's fair warning:

You must not be deceived by the seeming simplicity of the procedure. True, it is simple. But it is only simple enough to be effective—not automatic. This means that there is no substitute for work built into the formula. In fact, this creation of new ideas you so earnestly desire will very likely require greater mental effort, and more of it, than you have ever before invested in any endeavor. (Only men, not boys, need apply.)

Secondly, you cannot successfully omit any step in the procedure. Each step is essential to the whole of the structure and the success of each step depends upon completion of the preceding one.

Question 3. What is the first step in creative thinking?

      a. Finding a problem to be solved

      b. Leaving the mind open for ideas

First, forget about "ideas," as such. Instead, find out exactly what you are trying to get done.

What is your objective? Why do you want ideas? What is it you want to accomplish? What is the Problem to be solved?

If you attempt to start the creative process by indulging in a lot of random "looking around for ideas," or "keeping the mind open for ideas," you will only be defeating yourself. You will simply bog down in a quagmire of futility, and thus create only new barriers to new thinking. Why? Because the human mind doesn't work that way.

The mind cannot create new ideas merely by being made available to receive them. It cannot make worthwhile creations out of flotsam that drifts in accidentally through a hole in the head, any more than it can create just by being exhorted to do so. Merely keeping the mind "open," like an oyster lying torpidly in the mud, accomplishes nothing. As the famed G. K. Chesterton once put it, "The object of opening the mind, as of opening the mouth, is to shut it again on something solid."

Question 4. Where does one look for a problem to solve?

    a. He should discover what is wrong in his specialty.

    b. He should try to find a problem dealing with his greatest interest.

    c. He should look around for an interesting problem.

The "something solid" needed is something that will stimulate the mind into action; for creation is dynamic, not static. And the solid something that supplies both fuel and catalyst to start the creative process is, very simply, a problem. This may not be a glamorous beginning, but make no mistake about it—it's the only beginning that really works!

C. F. Kettering, one of the most creative men of our time, put it clearly when he said, "All research is simply finding out what's wrong with a thing, then fixing it."

So, pick a problem. Find out "what's wrong" in your particular specialty. Define the problem clearly, make sure you know what the problem really is. Then write it down and keep it before you throughout the remaining (or "fixing") stages of the idea-building process.

Question 5. What are the raw materials of the creative process?

    a. Opinions

    b. Known facts

    c. Random ideas

Ideas never suddenly materialize out of nothing. They must be painstakingly built out of some raw material, and that raw material is Knowledge.

Idea-building is a kind of "chain reaction" in which each tiny fact reacts against its neighbor to produce a new fact, thought or concept. The "atomic pile" out of which new ideas emerge is comprised of present, known facts. Your next step, therefore, is to accumulate a stock of "fact-atoms"—knowledge.

Where will you find it? Almost literally: anywhere.

It has been said, "All the world's knowledge is written in books." Whether you fully believe that or not, dig out and study whatever journals, books, magazines and other publications you can find that deal with your subject. And make a special effort to associate with informed people; by talking with them, questioning them and listening to them, you will learn directly of many thoughts, concepts, personal experiences and findings which otherwise might never reach you.

Question 6. What attitude should one have toward the facts he gathers in the creative process?

    a. Confidence in their worth

    b. A feeling of doubt

A word of advice: Beware of blind acceptance. Study your gleanings carefully, and be alert for contradictions. Match fact against fact. Little bits of knowledge are indeed "dangerous," because they are misleading alone, and are forever being rendered obsolescent by newer discoveries. Doubt your facts, therefore, and make them prove themselves before you accept them.

Question 7. In gathering information around the problem, how narrowly should one direct his search?

    a. Search as widely around the area of the problem as possible.

    b. Confine the search to immediate area of the problem.

Direct your search for knowledge over a broad field rather than a narrow specialty. One cannot tell at this stage exactly what information, or what kind and how much information, will be needed ultimately to build new ideas. But, obviously, the broader your knowledge, the better your chances for success and the easier your task. (Remember how many discoveries have been made accidentally during research into seemingly foreign fields? Penicillin, for example?)

In all this stockpiling activity, remember your objective—you are only trying to soak up information. You are not yet concerned with ideas; they will emerge later; as a natural, inevitable consequence of your becoming steeped in knowledge now.

Question 8. How can the facts dealing with a particular problem be conveniently preserved?

    a. Write them in a scrapbook or a card file.

    b. Make a listing of where the references may be found.

    c. Try to remember where you met them.

As you gather your "raw material" (knowledge) you must, at the same time, perform another key operation. You must organize your knowledge into such form as to make it useable.

One of the best and easiest ways to do this is simply to keep a scrapbook or card file of all the pertinent, significant items you uncover in your studies.

If you have ever read that classic of American humor, *Life in a Putty Knife Factory,* you will recall that Author H. Allen Smith told how his book resulted from the simple habit of jotting interesting little bits, incidents and observations on small scraps of paper and saving these scraps in an old cheese box on his desk. When he got enough scraps, he merely sorted them into the order he wanted—and proceeded to write a best-selling book from them.

You may have no desire to write a book. But, as an essential step in your preparation to create original ideas, you must preserve your information in a form that will later make sense to you.

Above all—write it down!

Question 9. What use should be made of the facts gathered during the creative process?

    a. Relationships and principles should be extracted from them.

    b. They should be screened and only the best kept.

Somewhere in the mass of knowledge you have built up are the "golden keys" with which to unlock the "idea vaults" of your mind. Your task now is to find these keys.

To do this, you must give your material a thorough refining—a process of fact-screening—in order to extract from it the significant Relationships and Principles it contains.

Relationships lead to the extraction of a general principle. The principle suggests the key to a new application, a new twist, a new combination. Result: new, creative thinking.

No "fact" is important in and of itself alone. It is important merely as a link in a chain of knowledge. The only reliable avenues that can lead you to ideas are principles. So, cultivate the habit of mind of always seeking to find what underlies facts.

The process of building ideas is plainly one of combining old, familiar elements to produce a new structure, a new concept, a new idea. And now is the time to match one bit of information against another, continually seeking to see what new meaning both together make.

As these new meanings take shape as principles, here again it helps to write them down; for the mere act of forcing yourself to express your thoughts in writing makes you think with greater logic, clarity and good sense.

Question 10. Once all of the facts are collected and properly assimilated, what kind of activity finally produces the idea, or tentative solution to the problem?

   a. A constant mulling over of the data and a search for solution

   b. A complete conscious withdrawal from the whole process or activity

Now comes a phase in the process to which you can contribute very little in a direct way. This step consists of removing the whole matter from your mind's "front burner" to its "back burner," where you let it simmer. You simply take the job away from your conscious mind, and delegate it to your subconscious.

No one understands exactly why the mind works as it does in this phase, and, for that matter, understanding the "why" of it isn't necessary to the use of the process at all. The important thing to know is that now you must let your conscious mind get its "second wind" while your subconscious mulls over the problems you've given it.

The best thing you can do here is "get away from it all"—go to a concert, see a movie, enjoy some mild diversion, sleep, have a good time—almost anything, so long as you don't think about ideas.

Question 11. What oftens happens if you refrain from active thinking about the problem?

  a. Ideas or solutions seem to appear.
  b. One will forget the point of the problem.

You won't be expecting this—hardly anyone seems to—but along about now, an IDEA will strike you. It might occur during a meal; perhaps you'll just be idly musing; you might be bathing (relaxation, curiously, seems to "trigger" the thing); it might even strike with such impact as to waken you from a sound sleep. However it may happen, it will happen.

If you have collected enough facts, organized them, refined them, extracted relationships and principles, and provided for good mental digestion, have no doubt about it—an idea will emerge, and it will be followed by others in rapid succession.

Question 12. Why do many people fail at this point of ideation?

  a. They fail to make a record of these new ideas.
  b. They don't trust these new ideas.

This is the end toward which you have been working all along. Peculiarly, this is also the stage at which many people fail. They fail (among other easily correctible reasons) because, once ideas begin to emerge, they keep coming with such rapidity that the memory cannot absorb them all; many of them—and these may be the best ones—are lost!

Obviously, the best protection against this pitfall is again, simply—pencil and paper. ("A short pencil will beat a long memory.") A sudden flood of new ideas can be expected to catch a person unawares, but there is no reason why it should also catch him unprepared.

So be ready. Carry paper and pencil with you. Spot writing materials in your home, your car, your workplace, your clothing. And when those ideas begin to smack you 'tween the eyes—write 'em down!

Question 13. How should these newly created ideas be handled?

  a. They should immediately be tested on the job.
  b. They should be critically appraised and reworked.

A new idea is like a new baby: it's wonderful; it's perfect—it's yours! Have you ever noticed, though, that the neighbors never seem to accord

your child the same unqualified adoration you give it? Rather, they tend
to judge it dispassionately, or even to disparage it. (After all, they have
"wonderful" babies, too.)

Let that knowledge guide you now in handling your new "brain
children." Put yourself in the neighbor's position and subject your progeny
to keenly critical inspection and appraisal.

Many an otherwise intelligent person has gone off half-cocked over
his new ideas and got himself labeled, "Screwball," simply because he
wouldn't take a little time to check his ideas objectively for flaws. That
need not happen to you.

Let that first great surge of joy over your accomplishment settle
down a little. Then, with all the detachment of which you are capable,
take each idea out into "the cold, gray dawn" and measure it for its true
worth.

The rest is obvious: Re-work each idea. Modify it. Re-shape it.
Adapt it to the practical situation.

> **Question 14.** In selling our ideas, which is the more im-
> portant emphasis?
>
> a. The practical application of the idea
> b. What the idea will do for the listener

Now comes the most important part of all—getting your ideas into
use.

If the situation is such that you can put them into use without having
to consult anyone else, then do it. Chances are, however, that most of
your ideas will involve others in some way, so you will have to do a job
of selling to get acceptance.

It is no secret that "people resist change." To get them to accept
your new ideas—and that is getting them to change—you will have to
give them compelling (or rather, impelling) reasons to do so. To help accomplish this:

Plan Your Sale—Assemble all the selling points for each new idea,
and plan in advance exactly how, when and where you will present it.

Allow Enough Time—Many people are made uncomfortable by new
ideas. If you try to rush them, you may never get them to "buy." It takes
time to get new ideas in the first place; it takes time to get "used to"
them, too.

Get Participation—Our human tendency is to be jealous of our accomplishments, to resent others tampering with our creations. But, invariably, better results are obtained by encouraging discussion of the

"pros and cons" of new ideas. So, allow some voice in decisions concerning them—minor modifications, how they shall be used, etc. (Note: Participation in development is best of all: those "owning a share" of a new idea are just as anxious as you are to see it succeed.)

Use "Samples"—Successful salesmen know that the "showing" of their products is often the key factor in making sales. In your case, the "products" are ideas—but the principle still applies. So, whenever feasible, show (demonstrate and illustrate) your ideas. Visualize them. Depict them with action, sketches, charts, pictures, models—whatever will let the "buyer" see their merits, and become "sold."

A special note: Whatever you use to help visualize any idea, make it neat! A messy, careless, sloppy job always implies sloppy thinking. But a neat job says, more eloquently than words can, "The originator of this work has put real thought into it."

Stress "Customer-interest"—Unflattering as the fact may be, it is nonetheless true that the other fellow is not half as much interested in you or your ideas as he is in himself. Why not use that truth? Soft-pedal your connection with your new ideas. Instead, show the other fellow what your ideas will do for him!

Reveal Your Ideas Where They Will Do the Most Good.

Key: 1. b   2. b   3. a   4. a   5. b   6. b   7. a   8. a
9. a   10. b   11. a   12. a   13. b   14. b.

Scanning in this article was probably more difficult than in the preceding article. The ideas were not as highly concrete and factual. The questions were more general and the facts you scanned for were harder to find. Answers often involved a paraphrasing or interpretation of the text. Thus this particular piece of scanning required somewhat more reading and more time than the first article. However, the process is still quite rapid. Each scanning should be completed in about ten to thirty seconds and the entire article should require about three to six minutes, if you were scanning efficiently.

We have deliberately varied the difficulty of the task of scanning in these two articles. Many of the materials you meet will not be as easy to scan as the article on absenteeism. As we suggested earlier, the speed at which you can scan, or the degree to which answers seem to pop out to meet you varies from one article to another. The concreteness of the fact you are seeking, the amount of interpretation demanded, and the amount of actual reading necessary vary from one situation to the next. But through practicing scanning in these various types of selections you will gradually acquire skill in using it whenever you need it.

ANOTHER KIND OF SCANNING

Sometimes a piece of reading matter may contain not more than one main idea. Editorials, essays, and short news articles often fall in this category. When this is true, scanning may be substituted for more thorough reading. Articles that lend themselves to scanning for the main idea should be quite short, and their content apparent from the title or headings. Having a fairly clear idea of the point of the article, you can scan rapidly for the sentence or two that clarifies this idea. Try this technique in this next article. First read the introductory paragraph under the title. Then see how long it takes you to discover what this training method is.

Training Method Tests Executive Judgment [3]

by Joseph M. Gambatese

New "Incident Process" stresses management development through discussion and digging for facts necessary to make sound decisions.

A new technique for developing executive skills is gaining the attention of American business. Based on the do-it-yourself principle, it is designed to sharpen management abilities in getting results with people, in organizational problems, in labor relations, and in other phases of leadership.

The new system, called the Incident Process, is the work of Prof. Paul Pigors and his wife, Faith. He introduced it at Massachusetts Institute of Technology, where he is an associate professor of industrial relations. Basically, Incident Process depends on group study, much like that of the Harvard case method of training which has been in general use

[3] Joseph M. Gambatese, "Training Method Tests Executive Judgment," *Nation's Business*, Vol. 40, No. 6, pp. 72-73. Copyright 1955, reprinted from the June 1955 issue of *Nation's Business*. Used by permission.

for almost half a century. Unlike the Harvard method, in which all the facts of a significant case are available for study, Incident Process presents only a bare incident. From this, those taking the course must make their own decisions, after digging for the facts on which the decision is to be based.

Dr. Pigors has demonstrated the Incident Process in many companies and to many groups of executives. Several firms are using or experimenting with this method in their training programs, sometimes as a supplement to the case method, often with variations of Dr. Pigors's formula. They include some department store members of the National Retail Dry Goods Association, the Goodyear Tire and Rubber Company, Bell System telephone companies, the Navy's civilian training office in Washington, Pratt and Whitney Aircraft, Aluminum Company of America, The Stanley Works, Koppers Company, and TransCanada Air Lines.

Considering or planning to use the Incident Process in some form are the Army Civilian Training Center, U. S. Bureau of Engraving, Giant Food Department Stores, American Airlines, and du Pont, among others.

Representatives of General Motors, General Electric, Inland Steel, American Can Company, Brown-Forman Distillers, Wyman-Gordon, U. S. Rubber and National Security Agency were also among the 75 executives who attended a three-day conference in Washington where the Pigors discussed the new method and introduced materials for using it. These materials are assembled in a manual published by the Bureau of National Affairs, Inc. Dr. Pigors will direct a two-week workshop on the Incident Process at M. I. T. beginning June 20.

Included in the manual are suggested incidents taken from arbitration cases or based on Dr. Pigors's experience as a management consultant in the personnel relations and communications fields. Many companies, adapting the plan to their own use, prefer to offer incidents from their own plants for study.

The Bureau of Engraving, for example, may use the $160,000 theft by an employee in 1953 as a study in its course for management training.

According to the Bureau of National Affairs, the new method duplicates the practical approach to decisions as they occur in everyday life.

Those who are being trained meet in groups of 15 to 20 to consider and decide on a course of action in a given situation. Typical of the incidents for study is the one, taken from Dr. Pigors's manual:

"Foreman McCrorie instructed Bell, a welder, to hook the cable of an overhead crane to a rack of finished work. Bell hesitated to pick up the lift. McCrorie insisted that this was an order. Bell turned to Shop Steward Harris: 'I think this is dangerous. What do you think? Should I pick up the lift?'

"Harris sympathized with Bell's fears, adding: 'If you feel it is unsafe or too dangerous, you don't have to do it.'

"You are Foreman McCrorie. What do you do now?"

A team leader who has studied the case in advance is prepared to answer questions or supply necessary documents. If a member asks, for instance, if the union contract (if there is a union) covers the subject of the incident, the team leader distributes copies of the pertinent section of the contract. Other documents might include the text of a notice posted on the bulletin board, a diagram of the area where the incident occurred, or a management organization chart showing line of authority.

An observer-reporter makes notes of the discussion and later gives a critical report to the group. He might report, as happened in one instance, that 97 questions were asked during a 30-minute fact-finding period, and that more than one third, or 35, were asked in the first five minutes. He might observe, critically, that the group was weak on follow-up questions, tending to wander at times in irrelevant directions.

All of the group members serve as fact-finders, with one of them summarizing the facts at the end of the fact-finding stage. Some become spokesmen for different viewpoints. They also take the parts of the principals involved in the incident and act out what they would have said or done.

Each member writes what his decision would be on the specific issue the group agrees must be decided. Majority and minority groups caucus to select their spokesman and to consolidate their arguments. Then the whole group debates the decision.

Finally, the group evaluates the case and the decisions that were made from the standpoint of hindsight and foresight, to see what generalizations can be drawn from the situation and their discussion of it that might apply to their everyday jobs.

Throughout the series of cases, the group constantly evaluates its own behavior and progress, and rotates leadership responsibilities in various roles. The complete course covers ten two-hour sessions.

Those who have had experience with the Incident Process generally cite some specific advantages over the established case-method technique.

Robert W. Fox of The Stanley Works, New Britain, Conn., says that supervisors in that company have improved their ability to obtain relevant facts and order them in such a way as to make an intelligent decision. The reasons given in support of a decision have also improved. (Dr. Pigors says that half the time management makes the right decision for the wrong reasons.)

Mr. Fox believes that the Incident Process could also be a valuable training aid in safety, scrap control, and quality control, in addition to employee relations.

George Plant, the manager of NRDGA's store management and personnel groups, likes the incident method as a leadership technique in sharpening skills of executives in defining a problem, analyzing it, and reaching intelligent conclusions.

Charles W. Potter, director of the Bell System Executive Conference, thinks the Incident Process has merit because, besides developing ability to find and weigh facts and consider the viewpoints of others, it brings the trainee as close as possible to actual situations as they occur from day to day.

Goodyear Tire Company has used the process to train 750 members of office management in Akron, from the department manager level to key staff personnel, and last month began giving it to 1,000 factory supervisors. W. R. Bryan, manager of Goodyear's conference and school programs, says:

"It stimulated more active discussion than any other method we have used."

Alcoa has no formalized program using the Incident Process, but it is using some phases of it, like fact-finding. According to R. J. Simonds of the training department, Alcoa has added a new touch to the new technique: use of a three-to-five-minute film to present a plant or office incident to the conference group for discussion.

One of the training directors at the Washington conference told of a real incident being used in his training program. It involved a "bull of the woods" type of manager who told the most efficient clerk in the office—a housewife guilty of frequent tardiness—that the next time she was late she was fired.

A few days later she walked into the office, late.

"Well, I guess I'm fired," she told the manager. "But I want you to know why I've been late."

She then explained that her husband worked nights, got home drunk, and insisted that she fix his breakfast before she left for her day-time job.

"We use that incident as a case study and learn three things from it," the training director said. "First, don't make a decision without knowing all the facts. Second, don't make a decision you are not prepared to back up. Third, don't short-circuit the chain of command. The manager should have taken the matter up with the woman's supervisor."

The training director hesitated, then concluded: "Incidentally, I was the manager."

Question: What is the Incident Process method of testing executive judgment?

    a. A method of forming a policy for personal procedure on the basis of one incident alone

    b. A group training method based on simple incidents for improving the judgment of management

    c. A method of training in forming judgments of personnel problems by presenting all the facts of a significant case from which the manager must reach a decision

    d. A method of individual manager training in which he is taught to deduce significant facts from a selected case history

How long did it take you to discover what the Incident Process method of testing executive judgment is? You should have been able to define it as given in answer *b* above in about 30 to 60 seconds. A complete description of the process is given in about a half dozen sentences scattered through the first six paragraphs. If you read only these sentences, you would have had the main idea.

Although you may find it interesting to note also the various companies that have adopted the process, or to read the illustrations given by the author, these were not necessary to the main idea. If, in intending to find the one major idea offered by the selection, you read all these details, you spent much more time than was essential.

FUTURE USES OF SCANNING

We have provided practice materials in scanning sufficient to give you a feel for this reading technique. You will find many opportunities for future applications in your daily work. Use scanning whenever you can to save reading time in finding specific facts or even main ideas. Scan instead of reading when: finding facts and figures, collating information, using an almanac, directory, or telephone book, or preparing materials for a report. Let the facts come out to meet you instead of searching for them laboriously, line by line. Use scanning for most reading situations where you are not trying to secure a continuous flow of ideas, or when you are searching for single ideas or facts.

If you are interested in reading other articles or books that deal with the topics treated in this chapter, here is a list of suggestions.

Fange, E. K. von, "Developing a useful imagination," *General Electric Review*, Vol. 58, September, 1955, pp. 52-55.

Ford, G., "Why they quit," *New York Times Magazine*, May 17, 1953, p. 28.

"G.E. plots strategy to combat absenteeism," *Business Week*, January 16, 1954, p. 94.

Hazzard, W. G., "Putting absence records to use," *American Journal Public Health*, Vol. 41, September, 1951, pp. 1087-1095.

Harris, H., "Three-year study shows how managers are made—General Electric's research study," *Nation's Business*, Vol. 44, March, 1956, pp. 90-94.

Newcomer, Mabel, *The Big Business Executive*. New York: Columbia University Press, 1955.

Newman, J. A., "Executive development: talent on tap," *Chemical Week*, Vol. 78, January 21, 1956, pp. 37-40.

Olsen, F., "Nature of creative thinking," *Phi Delta Kappan*, Vol. 35, February, 1954, pp. 198-200.

Shepard, D. A., "Management in search of men," *Atlantic Monthly*, Vol. 197, March, 1956, pp. 65-66.

"Survey shows how to reduce absenteeism," *Nation's Business*, Vol. 44, April, 1956, p. 104.

Thomas, C. A., "Creativity in science," *Chemical and Engineering News*, Vol. 33, August 8, 1955, pp. 3278-3281.

Warner, W. Lloyd, "Executive careers today: who gets to the top?" *Management Review*, Vol. 45, February, 1956, pp. 83-94.

Warner, W. Lloyd, and Abegglen, James, *Big Business Leaders in America*. New York: Harper, 1955.

What Makes an Executive? Toronto: Oxford University Press, 1955.

7

Critical Reading—Reading Propaganda

What You Will Do
  Try reading persuasive or propaganda writings and speeches

What You Will Learn
  To detect propaganda techniques and fallacies in logic in persuasive writings

  To read more critically for the author's purpose and accuracy.

This paragraph shows the need for skill in critical reading better than we could ever say it:

The sum of what we know through personal experience is small. In politics and economics, for example, where the facts are often not clear-cut and where rival authorities are common, all of us depend on sources outside ourselves for our opinions. Most Americans "know" their stands on Communism, big business, labor union, and international relations. You have opinions on all these things. But do you know any Communists? Have you ever administered a big business? Are you a member of a labor union? A screen lies between each of us and the world of events, through which we allow certain kinds and amounts of information to filter, and our term "propaganda" describes the way in which that filtering occurs.[1]

The writers go on to point out that, ". . . anything may be

---

[1] Hummel, William and Huntress, Keith, *The Analysis of Propaganda*. New York: Dryden Press, 1949, p. 3. Copyright 1949 by William Hummel and Keith Huntress.

labeled propaganda that attempts to make someone accept a fact or a point of view." The more you think about it, the harder it is to refute this statement. Anything you read, that you have not experienced firsthand, is merely someone's presentation of the facts as he sees them.

It would seem that when you lack the experience or knowledge to contradict the facts someone offers you, you have no choice left but to believe him. Fortunately this is not true. You still can use common sense and logic to analyze the writer's offering. You still can detect the means by which he attempts to influence your thinking, to convince you of his argument.

The first step in the analysis of a point of view is the comprehension of the writer's facts. You must first understand clearly his main idea—his proposal. What exactly is he saying? Can you summarize his ideas and state them fairly and clearly? This type of reading is not easy for most persons. They tend to read what they think the author says. Their ideas, their prejudices interfere with and influence their interpretation of the facts.

How many times have you stopped reading an article and thrown it aside because you felt that the writer was a crackpot? Did you really read far enough to understand what he actually was saying? Or were you disgusted because he differed so violently from your opinions?

Do you tend to read the same newspaper each day? Do you prefer a particular weekly news magazine? Why? Is it because you think they give an honest, objective reporting of the news? Isn't it true that you read these because they usually agree with you? You agree with the slant or interpretation they give to the news or you wouldn't enjoy reading them.

The ability to identify the facts, rather than to react emotionally to them, is the first requisite of intelligent, critical reading. Only after you are certain of what the author is saying, can you advance to higher levels of critical reading. If you understand what the author is saying, then you are ready to detect how he is saying it, and how he wants you to react. You are then ready to note omissions and distortions of fact, the appeal to emotion by the use of words chosen to arouse certain reactions in the reader and other professional propaganda tricks.

PROPAGANDA TECHNIQUES

What are some of the devices of speaking and writing that are used to influence your thinking?

Repetition. By continually repeating a statement forcefully, over and over again, the writer makes it take on the aspect of truth. Whether the claim is true or not is immaterial. If you hear or see it often enough, you believe it. Witness what the Nazi propagandists did with the word *Aryan.* There is absolutely no racial or scientific evidence of any kind to support the Nazi claims. But the concept of the master race of tall, blond gentiles who were to rule the world for a thousand years was swallowed by most Germans and by many anti-Semites in other countries. Here are a few such meaningless phrases which by constant repetition have made an impact upon the minds of the public:

> You can be sure—if it's Westinghouse.
> Chesterfields—they satisfy.
> The Republicans caused the crash of '29.
> The ———— party is the People's Party.

This technique of repetition is analogous to the blatant statement of personal opinion as though it were absolute fact—for example, "This country has been prosperous only under a ———— administration." (You choose the name of the party to insert.)

Confusing the Issue. This is a favorite device in political campaigns to discredit the opponent or his policies by linking them with an absurdity or incongruous characteristic. Lincoln was nicknamed "the baboon," Cleveland accused of having fathered an illegitimate child, Franklin D. Roosevelt of being a dreamer and "never having met a pay roll." The current version of this device, as so deftly used by the late Senator McCarthy and others, is to damn an individual by linking his name somehow with communism. Proof, or direct accusation, is unnecessary; the insinuation is sufficient.

On the positive side, this technique may be used to secure approval for a candidate or public person, by pointing out his attractive and acceptable traits. Goering, who directed the senseless bombing of Rotterdam, was characterized as "good-natured." Warren G.

Harding probably owed a large block of votes to his handsome appearance; Ulysses S. Grant, to his military accomplishments. The presidential administrations they conducted disillusioned a great many people.

This confusion device is often employed to clothe a candidate or party with traits acceptable to the general public. The professionals call it "soft soap" when someone starts talking about the "great American peepul," "the American way of life," "true Americanism," etc. For futher examples, listen to the speeches next Fourth of July, or read the advertisements and editorials in your favorite paper.

The Bandwagon.   This appeal is directed at the desire of the average person to be like all the others around him. If everyone is wearing wider collars, narrower pants, taller hats, or colored shirts, we too must follow in order to feel comfortable. The device is particularly flexible and lends itself readily to "snob appeal" as well as the opposite "home folks" appeal. You are advised to use "Pfapp's Mouthwash" or eat "Flap's Crunchy Crinkles" or vote for Joe Bloke because "everyone" or "the better people" or "all us plain folks" do it. Recently, "fireside chats" or "living-room" television broadcasts have been used to create a homey feeling toward presidential announcements. If this trend continues, we may expect to listen to one of the candidates in the next election or so deliver his appeal between strokes of an old-fashioned straight razor.

The appeals to power, size, or prestige are simply variations on the bandwagon theme. For examples, look at the advertisements in the "better" magazines of the distinguished gentlemen who drink only a certain whisky, or the socialite ladies who use a particular inexpensive face cream, or the prominent stage, screen, or sports figures who owe their entire success to chewing ———— or smoking ————. In other types of advertisements, it is the presence of the engineer, or white-coated scientist, or so-called expert, or the testimony of an eminent business figure that seeks to induce you to buy and use the product.

Emotionally Toned Words.   Probably the most common of all propaganda techniques is the use of words that carry connotations or feelings to the mind of the reader. Motion pictures today are not simply great but "colossal," "stupendous," or "magnificent." A mouthwash or toothpaste is no longer merely a pleasant-tasting substance but an "antiseptic" or "destroyer of cavity-forming bacteria." The federal government is no longer merely growing larger and more complex but "swollen," "monstrous," becoming "a hierarchy of bureaucrats," "socialistic," "an antagonist of the free, competitive system of American business."

Insufficient Evidence. Conclusions you are asked to accept, offered on inadequate or even irrelevant evidence, are common examples of this particular device. Typical of this type of reasoning is the conclusion that since a certain event followed another, it was caused by the first, or *post hoc ergo propter hoc.* It has taken Herbert Hoover years to regain the prestige he earned as presidential candidate and to overcome the blame for the world-wide depression that happened to coincide with his term in office. It was simple and logical to blame him and his predecessors for the events that occurred at that time.

False Dilemmas. The propagandist asserts that there are only two possible solutions to a given horrible situation—his and the wrong answer. You are invited to choose, as it were, between paradise and hell, when even a little thought would show that there are intermediate, fairly cool places to rest if you do not aspire to paradise. The conflict between labor and management is often presented in this light—with whichever side the speaker is representing being credited with offering the only program compatible with the "honest, decent, American way."

There are many other devices and twists in the propagandist's line such as outright lying, half-truths, evasiveness, false analogies, etc. But it is unnecessary to illustrate all of these here. We have emphasized a few merely to sharpen your critical faculties, to alert you to the need for thoughtful reading of any persuasive material.

Here are examples of persuasive writing or speaking on various topics. Read them, first to recognize the writer's major ideas and, second, to evaluate these ideas critically.

Should We Have More TVA's? [2]

There is an aspect of TVA which disturbs me more than its fiscal vagaries. It has operated as a federal corporation under a charter which has enabled it to do an incredible number of things and to escape government scrutiny. The federal charter is a comparatively new device to enable the Federal Government to expand its powers immensely. Mr. Lilienthal, in his book, *TVA—Democracy on the March,* calls attention to the vast growth of federal power. It has become so great that, he says, it cannot be wisely administered from Washington. But the power must not go back to the governors, mayors, legislatures and councils elected by the people. It must go to great regional areas administered by directors appointed by the President, to a corporation cunningly devised to accumulate power and to elude congressional authority. We will see the country split into a few great regional provinces run by corporate provincial governors. This is what Mr. Lilienthal calls "democracy on the march." I think it is democracy in retreat, a return to the European system of centrally controlled provincial governors. With TVA as a beginning the advocates of regionalism are planning under the guise of flood, navigation and forestry control and other excuses to blanket America with this new type of government which represents a complete revolution in our political system.

1. What is his main idea?
   a. To dramatize the danger of federal corporations like TVA
   b. To document the growing trend toward expansion of the powers of the federal government
   c. To describe a dangerous aspect of TVA fiscal policy
   d. To point out the need for greater local control of governmental projects

2. Which of the following devices does the writer employ to influence his readers?
   a. Emotionally toned words such as "cunningly," "elude"
   b. A false dilemma—regional provinces versus local control
   c. The bandwagon—"governors, mayors . . . elected by the people"

[2] Flynn, John T., "Hidden Red Ink in TVA's Books," *The Reader's Digest,* Vol. 308, December 1947, pp. 129-135. Extract reprinted by permission.

d. Confusing the issue—"democracy in retreat," "to blanket America"

Key: 1. a   2. a, b.

More Authorities for River Valleys [3]

Congress set up the Tennessee Valley Authority in 1933 to develop the resources of that region, and to help raise the standard of living in an area of general economic poverty. The "authority" was a frank experiment in regional planning and regional government. Flood control and soil conservation were desperately needed.

Because no one state could work out a successful program by itself, Congress took over the job, creating a new, unified planning agency. It seems the plainest common sense to extend this pattern now to other river valleys in similar need of large-scale development.

The Missouri River basin, spanning one sixth of the continental United States, is an excellent case in point. When rains flood the Missouri Valley, they strike at the heart of America's "Bread basket." One hundred million tons of irreplaceable topsoil wash away through the Missouri every year.

1. What is the writer's central idea?

   a. TVA solved the problems of that region.
   b. Regional planning authorities like the TVA should be set up to administer the Missouri River basin.
   c. The Missouri River basin is the site of costly floods which should be controlled.
   d. The TVA was an experiment in regional planning and regional government.

2. What questionable conclusion does the writer expect you to make?

   a. TVA was the best solution for the problems of an area of general economic poverty.
   b. There is no other solution for the Missouri River basin than an organization similar to TVA.

[3] Thompson, Carol L., "More Authorities for River Valleys?" *Senior Scholastic,* Vol. 54, May 4, 1949, pp. 6-7. Adapted from *Senior Scholastic* by permission of the editors. Copyright 1949 by Scholastic Magazines.

   c. Flood control and soil conservation are desperately needed in the Missouri Valley.

   d. Congress created the TVA in an attempt to solve the problems of flood control and soil conservation.

3. Besides the false dilemma offered in question two, what other propaganda techniques does the writer use?

   a. Use of personal opinion as though fact—"no one state could work out . . ." ·

   b. The plain-folks appeal—"It seems the plainest common sense . . ."

   c. The bandwagon—"America's 'Bread basket.' "

   d. Sheer repetition—TVA was a successful solution of the problems of flood control and soil conservation.

   Key: 1. b   2. b   3. a, b, c.

The following is a pro and con discussion of the tidelands oil question between Senators Spessard L. Holland of Florida and Herbert H. Lehman of New York. The question is whether Congress should return title to the submerged lands adjoining coastal states to the state governments. The critical point in the debate is the fact that oil deposits are present in part of this land.

Remarks by Senator Holland on Senate Joint Resolution 13, providing for giving the states "property rights in the submerged lands beneath navigable waters."

It will be noted that this joint resolution provides that nothing therein shall be deemed to affect in any wise the rights of the United States to the natural resources of the portion of the subsoil and seabed of the continental shelf lying outside the boundaries of the respective states, and it confirms the jurisdiction and control of the Federal Government over those natural resources. In other words, this measure clearly emphasizes that nine tenths of the submerged lands off the coast of the United States is under the control and jurisdiction of the Federal Government and that the other one tenth, which lies inside the boundaries of the states, and immediately adjoining the coasts of the states, should be owned and controlled by the respective states. . . .

In closing, it is interesting to note that many of those who oppose this proposed legislation are the very ones who have been active proponents of an ever larger Federal Government and who seem to think that an all-powerful Federal Government is a panacea for all the ills of the people of this country. Those of us who support the proposed legislation are strongly opposed to the nationalization of resources—and that is what they are attempting to do to us—in the five-thousand-mile shoestring of coastal waters which throttles the shores of our coastal states. The resources in this narrow belt are vital to the states and to local growth and prosperity, and we feel that the ownership and control of these resources should remain in the states and be subjected to state and local control where it will be very close to the people who are so greatly affected.

We are now talking about fundamental philosophy. We are talking about local self-government. We are talking about the opportunity of a citizen to see the very officials who serve him in the regulation of lands which may represent the total investment of his lifetime savings. We think it is sound government to keep such regulation, control, and ownership just as close to home as is possible.

We strongly feel that our position is sound and just, that it will receive as it has already received, the approval of the vast majority of our people who, we believe, as indicated by the result of the recent Gallup poll, agree with us that the important rights enjoyed by the states for a hundred and fifty years should be restored and safeguarded, and that such action would be in the interest of soundly economic and democratic government. These rights and the immense values already developed and to be developed in the coastal belt, plus the similar values in the inland waters and in the Great Lakes, involve problems which are so clearly local in nature that we shall continue with all of our strength to fight to prevent their transfer to a Federal Government which is already too big, too wasteful, and too far from the people.

Mr. President, there is not a senator within the sound of my voice who does not know that much of the body of ills which afflict us on the domestic front flows directly from the fact that the Federal Government is too big, and that there is no finite mind which can grasp all its implications or all its details, even though it is the responsibility of senators and representatives to make laws for the government of our huge, swollen Federal system, as well as of our people, and it is our duty to provide appropriations whereby those immense pieces of uncoordinated machinery can attempt to function.

It is our hope that the joint resolution will speedily pass the Senate and be enacted into law.[4]

Answer these questions to show how critically you read Senator Holland's arguments.

[4] Adapted from *Congressional Record* 99, 2848 and 2877, April 6, 1953.

1. Senator Holland suggests that his resolution refers to what portion of the submerged lands off the coast of the United States?
   a. Nine-tenths
   b. One-tenth
   c. One-half
   d. All

2. Why does he stress this point?
   a. To confuse his listeners
   b. To play down the magnitude of the transfer of the title
   c. Because the transfer of title affects only an insignificant portion of the submerged lands
   d. Because the lands being transferred are of little value

3. Where does Senator Holland claim that these lands really lie, and how does he use this claim as an argument for returning them to the states?
   a. Adjacent to the coast and hence part of the United States
   b. Within the navigable waters of the states, and should belong to the states
   c. Within the boundaries of the states and hence are part of the states
   d. Close by the states, and having once been their property should be returned to the states

4. What other arguments are offered by the Senator without sufficient proof of their validity?
   a. These are local lands and should be supervised locally.
   b. Local governments do a better job than state governments.
   c. Every man should be free to supervise his own business.
   d. What happens to these lands is the concern of only those living on or near them.
   e. All of these arguments.

5. How does the Senator try to gain the approval of his listeners for local rather than federal government of the submerged lands?
   a. By proving the inefficiency of a large government
   b. By referring to the Federal government as "swollen," "wasteful"

   c. By claiming that the lands are only a small part of the total area in question

   d. By failing to mention the presence of oil on these lands

6. How does the Senator attempt to help his listeners identify their interests with the small, local government?

   a. By claiming that everyone understands local government better than the federal system

   b. By drawing an analogy—the state and the submerged lands are like every man and his possessions

   c. By pointing out the advantages of local or state supervision

   d. By claiming that each person is first a citizen of a state

7. Which of Senator Holland's arguments would influence you most to agree with him?

   a. The area in question is only a small part of the submerged lands.

   b. The lands are within the boundaries of the states.

   c. Local lands and projects should be supervised locally.

   d. The federal government is too inefficient to administer these lands properly.

   e. These lands rightfully belong to the people near them.

   Key: 1. b   2. b   3. c   4. e   5. b   6. c   7. answer varies.

Before we point out the kind of fallacy by which you may have been influenced in answering question 7, read the following excerpts from a speech in opposition to this bill, then answer the subjoined questions.

Tidelands Oil [5]

by Herbert H. Lehman

We must not lose sight of the main question before us, much as the proponents of this legislation would like to have us lose sight of that question.

That question is: Why should we give these rights away? Why should we give these billions away?

[5] Adapted from *Congressional Record* 99, 3077, April 13, 1953.

Under the rulings of the Supreme Court these rights and this great wealth belong to all the states—to New York, and Connecticut, and Virginia, and Ohio, and Wisconsin, and Minnesota, and North Dakota, and Iowa—to all the forty-eight states and all the people of this country and to their descendants.

Why should Congress vote to take these rights away from all the people, from the nation as a whole, and give them to three states?

The proponents of this legislation have not given the answer. In my remarks today, Mr. President, I shall try to state why the Congress should not give these rights away. I propose to argue what I deeply believe, that the national interest and the national need require the retention of these rights, and that the alienation of these rights—this proposed giveaway—is a denial of the national interest, and a handicap to our national security.

What we should be doing, Mr. President, in the proper exercise of our obligations as members of the national Congress, is to be debating how best to use these rights to promote the national interest and to advance the national security—not what manner we can legally follow in giving away these rights which lawfully belong to the nation.

The Anderson bill offers a method of using the rights lawfully vested in the national government—to develop our oil resources, to expand our oil production, to promote the national defense, and incidentally to award to the states adjacent to these resources a very generous share of the benefits from the development of these resources, within the three-mile area.

The Hill amendment offers a way of using the benefits accruing to the national government to promote the general welfare of the nation by advancing the cause of education throughout our land, by investing part of the Federal Government's share of the proceeds from this development in the future of America, in the education of our young. In my opinion, nothing could possibly be more important.

The Holland joint resolution neglects these needs entirely. It concentrates on a confused and questionable formula for giving away what can be given away, and for paralyzing the national government's access to those rights which cannot, even under the most extreme stretch of the legal imagination, be given away.

The national rights of the three-mile belt are proposed to be given away. The bill proposes to give away title, but comprehends the strong possibility that title cannot be given away, and so provides for the contingency that this part of the giveaway will be declared illegal. So the Holland joint resolution proposes to give away the rights to the resources in the three-mile belt, even if the courts find that Congress could not legally hand over the legal title to this area.

Then the Holland measure goes further, and edges out beyond the three-mile zone, into the international zone, and seeks to give to certain states title to areas in the open sea beyond any limits which our country has ever claimed to be the exclusive territory of any country, even our own.

We have protested and resisted the claims of Russia, Ecuador, and Mexico, among other nations, to exclusive territorial rights beyond the three-mile zone off their shores; but today it is proposed to give to certain states proprietary rights to ocean areas far beyond our coasts—rights which we as a nation have never claimed to possess.

What a travesty on national responsibility. How irresponsible we will seem in the eyes of the world if we approve this legislation.

Try these questions based on Senator Lehman's remarks.

1. How does the Senator attempt to prejudice his listeners against the Holland resolution?
   a. By disproving all of Senator Holland's arguments
   b. By the use of satire and ridicule
   c. By describing it in such terms as "confused," "questionable," "irresponsible," "travesty"
   d. By offering the argument that the lands never did belong to the states

2. What emotional appeal does Senator Lehman use to sway his audience to approval of the Hill amendment?
   a. By showing the greater value of the Hill amendment
   b. By the emphasis upon the "future of America," "education of our young"
   c. By trying to anger the audience against his opponent
   d. By implying that the states are selfish in trying to secure these lands for their own ends

3. How does the Senator attempt to show that the lands do not belong to the states?
   a. By claiming that they should be supervised by the federal government
   b. By proving that the lands are not within the states

   c. By showing that supervision of the lands is not properly a local problem

   d. By citing the Supreme Court decision that they belong to the nation

4. What is Senator Lehman's main argument against giving the lands to the states?

   a. That administration of these lands is the concern of the entire nation

   b. That these lands do not belong to the states

   c. That the lands are too valuable to turn over to the states

   d. That the federal government would be more efficient in supervising these lands

   e. That passing this resolution would expose Congress to criticism from foreign countries

5. How does the Senator emphasize the importance of the exact area to be transferred?

   a. By disproving the assertion that only one-tenth of the submerged lands would be transferred

   b. By showing that such action would be contrary to the law

   c. By claiming that the land would include areas never claimed for the United States

   d. By demonstrating the tremendous value of these lands

6. Which of these facts would you like to know before agreeing with one of the Senators?

   a. To whom the lands originally belonged.

   b. How much money is likely to be realized from the oil on these lands.

   c. What would be done with the income derived from the oil rights.

   d. I have already decided against the Holland resolution.

   e. I am in favor of the Holland resolution.

   f. The detailed provisions of the Holland, Hill, and other resolutions.

   g. Why it was necessary to have a Supreme Court ruling on the ownership of the lands.

Key: 1. c   2. b   3. d   4. a   5. c   6. answer varies.

Now return to your answer to question 7, following Senator Holland's remarks. If you chose *a, b, c, e,* you permitted an argument with insufficient evidence to sway your thinking. The size of the lands, as in *a,* proves nothing about their real value or importance, or how they should be supervised. The fact that the lands immediately adjoin the state or, in a sense, are within the states' boundaries as in *b* does not necessarily prove that they belong to or should be administered by the state. The control and supervision of the coastal waters of a nation has long been considered the rightful province of the central government because of the international nature of the problem. States, counties, or other local political units have seldom been permitted to enter into agreements or treaties about such waters with other such units or with foreign nations.

Local supervision of local lands and projects as in *c* and *e* is a principle certainly not completely accepted in our country. Dams, state parks, canals, hydroelectric projects, flood control, the TVA, Indian reservations, and many other federal projects exist within various states but remain under federal control.

The efficiency of our central government can certainly be questioned in many details, as in *d* above, but, in our opinion, the raising of this issue does more to cloud the question under discussion than to clarify it. If the members of Congress were afraid of inefficient federal administration of the revenues to be derived from the lands in question, it was well within their power to direct the exact way the revenues should be administered. Senator Holland has created a false dilemma as though the only choice for Congress was between ineffective federal administration or local supervision, which presumably would be better. Several alternative courses are open, such as more detailed legislation concerning the administration of the lands, delaying action until a committee has explored all the problems in the situation, or leaving the lands under federal control with strict instructions from Congress regarding their administration.

Here are two viewpoints on the topic of price supports for agriculture. The first represents the view of business as interpreted by a businessman's organization. The second, although not a direct rebuttal, represents a defense of the policy of subsidies for farmers.

Business Looks at Price Supports [6]

Probably the most significant tool devised to aid the farmer has been the agricultural price support program of the Federal Government. Until a superior technique is developed it seems reasonable to assume that it will constitute the basis of our national agricultural policy.

But legislative history has well indicated that an agricultural support program can be used for two purposes. It can be used as a commodity floor to protect the farmer against devastating and abnormal declines in farm prices and incomes; or it can be used as a device artificially to peg farm prices, income and purchasing power at high levels. It is the growing emphasis on the latter purpose that is now of great concern.

During the recent war period, agricultural price supports were both extended and raised (thereby increasing their rigidity) in order to encourage maximum production on our farms. The results in this period of national emergency justified the means—the contribution of the American farmer to the war effort was no less significant than that of American industry and labor. Furthermore, the maintenance of supports at high and inflexible wartime levels, for several years after the war, seemed to many to be justifiable, since they protected agriculture from possibly violent price reactions during the postwar period of readjustment.

But surely the time has now arrived to formulate and adopt a permanent and workable price support program which will fit into a free, competitive enterprise system. Such a program should implement desired changes in order to place our farm economy on a basis where a minimum of government aid will be required. . . . This cannot be attained by a continuation of agricultural price supports at present high and inflexible levels. Nor . . . can it be accomplished by the adoption of the Brannan proposals, which embody extensive and relatively inflexible supports at high levels and a direct farm subsidy plan. Any agricultural program designed artificially to support farm prices, income and purchasing power at high levels is objectionable and contrary to the national welfare for three principal reasons.

First, it unnecessarily discriminates against other segments of the economy. The purchaser of farm commodities, who does not enjoy similar income assurances, has a legitimate complaint in protesting against

[6] From *The Farmer and His Government,* pamphlet issued by the Chamber of Commerce of the State of New York, Committee on Internal Trade and Improvements, October, 1949, pp. 20-23. Reprinted by permission.

the rigidity of high food prices. The proposal of Mr. Brannan to permit certain commodities to seek a market price while the government compensates for the difference between market and support price by the payment of direct subsidies does not vitiate this basic criticism. Such a plan merely transfers the consumer's food bill to the taxpayer. The consumer still pays, but in the form of enormous taxes.

No one has suggested that labor seeks its own price in the market to be supplemented by appropriations from the Treasury based on a cost-of-living index. Yet, there is more than a little similarity between this and Mr. Brannan's proposal. . . .

Secondly, a high level and inflexible support program can be effectuated only in conjunction with extensive and intensive production and marketing controls. . . . In our complex economy, full economic freedom is sometimes difficult, nevertheless, the farmer, as much as any other individual desires the maximum possible freedom to utilize his own talents and resources. It is axiomatic that intensive production controls lead to regimentation, or they fail. . . .

The third and possibly most important objection to inflexible supports at high levels is that they prevent prices from performing their normal market function of guiding production and consumption. Farming, despite its inherent production hazards should, to as great a degree as possible, be a competitive business, giving recognition to changes in demand.

There is no magic cure-all for the entire range of agricultural commodities. There are almost as many problems as there are products. But . . . to fit a prosperous and equitably treated agriculture into the over-all economy, agricultural price supports should be used as floor prices, with the primary objective being to provide a barrier against devastating price and income declines. Support programs should not be used as a means of price fixing, nor to assure a profit.

A soundly conceived support program, having as its primary objective this protection against abnormal declines, would permit the maximum freedom of operation, would rely to a minimum extent on public funds, and would permit a more normal relationship between prices and supply and demand.

Answer these questions to indicate how critically you read the first viewpoint.

1. What is the chief danger in a price support program, according to the author?

    a. Excessive governmental intervention because of the need for controls

b. The tendency to fix farm prices and income at artificially high levels

c. The discrimination against business and labor

d. The inflexibility of a price support program

2. What are the writer's three major objections to the price support program?

a. Discrimination against nonfarming elements of the population

b. The tremendous cost of the program

c. The possibility of actually creating rather than controlling surpluses

d. The difficulty of enforcing production and marketing controls

e. The artificial effect of price control upon production and consumption

3. Why does the author feel that subsidies to farmers are unfair to labor and business?

a. They are unnatural in a free, competitive business system.

b. Labor and business receive no subsidies from government.

c. Price controls involve undesirable governmental intervention in business.

d. The entire program is contrary to the national welfare.

4. Is the author's implication that labor and business enjoy no such advantages strictly accurate?

a. Yes, labor and business receive no direct subsidies.

b. No, labor and business are helped in some respects by the government.

c. No, labor and business receive indirect subsidies in the form of protective tariffs, loans at very low interest rates, and support for higher wage rates.

d. Yes, labor and business have had to operate in a highly competitive environment and to learn to exist solely by their own efforts.

5. Which of the following arguments of the author would influence you most to agree with him?

a. The discrimination against other segments of the population is undemocratic and unprecedented.

b. A great deal of governmental regimentation will be necessary to implement controls. This is undesirable and, furthermore, is unacceptable to farmers.

c. Price supports interfere with the normal relationships of production and consumption and are anomalous in a free, competitive market.

d. Price supports should provide merely floor prices to protect against abnormal declines in agricultural income rather than assure profits.

Key: 1. b   2. a, d, e   3. b   4. c   5. answer varies.

Before we discuss your answers to the last question, read the statements below in defense of price supports. See whether the proponent of this subsidy program refutes the logic and facts of the first viewpoint.

Justification for Farm Subsidies [7]

The farmer is at it again—or isn't it rather that the politician is once more courting the farmer's favors? The farmer looks for special dispensations from the laws of the market, backed by government guarantees of steady real income; the politician is busy interpreting, in his own partisan way, what he thinks the farmer's needs are. The farmer wants security and the politician wants votes.

There is nothing shocking or unpatriotic in looking for income security. This is a democracy; the cult of individualism does not mean that the individual is supposed to face the vagaries of economics in forlorn helplessness. Through association with others who feel the pinch of the same pressures and needs, he manages to have the group to which he belongs redress some of the handicaps that the accidents of occupation or of birth have imposed on him. The manufacturers, starting in the early days of the republic, achieved a large measure of protection in the internal market from the competition of foreign products. Why shouldn't the trade unions have struggled to give the workers a bargaining power equal to that of their employers?

The history of democracy is one of progressively democratized privilege or, if we prefer, of man-made political parities. The manufacturer has long obtained an advantage in the internal market for his products

[7] Ascoli, Max, "The Case of Our Kulaks," editorial, *The Reporter,* Vol. 1, July 19, 1949, pp. 2-3. Reprinted by permission.

against those imported from abroad—a parity with an edge in his favor; the trade unions have put the worker in a condition of parity around the collective-bargaining table. And why not the farmers? The chain reaction of man-made parities and of democratized privilege proceeds from one economic group to another, provided, of course, that each group has its claims backed by strong internal organization and by voting power. This is one of the facts of democratic life and there are no reasons to be squeamish about it. . . .

The price for political parities is government intervention, and government means, in our system, elected officers or public employes who keep an eye on the past and future election returns. It means politicians, and again there is no reason to squirm whenever we see politicians scurrying around and offering bigger and better parity schemes to farmers or to any other groups whose votes count. . . . In a democracy, the economic groups that feel aggrieved and have adequate voting power struggle to get from the consumers and taxpayers a share of what might be called the nation's surplus profit. And where in our country is the group so pure and unselfish as to behold the mote in the farmer's eye?

The real point of the matter is: What is the cost of each parity for the nation as a whole? Which price support and which type of parity should the farmers have? It is the point that marks the difference between acknowledging the facts of democratic life and deciding what we can do with them. The decision must be in terms of national policy, with a clear understanding that the vital interests of the nation cannot be found out by using an adding machine and summing up all the special interests that have received the benefit of the politicians' endorsement. Wise political decisions must be respectful of the facts and determined to make a dent on them. Specifically, from the incontrovertible facts represented by the "me too" trend and the now long tradition of political parties, we must derive an understanding of the farmer's case. But even this understanding will remain only a half knowledge unless we can add to it some criteria that may make us decide which farm law is best for the nation and the farmers themselves.

The subsidies should give the farmer a chance to grow into a better, more skillful producer, up to date on the latest technological improvements. The Russian Communists removed the farmer from the shocks of the world market by removing him from the farm. We, on the contrary, cannot leave the farmer so completely taken up by the care of his own acreage—plus the endorsement of government checks—as to have little interest in and little influence on the broad agricultural and social problems that go beyond the range of his own fence.

The whole of the non-rural community may accept not only as a fact of democratic life but also as a just debt the obligation to pay an inflated food bill, plus about 10 per cent in the form of farm subsidies. In all ways and as much as we can, we want to protect the individual from being tossed around by economic forces against which, alone, he has no defense; and so we have unemployment insurance, and terminal leave for homecoming soldiers, and farm subsidies. Subsidies should cushion the farmer against the shocks of sudden price falls and give him time to change crops according to the demands of the market without being stampeded by the market. . . .

If there is a danger in these plans, or rather in the trend they represent, it is of an entirely different nature. It is the danger that the great care for the individual and his individual income may lead us close to what could be called kept individualism.

1. The author's arguments for subsidies seem to be:

   a. The farmer is justified in seeking income security.
   b. Everyone is entitled to income security.
   c. It is the politicians who want to give subsidies to the farmers, rather than the farmers who seek them.
   d. The cost of subsidies is an obligation of the whole population.
   e. Subsidies would protect the farmer from sudden price changes.

2. What are some of the justifications for farm subsidies, according to the author?

   a. Many elements of labor and business receive some aid or protection similar to agricultural subsidies.
   b. Subsidies are justifiable in terms of national policy.
   c. Like business and labor, the farmer is entitled to protection against economic forces.
   d. The cost of a subsidy program would not be great.

3. Does the author consider his remarks a final answer to the problem?

   a. Yes, he would grant subsidies.
   b. He feels that subsidies to farmers are justified.
   c. No, the questions of the cost and best type of program are still unsettled.
   d. No, he is not certain that the nonfarming population is ready to accept the idea of subsidies for farmers.

4. Did you detect any element of humor in the writer's presentation of his arguments? If you scan rapidly over the material, you may find some humorous asides in the opening paragraph, and in the fourth and sixth.

Key: 1. a, e   2. a, c   3. c.

Now return to your answers to question 5 on the first abstract. Were you influenced to agree with the writer in disapproving a subsidy program? If you chose any of his arguments as presented in *a, b,* or *c,* you were jumping to conclusions without adequate evidence.

The author's argument as presented in *a* is inadequate because the giving of preferential treatment in one fashion or another to one type of business is certainly not without precedent in this country. For example, land grants to railroads, tariffs to protect young (and old) industries, direct subsidies to steamship and air lines, etc., have been in existence for quite some time. It is true that such programs reflect in increased taxes but this fact has seldom deterred political proponents of these measures when a sizable voting segment of the population would apparently benefit.

In *b,* we see reflected an attitude toward further intervention of government in business that produces strong feelings in many people. Some go to the extreme of decrying any governmental supervision, while others apparently wish for a nationalization of almost all business. Neither extreme is entirely logical or rational. The attitudes of the extremists present the problem as though there was no middle ground. This type of reasoning is often called a false dilemma—no choice between the frying pan and the fire. It is quite possible, however, that a price support program could be evolved with a minimum of regimentation of agricultural production and marketing controls.

In *c,* there is reason to doubt that a truly free, competitive system of markets exists throughout the world any longer. Restraints, subsidies, trade agreements, monetary restrictions, not to mention political influences have taken much of the "free" element out of world markets. Whether we agree with the principle of these restraints is immaterial, since they force modification of the actions of business in many ways. Production and marketing controls are common in many countries and it is probably impossible to argue them out of existence by claiming that they are antagonistic to a free, competitive system.

The writer's final argument, *d,* is probably an acceptable statement, at least to some, of the primary purpose of price supports—to protect the farmer against disastrous influences arising from world events—to make it economically feasible for the farmer to continue to contribute to the national economy. However, this argument is also only weakly supported. He implies, in the closing paragraph of his remarks, that a floor price program would be relatively free from regimentation and be more responsive to supply and demand. Does he really expect us to believe that, if guaranteed a minimum price for their crops, and production and marketing controls were loose, farmers would not attempt to increase production? Farmers are not responsive to the law of supply and demand (or there would be no problem here), nor do they refrain from increasing production of subsidized or other crops in the absence of controls.

CRITICAL READING IN THE FUTURE

We have introduced you here to the critical reading of persuasive and propaganda materials. We have illustrated some of the techniques used by writers and speakers to influence your thinking. We have tried to help you recognize some of the common logical fallacies present in much of the material presented to you. Whether you will be able to read critically and intelligently in the future depends largely upon your attitude, however.

The knowledge you have gained in this chapter can be no more than a foundation for future critical reading. Only if you are curious, questioning, and demanding of proof can you do independent thinking. Only by reacting objectively and evaluating what you read and hear can you be free from the constant, insidious influence of the propagandist and persuasive speaker.

Several other books offering suggestions on how to read critically are:

Altick, Richard D., *Preface to Critical Reading.* New York: Holt, 1946.

Howe, Quincy, *The News and How to Understand It, In Spite of the Newspapers, In Spite of the Magazines, In Spite of the Radio.* New York: Simon and Schuster, 1940.

Hummel, William, and Huntress, Keith, *The Analysis of Propaganda.* New York: William Sloane, 1949.

Irwin, Will, *Propaganda and the News: or What Makes You Think So?* New York: McGraw-Hill, 1936.

Lee, Alfred McClung, *How to Understand Propaganda.* New York: Rinehart, 1952.

8

Reading Statistics

What You Will Do
  Discover some of the statisticians' tricks

What You Will Learn
  How to read certain statistics and charts more critically

The reading of facts presented in mathematical form seems to bother many present-day adults. Graphs, tables, and charts are just so many lines and numbers to skip over, if possible. If you don't think so, ask the next person you hear using the word *billion* to tell you how much it really is. Or if he is talking in millions, ask him what a million dollars is, what it represents, what you can do with it. The chances are that he has little or no concept of how much a million dollars is or will do.

This ignorance of mathematical terms and concepts is quite widespread. As a result, those who present facts to the public through mathematics can easily deceive the average reader. Statistics and charts are manipulated to prove almost anything to the naïve consumer. Unless you learn to read mathematical materials critically, you too are at the mercy of the unscrupulous statistician or chartmaker.

THE DECEPTIVE SAMPLE

Many statistics are based upon a sample of the population. But no statistic is any better than the sample on which it is based. This sample may be too small, or biased by obvious or hidden factors, or deliberately chosen to prove the writer's point. Take the case of the *Literary Digest* poll of 1936 that predicted the presidential election of Alfred Landon. The sample was composed of ten million telephone and *Digest* subscribers who had been used in a correct presidential prediction in 1932. Such a sample seemed large enough and apparently free from bias. But the people who could afford telephones and magazine subscriptions just weren't representative of the American public in 1936. Most Americans were still struggling with the effects of the depression at the later date. Telephones and magazines were luxuries for many trying to make both ends meet. The sample was economically biased and reflected the voting preferences of a select group, not the general public.

To yield an accurate statistic, a sample must be representative of the total group. It should be selected by pure chance under circumstances in which every person or thing in the total group has an equal chance of being selected. This is called a random sampling. However, because it involves so great a cross section of the total population, true random sampling is almost prohibitive in time and cost. In its place, a stratified sample composed of a small group possessing those traits characteristic of the general population is commonly used. Public opinion polls, surveys of users of a certain product, sales predictions for a proposed new product, views of magazine-readers, preferences of radio-listeners and televiewers are commonly based on this stratified sampling technique.

But how does the researcher know that his stratified sample is really a random sample of the total population? The truth is, he doesn't. His conclusions may be distorted by any of a dozen factors such as the very questions asked, the emotional reactions of those interviewed to the questions or the interviewer, the extent to which social prestige or the ego of the respondent is challenged, etc. How accurate, for example, can a survey of such personal matters as income, church attendance, racial discrimination, or wife-beating really be?

By this time, you have recognized that our purpose is to make you look more critically at any statistic based on sampling. Most poll results are apt to be biased, even when they are not deliberately distorted. This bias is likely to be toward reflecting the thinking and actions of the person with better-than-average economic and social status. As Darrel Huff expresses it, if you were the interviewer waiting outside a factory, which man would you stop—the surly-looking fellow plowing along with his head down, or the clean-cut, smiling chap walking leisurely homeward?

To help you read and interpret statistics based on sampling, we suggest you "ask" the writer such questions as: How many people are involved in these data? What kind of people were they? How were they selected? What are some of the factors that may have influenced the results? What do the results prove, if anything? What kind of sense do they make? For example, the manufacturer of a popular brand of cigarettes claims that more doctors smoke this brand than any other. Are doctors better judges of taste, mildness, and other cigarette qualities than other people? Aside from the fact that we don't know how many doctors were sampled, just what does this statistic prove? The implication is, of course, that medical training makes one a better judge of cigarettes and more aware of the possible harmful effects. Therefore, if more doctors smoke X brand, it must be better and less harmful than other brands. Only a moment's thought will demonstrate that if X is a widely sold brand, it is likely to sell well among most groups, plumbers as well as doctors. This is a common type of two-pronged propaganda device, this use of the prestige of the medical profession in impressing the public, and questionable statistics.

Or take the claim of a toothpaste manufacturer that six out of eight people prefer the taste of his product to that of others. Does he tell you how many people were sampled before these results were secured? Usually not, because his researchers probably waited until they found such a result in one small group rather than reporting on the preferences of the entire population sampled. If two toothpastes were being compared, we would expect five out of ten people to prefer Z paste, purely on a basis of chance. Flipping a coin several hundred times is likely to result in half heads and half tails. But in a small sample, the law of probability does not operate in the same fashion. The first ten tosses of your coin may all be heads. Thus, if the surveyors for Z toothpaste took a number of small samples, it is quite possible that they would find one in which the results were the kind they wanted. This may not be dishonest reporting of research but it certainly is rigged to produce the desired results.

THE MISLEADING AVERAGE

What is an average? Is it the most common characteristic of a relatively large number of people, or a point that divides the population into two equal halves of "haves" and "have-nots"? Or, is it the total amount of a certain trait divided equally among the entire population? Well, it is and it isn't. It may be any or all of these.

The word *average* is used loosely to describe any of three measures known technically as the mode, the median, and the mean. When we discuss such human traits as height and weight, it doesn't matter much which we use, for these characteristics are distributed normally throughout the population. But if we talk about incomes or income taxes, wattage consumption or divorce rates, it matters a great deal which average is selected.

Let's take a case in point. The ABC Electronics Company tells us that their average employee earned $4,000 last year. Sounds fairly good, doesn't it? But what does this average mean? Was $4,000 the most common salary among the employees? No, because the greatest number of employees earning any one salary, or the mode, is found at $2,500. Did half of the help earn more and half less than $4,000? Is this a median? No. All but about a half-dozen employees are hourly workers at a basic wage of $2,500. Then what does the $4,000 mean? It must be an average of the salaries paid to the two partners who own the company ($23,000 each); the two engineers ($12,000 each); a technician and a production manager ($8,000 each); two foremen ($3,000 each) and the forty hourly workers who earn about $2,500 per year. All these salaries add up to $192,000 which divided by forty-eight employees averages $4,000. Neat, isn't it? Would you have thought of adding in the owners' shares to raise the average yearly salary? But the labor union isn't likely to use this mean in asking for a better salary scale. They are more apt to use the mode, the point at which most of the employees fall on the scale of $2,500. In this case, the union could also use the median of $2,500 since more than half of the workers earn this amount or less.

Graphically, these data could have been presented something like this (but of course no statistician attempting to please the owners of the ABC Electronics Company would have used such a method of presenting the facts):

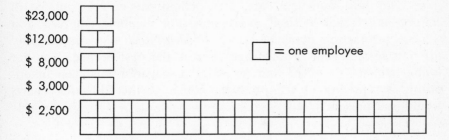

Fig. 1. Average Yearly Salary—ABC Electronics Company.

The next time you read something about an average, ask yourself, "What average—mean, mode, or median?" or "Average of what? Who and what is included here?" Here are typical "average" figures found in a recent publication. Just what do they mean?

Changing Times for June, 1956, reports an average of 6.02 hours of televiewing per day in the American home. Last year's figure is given as 5.81 hours per day. It concludes, "The glass screen is really taking over."

These figures have an artificial note of authenticity because of the use of the decimal figures. It sounds much more accurate to say 6.02 hours rather than simply 6 hours. But how many homes were involved in this survey? The fine distinctions implied in the decimals are absurd unless the sample was quite large.

How was the survey done? By whom? By calling on the phone and asking how many hours a day the TV set was used? Were reliable time-sampling measures used to determine actual amount of televiewing? Are these figures offered by TV manufacturers or broadcasting chains who, perhaps, have an ulterior motive? As for monopolizing the televiewer's day, how much of a real difference is the .21 of an hour (thirteen minutes)? Is the conclusion based on a significant difference? Do these facts actually add up to anything at all? Do they even indicate a reliable trend?

PLAUSIBLE CHARTS AND GRAPHS

In the effort to make mathematical concepts more palatable, or more shocking, writers often employ a pictorial or graphic presentation. Like most statistical data, this method can be manipulated to convey almost any desired impression. For example, suppose you were a production manager trying to show top management why the unit cost of your product had risen in the past decade. You are trying to convince them that the sales manager is mistaken in opposing a repricing of the product. Which of the following charts would you present?

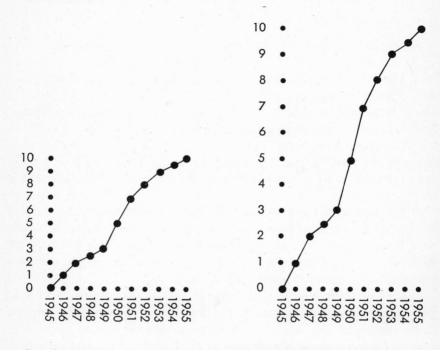

Fig. 2. Increase in Unit Cost in   Fig. 3. Increase in Unit Cost in
Per Cent, 1945–1955.   Per Cent, 1945–1955.

These graphs are all accurate and honest but there is a great deal of difference in the impression they create. Figures 2 and 4 imply a fairly constant but gradual increase in unit cost. In figure 3, the rate of increase seems terrific. The trick, of course, is merely to narrow the horizontal interval in the graph. If you do this, you automatically come up with a startling picture. Push the base line closer together, and your line shoots up. Or, to produce the opposite effect,

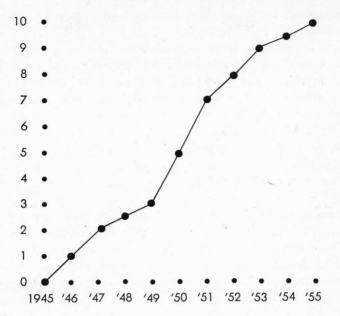

Fig. 4. Increase in Unit Cost in Per Cent, 1945–1955.

Fig. 5. Frozen Food Consumption. (From an advertisement by Marathon, a Division of American Can Company, in *Business Week*, January 7, 1956.)

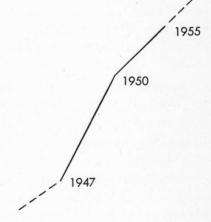

merely lengthen the base line. What do you want to prove? Pick your own chart.

There is another technique of manipulating graphs that isn't quite as obvious but helps to strengthen your data. This is presenting the facts without a reference point. If the possible range of data and the zero reference point are omitted, it becomes much easier to prove your point, whatever it may be. Figure 5 is an example of this type of graph. Visually, you are led to believe that frozen food consumption has grown tremendously in the period from 1947 to 1955. But how much actual increase does this represent? One per cent? Ten per cent? One hundred per cent? There is no way of knowing from the graph.

There is nothing wrong with this chart from the advertiser's viewpoint. Or, from the naïve reader's interpretation. He gets the point. But from the standpoint of accuracy and sincerity, there is much to be desired. But no one would stoop so low, you say. Darrel Huff gives numerous samples drawn from reputable newspapers and magazines in his interesting book, *How to Lie with Statistics*. This is a common method of producing striking statistics with weak data.

This brief review of questionable statistics has been intended to sharpen your critical attitudes toward materials presented in this fashion. We have not attempted a thoroughgoing study of the subject of statistics as such. Our purpose has not been to teach you all you should know about statistics, or even all you may need to know to read them intelligently. If you are really interested in examples of plausible but deceptive statistics, these articles and books will be useful.

Dornbusch, Sanford M., and Schmid, Calvin F., *A Primer of Social Statistics*. New York: McGraw-Hill, 1955. Pp. 230-234.

Huff, Darrel, *How to Lie with Statistics*. New York: Norton, 1955.

Knight, M., "Figures Can Lie," *Science Digest*, Vol. 30, September 1951, pp. 52-55.

Neyman, J., "Statistics, servant of all science," *Science*, Vol. 122, September 2, 1955, pp. 401-406.

Walker, Helen M., "Allergic to statistics?" *National Education Association Journal*, Vol. 43, October, 1954, pp. 419-420.

9

Building a Better Vocabulary

What You Will Do
  Evaluate your vocabulary

What You Will Learn
  Ways of improving and increasing your vocabulary

Vocabulary development follows a fairly common pattern for most individuals. It is more rapid during infancy and early childhood. After a child is a year or two old, new words appear in his vocabulary so rapidly that it is almost impossible for an observer to count or keep track of them. As most men know, speech develops earlier for girls and progresses more rapidly. This stage of rapid growth persists through the early school years. Even foreign languages are learned easily and rapidly during this period. As the child matures to high school age, the relative rate of increase of vocabulary gradually diminishes. New interests and demands take precedence over interest in words and vocabulary development continues at a much slower rate.

After formal education is completed, there is relatively little vocabulary growth in the average adult. Because there are no demands for study, he does little reading in new fields and hence, learns few new words. If reading is demanded by his vocation, it is more likely to be confined to one or two major areas and there is no real contact with unknown areas of vocabulary. The average adult shows little interest in acquiring the new words he does meet. He seldom attempts to transfer the new terms and expressions from his reading vocabulary into his own speech and writing. His techniques for learning new words are primitive. Occasionally he looks for the meaning or spelling of a word in the dictionary. More often he depends upon guess or feel for the meaning of an unknown word encountered in reading rather than using the context in any of several ways to help determine the exact meaning. He has little knowledge of word structure or structural parts such as prefixes, suffixes, and roots and makes practically no use of these in analyzing new terms. He shows only slight interest in diction or careful choice of words to express exact meanings. His speech and writing vocabularies are dependent upon hackneyed words such as *got, nice, thing, take, very, swell,* and upon clichés and commercial expressions.

There is, of course, considerable individual variation from this pattern of gradual stagnation of vocabulary development. Some widely read and highly verbal individuals expand their knowledge of words far beyond the average adult. Their interests and reading may lead them to know and use literally hundreds of thousands of words beyond the relatively few known to the average person. As a result, their capacities for understanding ideas and communicating with others are outstanding. Because of their fluency and clarity, they invoke respect and advance professionally and vocationally. Some research has shown that one of the major differences between executives and their employees is the skill with words exhibited by the former. This does not necessarily imply, as some have assumed, that self-improvement in vocabulary results in immediate capacity for and advancement to executive rank. But, in this business world, ability to express oneself and to transmit ideas to others is an essential for successful management. Lack of skill in communication makes the direction and guidance of others almost impossible.

IS YOUR VOCABULARY REALLY POOR?

Undoubtedly some of you feel that your vocabulary is weak or that it is a handicap in your reading. Trouble with vocabulary is a common complaint of adults who feel that their reading skills are not good. Quite often, however, this self-criticism is not based on any real grounds. Some individuals feel that they should know practically any word they meet in reading. It disturbs their self-confidence to encounter an unknown word. If we realize that the English language may have as many as three million words, according to the semantic word count of some authorities, it becomes obvious that no one knows all of these. In fact, a well-read college graduate probably doesn't know more than fifty thousand to seventy-five thousand different words. If these rough estimates are anywhere near correct, then the average reader can certainly expect to find some unknown words in almost any difficult material he tries to read.

Some of those who complain of poor vocabulary are really handicapped by a tendency to vocalize words as they read. They read slowly, carefully, saying words perhaps audibly, perhaps inaudibly. Or they have the feeling that they are thinking over each word, even when their lips and tongue are still. Because of their caution, and concern with words, they feel handicapped in vocabulary, they say, when the true difficulty is that they are not reading for ideas. Those who read word by word often have the feeling that their vocabulary is poor. The real culprit is lack of speed and overconcern with words.

Some of those who do this mental pronouncing of words are disturbed by new terms simply because they can't pronounce them. If the word is not included in their auditory vocabulary, they are upset and somewhat disorganized by the experience. Auditory vocabulary consists of those words we readily recognize by ear. But this group of words is not the same as those we recognize in reading. For numerous reasons, our auditory is much smaller than our reading vocabulary. We can read intelligently literally thousands of words that we could not recognize easily if someone used them in conversation. This difficulty with pronouncing words met in reading accounts for the complaint of many of those who feel inadequate in vocabulary.

Such individuals fail to realize that it is normal to be able to read fluently many words that one cannot pronounce. They fail to make use of the context, or the sense of the sentence, to help them over new words or expressions. They stop, fumble over the mental or audible sounds of the term, and feel that the reason their reading is so labored and slow is that their vocabulary is scanty. To illustrate, can you read straight through the following sentence without stopping to puzzle over any of the words?

The executioner gave the *coup de grâce* to the condemned man by a final bullet in the head.

Did the French expression bother you or did you read all of the sentence and thereby understand it? Actually, the term is thoroughly explained by the sentence. A *coup de grâce* is a final blow, a death blow, often by a bullet in the head of an executed person. If you fumbled with the expression, or felt uncomfortable about it, you would logically conclude that such feelings were due to your poor vocabulary. The real reason for your discomfort is lack of skill in using the context to find meanings for new terms. As we pointed out before, you cannot expect to know the thousands of new terms you will meet in your future reading. But you can be expected to develop skill in using the thought to help you understand these unknown words and to help you build your vocabulary from day to day. This skill will be one of those emphasized later in this chapter.

EVALUATING YOUR VOCABULARY

We have not included a test of vocabulary to help you evaluate your ability because vocabulary is not a unitary trait. Like rate, it varies considerably from one reading situation to the next. There are many kinds of vocabulary, such as speaking vocabulary, writing vocabulary, and listening vocabulary. Knowledge also varies from one field of interest to another. One commercial test, for example, includes separate tests in the areas of human relations, commerce, government, physical sciences, biological sciences, mathematics, fine arts, and sports. Other tests measure vocabulary in literary and social science terms, as well as general vocabulary. Accurate evaluation of your vocabulary needs just isn't feasible without extensive testing, for which we have little time here.

Furthermore, evaluation of growth in vocabulary is not accurate with present available tests. The sample of a few words in the average test does not reflect the individual's actual growth in learning new words. Tests are built by stratified sampling of a dictionary and each test word is assumed to represent perhaps hundreds or even thousands of other words. An individual attempting to improve his vocabulary might learn many words but unless some of these happened to coincide with test items, his progress would not be manifest from the test score. This inability of common tests to reflect progress in vocabulary building has been observed in the test results of many college and industrial reading training courses. While gains in rate and comprehension are often very marked, vocabulary seldom shows any real change, insofar as tests can detect it.

SIGNS OF POOR VOCABULARY

Rather than attempting the evaluation of your vocabularies by inadequate or time-consuming tests, we suggest that you use the following check list in judging your own need for vocabulary building. Check those that apply to you.

Do you:

Have difficulty in conveying your exact meaning to others

Often feel the need for a better word to express precise meanings

Seldom use syllabication to work out pronunciation and meanings

Depend largely on guessing for meaning of unknown word in reading

Use dictionary only rarely

Use dictionary only for meanings and spelling

Have to look up a word in dictionary several times

Seldom consciously analyze parts of a word to discover meaning

Fumble with words when reading

Often feel that comprehension is hindered by lack of understanding of certain words

Feel that your understanding of word meanings is hazy or inaccurate

Have difficulty remembering meaning or spelling of words

Meet words you don't immediately recognize in almost everything you read

Sometimes avoid using a word because you're not sure of it

Seldom try to learn a new word and use it in speaking or writing

Often feel inadequate in trying to explain something to others

Feel dependent upon the dictionary for word meanings

Pay little or no attention to new words other than to secure a temporarily satisfactory meaning

This check list includes reading behaviors that are indicators of weakness in vocabulary, as well as behaviors that reflect your flexibility in learning new words. If you checked five or more items in the list, either your vocabulary is weak or your attitudes toward vocabulary building are poor. Such poor practices or unfavorable attitudes will prevent any real growth in this highly significant skill of communicating with others. If you checked five or more items in this list, or feel the need of improving your vocabulary, you should certainly read the rest of this chapter.

HOW TO INCREASE YOUR VOCABULARY

Before you begin this effort, let us point out that significant vocabulary growth is not easily and quickly achieved. You are not going to witness a tremendous broadening of your stock of words in a few weeks or even months. After all, it has taken you all your life to learn the relatively few words you now know. There is no magic series of exercises that will suddenly change this situation. You will probably add only a few new words a day, or perhaps a thousand a year, to your total inventory. Although this isn't a very rapid rate of learning, it is decidedly faster than that of the average person. If you work at it, you will show real progress, even though it won't be quite as dramatic as you would like.

More important, however, than the number of new words you will learn, will be the changes in your attitudes toward words and your increasing flexibility in handling them. If you conscientiously work through the rest of this chapter, you will learn a number of techniques for vocabulary building. Your interest in new words will awaken and your skill in dealing with new, difficult terms and expressions will continue to grow.

SHOW INTEREST IN NEW WORDS

In order to promote continual vocabulary growth, you must cultivate an interest in new words for their own sake. Try to be aware of them when you meet them. In fact, look for interesting words each time you read. These new terms and expressions are to be your means of communicating with others. Your vocabulary will grow only if you are alert to these new tools.

The recognition of new words as unknown is not quite as simple as it seems. Studies of college students and adults tend to show that they do not realize when a word is unknown to them. They think they recognize and understand more words than they actually do. For this reason, some self-criticism and questioning of your own vocabulary is necessary. Do not assume that you know a term simply because you can hazard a guess as to its meaning.

Check your impressions by use of the dictionary. Use this reference tool to study the meanings, pronunciation, derivation, and spelling of each new word. Don't make the mistake of simply finding a meaning which fits temporarily, and then dismissing the term as thoroughly understood. Try instead, to make as many mental notes about the word as you can, such as the appearance, peculiarities of pronunciation or spelling, as well as some unusual or interesting fact about its history and origin. For example, suppose you meet a reference to the "halcyon days of childhood." Does this refer to nostalgic memories for this period, or the freedom from responsibility, or the peacefulness and serenity of the early years? Your dictionary may tell you that this is the Greek word for the kingfisher. This bird built a nest on the sea at the winter solstice and magically calmed the waves during its nesting time, or so the Greeks believed. Hence, the word came to refer to a calm, peaceful period called "halcyon days." This information concerning the derivation of the word plus attention to its unusual spelling should help in retaining it.

Try to broaden your vocabulary by seeking new fields of reading. If you are a lawyer, try reading psychology, sociology, or anthropology for a change. Ralph Linton's *Tree of Culture* or C. Wright Mills' *The Power Elite* may give you different views of the people you deal with. If you are an accountant, you might enjoy a change of diet to *Scientific American*'s *The New Astronomy,* or to Peter Hood's *How Time is Measured.* Read fiction and biography as well as nonfiction to enlarge your reading tastes and to bring you into contact with other vocabularies.

When reading in an unfamiliar technical field, you may find it useful to build a vocabulary card file. This systematic approach to learning new terms has amply demonstrated its effectiveness. In this system, you write the new word and the sentence in which it occurred on one side of the card. On the other, write a brief dictionary definition, and the word itself. If it is difficult to pronounce, use the diacritical markings given in the dictionary. If there are recognizable parts such as the stem or prefix, indicate the meanings of these also to aid your retention of the word.

To support your new interest in words, put some of the following next to the dictionary on your desk:

Barnes, Duane Clayton, *Wordlore*. New York: Dutton, 1948.

Funk, Wilfred, *Word Origins and Their Romantic Stories*. New York: Funk, 1950.

Mencken, H. L., *The American Language*. New York: Alfred A. Knopf, 1945.

G. C. Merriam Co., *Picturesque Word Origins*. Springfield, Mass.: Merriam, 1933.

Myers, E. D., *The Foundations of English*. New York: Macmillan, 1940.

Radford, Edwin, *Unusual Words and How They Came About*. New York: Philosophical Library, 1946.

Shipley, Joseph T., *Dictionary of Word Origins*. New York: Philosophical Library, 1945.

Finally, to implement your continued growth in vocabulary, attempt to use the new terms as often as you can in speaking and writing. Increasing ability to express your ideas precisely and understandably is the real goal of all your efforts in vocabulary building. Think of the new additions to your knowledge as tools to express ideas better. If you fear embarrassment or being thought pedantic when you use a new term in speech, then try it first in your writing. But use it again and again until it becomes part of you.

USING THE CONTEXT

The average adult has one favorite technique for determining the meanings of unknown words—the guess. It may be sheer intuition in which the reader tries to sense the meaning implied by the rest of the sentence. Or, the meaning may actually be given in a phrase or clause following the word so that no real analysis is necessary. But such use of the context is apt to be a fumbling, hit-or-miss process that works only occasionally. Tests show that even when the sentence is carefully constructed to give the meaning, the average person can recognize the meaning only about half the time. Because of this lack of ability to use the context efficiently, we will offer some suggestions and illustrations of this technique.

Here is an opportunity to demonstrate your skill in deriving meanings from context. Try to match each of the words with the correct definition. Score yourself on this trial. Then read the sentences that use the key words in context. Try the test items again. See whether you can correct your errors by using the sentence to help you grasp the meaning. If you really use the context effectively, your second trial should result in correcting more than 50 per cent of the errors in your first trial.

1. *perusing* means
   a. amusing
   b. reading carefully
   c. looking at
   d. for use

2. *accosted* means
   a. easy to reach
   b. blamed
   c. stopped
   d. spoken to

3. *ogre* means
   a. monster
   b. giant
   c. desperado
   d. evildoer

4. *peculation* means
   a. gambling
   b. arguments
   c. theft of money
   d. petty criticism

5. *decry* means
   a. to speak loudly
   b. to deny
   c. to be against
   d. to believe in

6. *largess* means
   a. generosity
   b. nobility
   c. greatest
   d. respect

7. *expropriated* means
   a. budgeted for
   b. improper
   c. confiscated
   d. stolen

8. *orison* means
   a. the source
   b. edge of the earth
   c. a prayer
   d. a talk or speech

9. *reciprocity* means
   a. the opposite
   b. lowered tariffs
   c. cooperation
   d. cancellation of debts

10. *malfeasance* means
    a. wrongdoing
    b. ill-will
    c. bribery
    d. robbery or theft

11. *contumacious* means
   a. secretive
   b. rebellious
   c. despicable
   d. incorrigible

12. *colophon* means
   a. a type of column
   b. an emblem
   c. human organ
   d. punctuation marks

13. *lethal* means
   a. a gas
   b. sleepy
   c. deadly
   d. a fuel

14. *importune* means
   a. to extort
   b. significant
   c. to flatter
   d. to request

15. *intestate* means
   a. without a will
   b. between states
   c. to import
   d. internal organ

Score yourself on these fifteen items. The answers are:

1. b.	6. a.	11. b.
2. d.	7. c.	12. b.
3. a.	8. c.	13. c.
4. c.	9. c.	14. d.
5. c.	10. a.	15. a.

Now read these sentences to improve your understanding of these words. Try to use the context to secure the meanings.

1. After perusing each line of the poem, he believed he had a clearer understanding of its meaning.

2. As the man attempted to jaywalk at the intersection, he was accosted sharply by the traffic policeman.

3. Many stenographers conceive of their bosses as ogres whose only purpose is to squeeze as much work as possible from them.

4. The bookkeeper was arrested after the auditors found evidence of peculation in his accounts.

5. In recent months, anti-Negro groups of certain states have loudly decried any efforts at integration of Negro and white children in school.

6. It was only through the largess of his patron that Fra Angelico was able to continue his painting.

7. Those who have been upset by Egypt's nationalization of the

Suez Canal have forgotten how successfully Mexico expropriated American oil equipment a few years ago.

8. As twilight descended, the monks lifted their voices in a quiet orison to their Maker.

9. The principle of reciprocity among nations has resulted in preferential tariffs and, in many instances, increased trade exchanges.

10. Not all types of malfeasance are necessarily punishable by law, however unethical they may be.

11. There is a period in the childhood of most American children when their contumacious behavior toward any adult suggestion is almost unbearable.

12. Logically enough, the colophon of the Cardinal editions of Pocket Books, Inc., is a male bird of that species.

13. In some parts of our country, smog has, upon occasion, become a lethal danger to local inhabitants.

14. The man begged an opportunity to present his case before the king and importune the king's forgiveness.

15. Many businessmen who are highly efficient in their occupations cause great difficulties for their families by dying intestate.

Now try for a better score on the list of words.

Meanings by Inference.   The most common way of finding a meaning from context is by inference, or reasoning out the probable meaning from the sense of the sentence. The average person does this so unconsciously that he isn't even aware of it. In fact, unless the new term makes him pause to notice it, he reads past it assuming a probable meaning without conscious effort. This process can be sharpened and improved, obviously, by a little conscious attention.

Here are two words or expressions you may not know. They were used in some of the reading materials in other chapters. First try to choose the correct definition. Then read the sentence to see whether you can discover a more accurate meaning from the context.

1. *redress* means   a. to maintain   c. to alter
                      b. to correct   d. to guess

To *redress* that attitude, the executive who wants to know what the facts are—rather than looking for something to blame the facts upon—may well take a long, careful look at a new publication . . . of the Survey Research Center at the University of Michigan.

2. *acumen* means   a. effort   c. slyness
                               b. decisiveness   d. keenness

More than one businessman has applauded his own *acumen* when he has bought off certain union demands by the single expedient of making concessions on issues which appeared to cost very little or meant very little to the company at the time.

Key: 1. b   2. d.

If either of these words was unknown to you, careful reading of the context would have clarified its meaning. Or, you may have recognized the exact meaning of *redress* by reasoning from the significance of its structural parts. *Dress,* when used as a military drill term, or to refer to polishing a stone or trimming lumber means to align or straighten. *Re* means again, or to repeat. Therefore redress must mean to restraighten or to correct. *Acumen* obviously resembles *acuity* or *acute,* which connote sharpness or keenness. Bringing to bear your knowledge of word parts, reasoning by analogy with cognates or words having the same root, can add to the inferential or intuitive hints given by the context. With a bit of thinking and effort, many apparently new or difficult terms and expressions will lend themselves to relatively easy interpretation.

Meanings by Direct Explanation. It may seem too apparent even to mention, but many terms are actually explained by the author in his text. This is a common practice among technical and textbook writers who are aware that the reader may not be familiar with their vocabulary. Try to identify the correct definition of these two words, and then see how clearly the author explains the exact meaning.

3. *scarab* means   a. an isolated rock   c. shoulder blade
                               b. an Italian design   d. a large black beetle

The ring on his left hand bore a carved stone resembling a scarab or beetle.

4. *aggregate* means   a. the sum or total   c. the value
                                 b. partial   d. marble material

Loss of profits and increased costs due to interrupted business, terminated leases, and destroyed records may produce an embarrassing loss. The aggregate or total loss may be far greater than the separate values of all the property destroyed.

Key: 3. d   4. a.

If these words *scarab* and *aggregate* were unknown to you when you began to read the sentences, they became familiar as you read. In each case, the meaning of the word was actually explained in the context. If you read attentively, you could not help but understand these terms.

Meanings from Structural Clues. The meaning of an unknown word may be discernible from the structure of the word itself or the nature of the sentence. A definition of the term may be given in a phrase or clause following the word. Or, the author may show its meaning by contrasting or comparing it with a simpler word. Try your knowledge of these words first, then read the illustrative sentences to see how their structure helps you.

5. *nominal* means   a. to name   c. to name for office
                               b. not real or actual   d. single or only

The transfer of the land was concluded by a nominal fee, or the token payment of one dollar, in order to make the transaction appear to be a sale rather than a gift.

6. *accrue* means   a. date of payment   c. admission to
                              b. to accept as valid   d. increase in orderly
                                                       fashion

If you retain these shares, their dividends will accrue and grow into a reasonable return on your investment.

7. *patronage* means   a. to guard or protect   c. owner of large
                               b. to treat with   tracts of land
                                     condescension   d. control of nomination to public office

Patronage, which involves the giving of jobs to minor politicians, makes an efficient civil service system based on merit almost impossible.

Key: 5. b   6. d   7. d.

In each of these sentences, the unknown word is compared or contrasted with a simpler word, or clarified by an explanatory phrase. Thus its meaning becomes apparent provided the simpler term of the explanation is understood. You will find that explaining terms by contrast or comparison is a fairly common practice among technical and textbook writers.

Meanings from Figures of Speech.   Figures of speech are often used, particularly in speeches or literary works, to provide color and variety. Most of them are basically a comparison, such as "angry as a bear" or "snake-like" or "hawk-nosed." Try your knowledge of the three following words. Then see whether the figures of speech in the sentences that follow help your understanding of the words.

8. *stealthily* means   a. strongly   c. illegally
                           b. secretly   d. taking unlawfully

Moving as a sneak-thief might, he stealthily hid the unfinished work under his desk and left the office.

9. *pecuniary* means   a. small, tiny   c. miserable
                          b. pertaining to   d. contemptible
                             money

The average individual is likely to think of bankers and financiers as possessing the Midas touch that turns all their activities into pecuniary profit.

10. *specious* means   a. money   c. unusual
                           b. kinds or types d. deceptively
                                                 plausible

The speaker's arguments were as specious as those of the snake in the Garden of Eden.

Key: 8. b   9. b   10. d.

Recognizing meanings by means of the author's figures of speech makes more demand upon the reader's background than other contextual clues. The reader must be familiar with mythology (the Midas touch), ancient history, religion (the Garden of Eden), and many other areas. He must also be familiar with the human traits attributed to animals and other unhuman figures. This type of use of the context is the most difficult of all those we have discussed, but with imagination and effort it can be made to help the reader.

Meanings from Tone or Mood.   In subjective types of writing, such as essays, biography, advertising, novels, etc., authors often attempt to create a feeling or emotion in the reader. Their words are chosen carefully to create the tone or mood of the piece and produce the desired effect in the reader. If you can sense the underlying tone of the author, his terms become more clearly understood. Test yourself on these words. Then read the sentences to feel the tone that gives meaning to them.

11. *sawdust trail* means   a. a way of re-
                                   pentance
                              b. a trail around a
                                   sawmill

   c. a church aisle
   d. any path of
        sawdust

   Tonight, I am going to mention plenty of bad practices by labor; and plenty by management also. I think we all ought to hit the sawdust trail together.

12. *irascible* means   a. shining
                         b. sarcastic

   c. angry
   d. lit up, illuminated

   His visage changed until he appeared ready to jump upon us. As his irritation mounted, his voice became increasingly irascible and strident.

Key: 11. a   12. c.

   This has been a very brief introduction to five ways of using the context. These illustrations should serve, however, to prove that many unknown or difficult words may be understood if you dig into the context. If used as the first step in attacking an unknown word, active use of the context can save many unnecessary trips to the dictionary and speed up comprehension as well. Whenever possible, make the written material work for you to aid your understanding of its terms and ideas.

AFFIXES AND ROOTS

Another method of increasing vocabulary and discovering word meanings while reading is dependent upon knowledge of affixes and roots. We have already alluded to this technique in discussing structural clues to meaning, but the practice can be expanded with profit. You are aware, of course, that most English words are formed from a base word and perhaps another word part attached to the front or rear of the word. But, can you use these facts when reading? How often are you able to deduce the meaning of a word from its root or stem? Can you recognize how the meaning of the word is modified by the affixes—that is, the prefixes, or suffixes? Can you do this often enough for it to become a real aid in discovering word meanings, or do you read so inattentively that the structure of words escapes you?

Here is a paragraph that might have been drawn from a text. You will find that there are several word parts that are used a number of times. If you can figure out the meaning of these parts, you should have no difficulty in comprehending the technical terms used in the paragraph.

Some conceive of a discussion merely as an opportunity to contradict another's opinions as soon as he stops for breath. In contradistinction to this, the effective listener does just that before he offers a contraposition. He does not argue purely for contrariness sake or contravene the speaker in order to have something to say. On the contrary, his attention permits him to recognize the other's viewpoint calmly and clearly before deciding whether he shall offer a contradictive statement.

Did you recognize the recurring prefix? Were you able to detect its significance in each of the words in which it appeared? Show whether you understood all these words by matching each with the correct definition.

1. contradict   a. the opposite
2. contradistinction   b. to deny, to speak against
3. contraposition   c. opposing or against
4. contrariness   d. to oppose or contradict

5. contravene
    e. distinction by contrast, in contrast to

6. contrary
    f. in opposition, or opposing position

7. contradictive
    g. being opposed for the sake of being opposed to

Key: 1. b   2. e   3. f   4. g   5. d   6. a   7. c.

The prefix *contra* and its meaning, opposed or against, run through all these words like a central theme. The meaning of these words is so strongly dominated by the common prefix that it is very difficult to write definitions that clearly distinguish the words.

There are literally thousands of such affixes and roots in current English. Learning all of these would obviously be uneconomical. We have attempted to combine the results of a number of studies of the importance of various affixes and roots into a practical, brief list. The list includes those word parts that research indicates are significant because they occur relatively frequently. Furthermore, we have reviewed the list of important affixes and roots to eliminate those related to technical areas other than business.

LIST OF AFFIXES AND ROOTS

FROM LATIN

A. Roots

1. *annus* = year
    (biennial, annuity)

2. *audio* = to hear
    (auditor, audience)

3. *bene* = well
    (beneficiary, benediction)

4. *caput* = head, chief
    (capital, capitalism)

5. *cede, cess* = to go or move
    (proceeds, concession)

6. *corpus* = body
    (corporation, incorporate)

7. *credo* = to believe, trust
    (credit, credential)

8. *dic, dict* = to speak
    (indictment)

9. *duco* = to lead
    (inducement, conducive)

10. *facio, factus* = to do or act
    (fact, factor)

A. Roots (cont.)

11. *integer* = whole
    (integration, integral)
12. *jungo, junctum* = to join
    (junction, injunction)
13. *jus, juris* = law
    (jurisdiction, jurisprudence)
14. *lis, litis* = dispute, lawsuit
    (litigation, litigant)
15. *locus* = place
    (locate, locale)
16. *mitto, miss* = send
    (remit, commission)
17. *mors, mortis* = death
    (mortality, mortgage)
18. *omnis* = all, entire
    (omnipotent)
19. *pono, positum* = to place
    (position, positive)

20. *potior* = to be able
    (potential, potent)
21. *rogare* = to ask
    (surrogate, interrogate)
22. *scribo, scriptum* = to write
    (script, inscription)
23. *sequi* = to follow
    (executive, prosecute)
24. *solus* = alone, whole
    (solicitor, solo)
25. *ulter* = last or beyond
    (ultimo, ulterior)
26. *utilis* = useful
    (utility, utilize)
27. *verto, versum* = to turn
    (conversion, invert)
28. *video, visum* = to see
    (supervise, visible)

B. Prefixes

29. *a, ab* = away from
    (absenteeism, averse)
30. *ac, ad* = toward
    (adverse, advance)
31. *ante* = before
    (antecedent, anteroom)
32. *circum* = around
    (circumstantial, circumnavigate)
33. *com, con, co, col* =
    together with
    (converse, collaborate)

34. *contra, counter* = against
    (contradictive, counteroffer)
35. *de* = down from
    (deduction, debase)
36. *dis, di* = apart
    (disposal, disassemble)
37. *e, ex* = out of
    (export, evoke)
38. *in* = into or not
    (invalid, intake)

B. *Prefixes* (cont.)

39. *inter* = between
    (interrupt, interaction)
40. *intra, intro* = inside
    (introduce, intrastate)
41. *mal* = ill, wrong
    (malfeasance, malefactor)
42. *per* = through
    (permit, per annum)
43. *post* = after
    (postscript, postdate)
44. *pre* = before
    (prewar, premium)

45. *pro* = in front of
    (proceed, procure)
46. *re* = again
    (revolve, revenue)
47. *sub* = under
    (subscribe, subcontractor)
48. *super* = above
    (superimpose,
    supervision)
49. *trans* = across
    (transaction, transgress)

C. *Suffixes*

50. *al, ic* = relating to, like
    (industrial, economic)
51. *able, ible* = that may be
    (marketable, visible)

52. *ance, ion, ty* =
    state, condition, or quality
    (perseverance, automation,
    certainty)

FROM GREEK

A. *Roots*

1. *aer* = air
   (aerial, airplane)
2. *autos* = one's self
   (automation, automatic)
3. *grapho* = to write
   (graphic, diagram)
4. *heteros* = other, diverse
   (heterogeneous)
5. *homos* = alike
   (homogeneous,
   homocentric)

6. *logos* = speech, science
   (technology, logic)
7. *phone* = sound
   (microphone, telephone)
8. *techno* = art, craft
   (technocracy)
9. *tele* = far off
   (telegraph, telephone)

B. Prefixes

10. *anti* = against
    (antilabor)

11. *dia* = through
    (diameter, diagonal)

12. *epi* = upon
    (epigram, epitaph)

13. *sym, syn* = together
    (synchronize,
    symmetrical)

How to Use This List

1. As a reference list. When you meet a word containing an unknown root or affix, look it up in this list first. The list is certainly not all-inclusive but it does contain the most important and most frequently used word parts. If the root or affix is not given in our list, then look up the word in the dictionary.

If you find the base of the word in our list, pay particular attention to this word part. Try to think of other common words with similar derivation. Try to associate the known words with the new word to help you remember the latter.

2. To promote learning new words. Try to learn one or two of the word parts in the list each day. As you read, look for examples of this root or affix. Try to discover how it conveys meaning through each example. Notice changes in spelling or pronunciation from one use of the root to another. Try to acquire a curiosity about words, their parts and their meanings.

As you become more familiar with each root or affix, try to transfer this information into your writing and your speech. Use the words you have learned as often as you can until they begin to appear spontaneously in your speech or dictation. Ignore the fact that these new words seem strange at first. Continued use of them will wear off the newness and they will become integral parts of your vocabulary.

3. Practice using and understanding each word part by asking yourself such questions as these:

   1. How do the prefixes change the meanings of these common words?

fame + de =
stimulate + contra =
secure + in =
version + a =

2. What are some of the variant spellings of *sub, ex,* and *in?*

ex + face =
sub + press =
in + passable =
sub + fix =
in + legal =
in + rational =

3. What are the literal meanings of the roots and affixes composing these words?

interpose =
procession =
controversy =
subscription =
postscript =
photograph =

4. Try to think of three or four words containing each of the following roots.

credo
autos
mitto
annus

5. What other words do you know that resemble (have the same root) as:

fact
potential
prologue
automatic
junction

If you are interested in further detailed study of word parts, you will find useful materials in any of the following books.

Davis, C. Rexford, *Vocabulary Building*. New York: William Sloane, 1951.

Gilmartin, John G., *Increase Your Vocabulary*. Englewood Cliffs, N. J.: Prentice-Hall, 1950.

Greene, Amsel, *Word Clues*. Evanston: Row, Peterson, 1949.

Hart, Archibald, *Twelve Ways to Build a Vocabulary*. New York: Dutton, 1948. Chapters VII, VIII, IX, and XII.

Jones, W. Powell, *Practical Word Study*. New York: Oxford University Press, 1952. Sections Two and Three.

Mallery, Richard D., *Workbook for English Vocabulary Building*. Boston: Heath, 1948. Part Three.

Mathews, M. M., *Words: How to Know Them*. New York: Holt, 1956.

Miller, Ward S., *Word Wealth*. New York: Holt, 1948. Appendix One.

Norwood, J. E., *Concerning Words*. Englewood Cliffs, N. J.: Prentice-Hall, 1950. Sections Two, Three, and Four.

Nurnberg, Maxwell, and Rhodes, W. T., *How to Build a Better Vocabulary*. Englewood Cliffs, N. J.: Prentice-Hall, 1949.

Smith, S. Stephenson, *How to Double Your Vocabulary*. New York: Crowell, 1947. Chapter VI.

USING THE DICTIONARY

Few of those wishing to improve their vocabularies realize how helpful a dictionary can be. It is true that most of us use a dictionary occasionally to find out the meaning of a word. Some even know how to determine the spelling of an unknown word or how to resolve their spelling doubts with the aid of a dictionary. But these casual uses are about the limits of a dictionary for the average individual.

The dictionary is usually the last place we look for a meaning after exhausting the possibilities of guessing it, or trying to deduce meaning from the structural parts, or asking someone what the word means. Even when we do turn to the dictionary as a last resort, we are satisfied if all we find or learn is a meaning of the word that can be used in the particular sentence we are reading. Unfortunately, this kind of dictionary-use leaves us with no permanent knowledge of the word. As one of our students once remarked, "I get tired of looking up the same words again and again. Isn't there some way of learning new words?"

If used effectively, the dictionary can be a distinct aid to vocabulary building. Since it provides much more than a temporarily important meaning, the information offered by the average dictionary can strengthen retention of new or unknown words. The pronunciation, spelling, derivation, and correct usage of each word are usually offered in a high-quality dictionary. These additional facts buttress the understanding and memory for a word, if they are utilized.

If we are to grow in vocabulary, we must transfer the words we learn into our own speech and writing. These ultimate uses of words cannot be accomplished without attention to spelling, pronunciation, and correct usage. We hesitate to use words in speech when we are doubtful of their correct pronunciation. Similarly, few would attempt to write a word, despite its precise appropriateness, if we were doubtful of its spelling. Knowledge of the derivation and structural characteristics of words further supports our command of both spelling and pronunciation, as well as meaning. Thus effective use of all the information commonly offered in a dictionary entry promotes permanent vocabulary growth.

WHICH DICTIONARY DO YOU NEED?

Thus far we have discussed dictionaries as though there was only one kind. Fortunately for the varied needs we have throughout life, there are many kinds of dictionaries. For example, there are a number prepared especially for the use of the college student. These include *Webster's New Collegiate Dictionary, Funk and Wagnall's New College Standard Dictionary,* and the *American College Dictionary.* Others often used in college are the *Winston Dictionary, College Edition, Macmillan's Modern Dictionary,* and *Webster's New World Dictionary.*

The *Webster's New Collegiate* and the Funk and Wagnall's are abbreviated versions of the more comprehensive *Webster's New International* and the *New Standard Dictionary,* which are preferred by some in postcollege life. A relative newcomer to this type, the *Thorndike-Barnhart Comprehensive Desk Dictionary,* is also issued in a pocket-sized edition. The *Pocket Oxford Dictionary of Current*

English though following British spelling and usage, is also available in a convenient size.

For those particularly interested in the history of usage and meanings, the ten-volume *Oxford English Dictionary* is a standard source. This, again, is British. For words that are strictly American, the *Dictionary of American English on Historical Principles* and the *Dictionary of Americanisms* are particularly useful.

In addition to these collegiate and historical dictionaries, there are a large number of specialized works related to specific professions or areas of interest. There are, for those who need them, separate dictionaries in the areas of music, psychology, science and technology, political economy, the arts, literature, and many other fields. Any competent librarian can aid in the selection of those for which you feel a need.

For those in business the following are particularly appropriate:

Ballentine, James A., *Law Dictionary with Pronunciations*. Rochester: Lawyers Cooperative Publishing, 1948.

Benn, A. E., *The Management Dictionary*. New York: Exposition Press, 1952.

Encyclopedia Dictionary of Business. Englewood Cliffs, N. J.: Prentice-Hall, 1952.

Munn, Glenn G., editor, *Encyclopedia of Banking and Finance*. Cambridge, Mass.: Bankers Publishing, 1949.

Van Nostrand's Scientific Encyclopedia. New York: Van Nostrand, 1947.

Besides these general works, there are separate dictionaries for a number of industries such as petroleum, textiles, radio, and television, as well as for branches of business as marketing, accounting, advertising, and many others. If you are interested in improving your vocabulary in general or in a specific branch of business, you can find a dictionary to suit your needs.

There are, of course, a great many other aids to vocabulary building that can be recommended. Some of these, like *Roget's Thesaurus of English Words and Phrases* and *Webster's Dictionary of Synonyms* help to deepen vocabulary and to improve diction and choice of words. These sources will suggest synonyms or alternative words for conveying a concept, thus adding variety and interest to your speech and writing.

WHERE DO WE GO FROM HERE?

We have outlined four ways of promoting vocabulary growth. Perhaps the most important of these will be your efforts to cultivate an inquiring attitude toward words. If you become keenly aware of words, and learn to enjoy manipulating and using them to express yourself, your various vocabularies will undoubtedly increase. You will spontaneously use the context as a real aid to word meaning, note and understand recurring word parts, and learn to appreciate the dictionary as an aid to self-expression. As your skill in expressing yourself precisely and fluently improves, you will experience a feeling of confidence in yourself that will more than repay you for the slight investment in time you have made in vocabulary building.

10

Using Your Reading Skills

What You Will Do
    Try out your various reading skills

What You Will Learn
    How flexible your reading is

Space does not permit us to provide all the reading matter we would like to offer for practice in your new reading skills. Instead, we have continually stressed the necessity for your trying your techniques in materials of your own choosing. If you are to secure any improvement in your reading, it will come only as a result of real effort to use your new skills intelligently in your actual reading situations.

But, of course, some of you will not take the time to find practice materials of your own. For that reason, here is a final group of selections we have assembled for your practice. The articles vary considerably in type and content to permit you to demonstrate your flexibility. Evaluate each by previewing to determine an appropriate reading approach. Look over the questions to determine how carefully you should read. For example, the article on collective bargaining is long and technical. Hence, it has been assumed that you will both preview and read completely, and questions of both types have been prepared. Make your own decisions as to how to read the others. Time yourself for each selection and check your comprehension. Let's see how much you have improved.

A Warning to Labor—And to Management [1]

by Eric A. Johnston

Eric A. Johnston, four times president of the Chamber of Commerce of the United States and now head of the Motion Picture Association of America, Inc., is one of the frankest speakers in American public life. When many an industrialist would not admit, even to himself, that management had ever made a mistake, Johnston talked openly about the mistakes of management. When others avoided labor leaders, Johnston cultivated their personal friendship, spoke to them privately and publicly.

This speech shows Johnston at his best. It was delivered at the Founder's Day Dinner of Boston University on March 13, 1944; but Johnston was not talking to the diners who sat before him that evening. He was using the occasion to talk to labor, and, over his shoulder, to management throughout the country.

This is a talk about labor and management and their place in meeting American human needs.

I remember a strike out my way in the West. The strike leader was a smart man. When the newspaper reporters asked him what all this labor trouble was about, he said:

"Labor trouble? There's no labor trouble. The employees in this plant are just having a little *management* trouble."

And he was right. That particular strike was management's fault.

Tonight, I'm going to mention plenty of bad practices by labor; and plenty by management also. I think we all ought to hit the sawdust trail together.

But, gentlemen of labor, I'll tell you something straight. Right now you have a priority at the mourner's bench. Right now you're just where we of management were ten years ago.

What a chance we in management missed! From 1921 to 1930 we had everything our own way. A friendly administration in Washington. Low taxes. And a friendly public. And what did we do with our power? On the economic side we gave this country a balloon boom that had to burst. On the moral side we produced men like Insull and Hopson and Musica, who undermined confidence in business.

So what did we get? Beginning with 1933, we got the biggest public beating that any group of Americans ever took. Congress socked us with

[1] William Norwood Brigance, *Speech Communication*, New York: F. S. Crofts and Co., Inc., 1947, pp. 206-214. Used by permission.

a new law just about every other day. It socked us with good laws. It socked us with bad laws. It socked those of us who were criminal. It socked those of us who were decent. Who cared? The public wanted us socked, and socked we were.

Gentlemen of labor, I must accuse you of not being very original. How faithfully you have imitated us of management. From 1933 to 1942 you rode high. You were tops. A friendly administration in Washington. All sorts of favors fed to you daily from the Washington political table. Management weak and intimidated. So what did you do with your power? On the economic side you gave yourselves a labor boom, regardless of the consequences to any other element in the population. On the moral side you produced men like Browne and Bioff and Scalise who gave all labor a black eye.

You forgot the very thing we forgot: In the architecture of American society it's just three jumps from the master bedroom to the dog-house.

Now the dog-house is yawning for you. The Federal Government and many of the State Governments are beginning to sock you with laws. Some of these laws may have too many teeth. Some of them may bite chunks out of good unions as well as out of bad unions. Who's going to care? If the Public wants you socked, why, socked you will be.

And don't think that you can duck any of it by yelling "anti-labor" and "reactionary" and "Fascist." We didn't escape any blows coming our way by yelling "anti-business" and "bureaucrat" and "Communist." You can't stop hell with vocabulary. When the devil is after you the only recipe is repentance and good works.

So how about a few good works?

Let's take a look at seven deadly sins in a spirit of frank helpfulness and with full recognition that they do not apply to all unions and all management at all times.

Sin one. Arbitrary refusals to accept workers in membership. This can be a most devastating sin. When a union has a closed shop contract, a refusal of membership means that the worker is deprived of his livelihood. That is intolerable.

These refusals of membership take many forms. Sometimes a man is refused by putting the initiation fee so high that he cannot pay it. Sometimes he is refused by being given a temporary "work permit," under which he can work for a while but is never admitted to the union's permanent benefits. Sometimes he is refused by being shunted into an "auxiliary" local or a "subordinate" local where he is obliged to pay dues but gets no chance to share in electing the union's officers or in deciding the union's policies. In such cases the democratic principles on which true unionism is based are discarded and a great multitude of workers become an inferior caste. Do you gentlemen of labor really think that you will be allowed to establish a caste system in America?

It didn't work that way with *us*.

Moreover: All these refusals of membership are designed to create a monopoly of jobs for the workers who already possess the privilege of union membership. How popular do you think the idea of monopoly is with the American people?

Gentlemen of management, you tell them. You know the answer out of private behavior and public experience. Did you ever hear of monopolistic practices in business? Did you ever hear of cute little schemes for preventing new competitors from getting into your industry? Did you ever hear a business man shout himself hoarse in favor of "free enterprise" and then squawk and squall just as soon as the Anti-Trust Division puts him on the fire for trying to destroy freedom in his own industry by means of fixing prices?

Gentlemen of management, monopolistic practices have helped to make us unpopular. Monopolistic practices are now helping to make organized labor unpopular. Gentlemen of labor and gentlemen of management, when we wash our hands, the right hand washes the left and the left the right. How about a little joint hand-washing to cleanse both sets of hands of monopolistic practices? It wouldn't be a bad idea, in case you both want to get in right with the American people.

Sin two. Arbitrary crushing fines imposed upon union members. Arbitrary suspensions from the union. Arbitrary expulsions. When the union has a closed shop contract or a union shop contract, the expulsion from the union means that the worker must be discharged by the employer. He loses his job. He and his wife and children lose their bread and butter.

Sometimes expulsions happen just because workers criticize the union officers and oppose them in union meetings. Don't tell me that such things don't happen. The records of our courts contain plenty of instances.

Sometimes, too, although a member may not be suspended or expelled, he cannot in practice get a job unless he has the union business agent's personal okay on his union card. Thus the business agent can tell the worker whether or not he can eat.

The parallel in management was when a firm in an industry felt free to throw other firms out of the industry by unfair competition. There were hundreds of forms of unfair competition, in advertising, in secret rebates, in preferential discounts, in pricing tricks in sales contracts. Don't tell me that such unfair competitive practices did not happen. The files of the Federal Trade Commission hold the evidence. But when they happen today, the law exacts a penalty.

Gentlemen of management and gentlemen of labor—if you really want a free and fair America, you have got to go after it *together*.

Sin three.   Some unions do not hold regular meetings or regular conventions or regular and free and fair elections of officers. In such unions we often get union bosses who pay themselves big salaries and perquisites and who can't be dislodged.

And I have heard of top-flight corporation executives who by proxies and other devices get such a control of the meetings of their stockholders that they become corporation bosses who vote themselves big salaries and bonuses and who can't be dislodged.

The American people are against both of these evils. Union autocrats, corporation autocrats, political machine autocrats, all of them are contrary to American democracy.

Sin four.   Failure to make public proper financial accounts. On this point I think that we of management have done better than you of labor. Some of it has been forced on us by law. For instance, our banking, railroad, insurance, and public utility managements must all by law render detailed financial accounts not only to their stockholders but to the public authorities.

The principle is correct and should include all corporations and all unions. Corporations and unions are not bingo and fish-fry clubs. They are agencies of the general national economic welfare. They should disclose their affairs fully.

Some unions do it admirably now. They will send you their latest financial report by return mail. In it you will see their receipts and expenditures detailed to the last dime and verified by a certified public accountant. Other unions, on the contrary, protest that they do not want to reveal their financial condition. It is an alibi, I think, which will soon go down the drain.

There are corporations today which circulate among their employees an annual statement showing exactly what happens to each dollar of the corporation's income. So many cents of it to raw materials; new machines; to the stockholders; to the employees. Then the employees do not need to rely on rumor and suspicion. They know the truth.

I think that employees should know the truth about the firm for which they work. I think that the firm should know the truth about their employees' unions. I think that there can be mutual confidence between a firm and a union only when they come clean with each other. I hope to see the day when all firms and all unions will wholly abandon the sin of financial secrecy.

Sin five.   Too many strikes. Strikes called arbitrarily by dictatorial business agents. Strikes called without warning, even to the mass of the members of the union, at a meeting attended by a few hotheads. Strikes called for reasons that the strike leaders will not even disclose to the employer. Strikes called against employers who have nothing at all to do with the strike. Jurisdictional strikes.

I have already said that strikes can be the fault of the employer. Just the same, gentlemen of labor—if you fail to support the no-strike pledge given by your leaders at the beginning of the war—you will get what you got after the great disastrous strikes that followed the last war. Public resentment set your program back a decade.

I think that you should resolve on fewer strikes. And so should management.

A strike by a union is a withholding of labor. But there can also be a strike that is a withholding of product. When a corporation gets a new invention and declines to use it and declines to let anybody else use it and thus withholds a product from the market, that's a strike.

I'm for fewer strikes all around.

Sin six.   Violence on the picket line.

This sin is clearly seen by the public and makes unionism a host of enemies. But I want to be fair. There are three kinds of picket-line violence. First, violence by the pickets themselves, and plenty of it. Second, instances of violence in a dark past incited by thugs hired by employers to start trouble and make the strike unpopular. And, third, violence incited by "energetic" policemen who start cracking the skulls of pickets who are peaceful.

Nevertheless, gentlemen of labor, in this matter there is one reform that you can accomplish all by yourselves. You often send your pickets four or eight abreast in a closed circle around a factory so that nobody can get in, while the pickets sweetly and innocently sing songs. Well, don't think that you fool anybody when you call it peaceful picketing. It is forbidden by law in Britain. It is beginning to be forbidden by law here, and with frills that you won't like.

It is only a step from mass picketing to the sit-down, and only a step from the sit-down to revolution.

Watch your step, gentlemen of labor, stop mass picketing.

Sin seven.   From the economic point of view, this one is the worst. Restraints on production.

As developed in the rules of some unions, these restraints are called "feather-bedding," and "slow-downing." More men than are needed for the job. Each man doing less than he could do. Waste of man-power.

Waste of human resources. It is a grievous wrong to the whole American economic system.

But there are two comments to be made on it.

In the first place, some enlightened unions have turned their backs on all this kind of thing and are earnestly helping their employers to increase output. They realize that if the workers are to have the good things of life, those things must be produced and produced more abundantly.

In the second place, some employers are themselves to blame. For what is the basic cause of "feather-bedding" and of "slow-downing" by workers? It is this:

The workers say to themselves—and they say it in non-union factories as well as in union factories:

"Listen! As soon as this job is finished, we're going to get laid off and thrown into the street. So let's go slow and make the job last."

Gentlemen of management—you don't get laid off. You're part of what we call the "overhead" of a business. The "overhead" has to go on even between jobs in order to hold the business together.

But doesn't it occur to you that the worker also has an "overhead"? He has his family to hold together. He has to keep on paying the landlord and the grocer and the butcher. His costs don't stop just because he is laid off.

We have to have more job security in America.

We must strive to give our workers continuous employment; and, where that's impossible, we must develop a sane and sensible program for adequate unemployment insurance which will take care of the worker's "overhead" during his times of being laid off.

Then the unions must do their part. They must abolish rules that keep a man down to doing half a man's work. You can't build a strong America on half-men.

Gentlemen of labor—in this matter as in the other six matters I have mentioned, are you ready to do *your* part?

I'd like to see a pact of non-aggression and mutual assistance between management and labor. You can't get rid of management and you can't get rid of unionism in a free country. Both are social economic facts. The right of labor to organize into unions is the legal right of American citizens. I calculate labor will exercise that right.

We of management, having gone through our dog-house, are still here. You of labor unions, when you've barked and yowled your way through *your* dog-house, will still be here.

I admit that we of management might become more labor-minded. But I also think that you of labor might become more business-minded.

A basic need of business is profits. Without profits business cannot continue, cannot expand, cannot improve. Yet you are always running about Washington encouraging Congress to put the kind of taxes on us that would destroy our whole ability to make economic progress for America. If we are going to meet, we've got to meet half-way.

So, to summarize:

What about agreeing, more or less roughly, as follows?

We of management will try to repress monopolistic practices, unfair treatment of competitors, and business racketeers. You will try to repress monopolistic practices, unfair treatment of fellow-workers, and labor racketeers.

We will tell you the financial facts of life about *us*. You will tell us the financial facts of life about *you*.

We will try to reduce the number of our "strikes" which withhold inventions and products. You will try to reduce the number of your strikes which withhold labor and service.

We will try to give you job security and basic income security. You will try to give a full honest day's work every day.

We will recognize you and refrain from trying to cripple you with unfair regulatory laws. But you will recognize us and refrain from trying to destroy us by unfair and ruinous laws.

The United States can be strong only by acts of popular free-will.

That is why I say in conclusion just two things to you of management and to you of labor.

One. Go ahead and turn this country into a continuous brawl, and government will chain you both.

Two. Make a better choice. Work together and stay free.

If you stay free, I have no doubt of the result—a strong America, an *America Unlimited*.

Questions on "A Warning to Labor— And to Management"

Since the answers to these questions often refer to either labor or management, note carefully whether several answers to each question are possible.

1. Johnston accuses labor or management of monopolistic practices such as:

    a. refusal of union membership.
    b. price fixing.
    c. a closed shop contract.
    d. under-the-counter agreements.

2. Labor and management are guilty of unfair, arbitrary practices such as:

   a. unwarranted strikes.
   b. secret, shady competitive practices.
   c. expulsions and fines instigated by the union officers.
   d. price fixing.

3. Autocratic control is achieved in unions and management by:

   a. rigged elections of officers.
   b. big salaries and other perquisites.
   c. control of stockholders meetings.
   d. manipulation of stock issues.

4. The sin of financial secrecy is:

   a. more common among labor unions.
   b. not true of management as a whole.
   c. committed by very few labor unions.
   d. almost impossible for management.

5. Johnston feels that strikes:

   a. are often the fault of the employer.
   b. are a weapon of labor only.
   c. may be committed by both labor and management.
   d. should be entirely abolished.

6. Johnston suggests that picket-line violence:

   a. can be lessened by eliminating mass picketing.
   b. is almost always started by the strikers themselves.
   c. could be eliminated by more energetic police action.
   d. is the result of mass picketing.

7. Restraints on production:

   a. include such practices as "feather-bedding" and "slow-downing."
   b. are caused by management's failure to provide job security.
   c. could be removed by more and better production.
   d. may include withholding new inventions from the market.

   Key: 1. a, b   2. b, c   3. a, c   4. a   5. c   6. a   7. a, b.

How did you read this straight-from-the-shoulder 2,600-word speech? Probably fairly rapidly, especially if your background in industrial relations is strong. There were really only seven major ideas in the speech, "the seven deadly sins" of labor and management. These might have been read by skimming, although the informal style of the speech doesn't lend itself too readily to this approach.

Mr. Johnston's speech certainly lends itself to reading for ideas. There is a constant stream of related ideas, the flow of which leads to easy, rapid reading. If you have profited from the suggestions given earlier in this book, you certainly should have read this speech rapidly and with good comprehension.

The Human Side of Management [2]

by Leslie F. Robbins

"Until management realizes that employees are infinitely more complicated than the machines they operate, maximum cooperation and working efficiency will seldom be achieved."—ALFRED B. HOWE

The Author has for many years directed the purchasing department at the University of Colorado and has taught the course in purchasing at that institution. He is an active member of the Denver P. A. Association, and has served on the National Executive Committee of N.A.P.A. He has also been active in the affairs of the National Association of Educational Buyers and has been a valuable leader in its training conferences.

Management is as much an art as it is a science, maybe more so. This applies to the management of even a purchasing department. There may be those who regard management primarily as a set of procedures, backed up by official regulations and flanked by a sound statement of policies, staffed by a contingent of selected personnel, each person with his official title and designated function. That is only part of management. In the ultimate analysis, management consists of having each one in the department know what the boss wants done and then getting it done. The better sort of management includes more than just barely getting the job done. It involves getting the people to do their work creatively and constructively.

[2] Leslie F. Robbins, "The Human Side of Management," *Purchasing*, Vol. 38: (February, 1955), pp. 85-87, 324. Used by permission.

WHO IS THE BOSS AND WHAT DOES HE WANT DONE?

In this usage, the boss is not just one specified person in each firm, but rather the term represents the whole chain of command,—those with authority and concurrent accountability, up and down the ladder. To a janitor the head custodian is the boss; to the president the Board of Directors is the boss. Most bosses take orders from someone.

It is understandable that occasionally the boss does not know exactly what he wants done, in definite terms, or all that he wants done at any one time. He usually knows in general terms at least some of the things he wants done, and, of course, he knows that he wants all departments and individuals under his supervision to function with a high degree of effectiveness. But the choice of specific procedures for the work may be subject to differences in judgment. He may be qualified to judge what constitutes the currently best procedures and performance, but again he may not, especially if his supervision extends over a wide range of technical processes. The comptroller or general manager to whom the purchasing agent reports may have been trained in purchasing, but he may not have. He may know good purchasing performance when he sees it, but he may not be as well qualified to make purchasing decisions as is the purchasing agent. Nor is the president necessarily the best judge of a program of floor maintenance.

THE ART IN MANAGEMENT

It is the afore-mentioned stipulation of 'doing their work creatively and constructively' which separates the men from the boys in management Procedures, regulations, policies, official titles—these are not living things; they are but channels, guideposts, and implements. It takes people, all kinds of people, to give life and meaning to the mechanics of operations. Sometimes people act according to a prescribed pattern but often they do not.

A study which deals with the patterns of actions of people is usually thought of as being in the realm of the social sciences. But social science, as a science, can only apply to large enough masses of people to be subject to analysis and prognosis. Individuals are often unpredictable and must be dealt with on an individual basis, or at most in small groups with a definite consciousness of the individuals in the group. The management of most departments in a business, and probably of the business as a whole, therefore is an art as well as a science.

It is the art of human relations.

Each of the arts has its own media. Among the media of the art of human relations are ideas and the communication of ideas. There are other media in this art also, such as emotions, attitudes, interests and ideals, but there is not enough space in this article to touch upon them all. Anyone who aspires to become proficient in this art of human relations must understand something of these media and how to use them effectively. Much of this understanding is not obtained from books and lectures. Mostly it is acquired in the school of life. Some say the talent for it is inherited.

COMMUNICATION

By and large, the point of most frequent failure of effective management, it seems, is in the area of communication We don't make ourselves understood. In spite of the many schools and colleges, only about one in every fifty persons can express himself easily and adequately. The difficulty apparently starts with a weakness for condoning incomplete and inexact information; it is compounded in sloppy thinking, and the process of communication is finally wrecked by the inexpert use of words and terms. We tend to presume that the mental image we have associated with a certain word or expression is the one correct and universal meaning for that expression regardless of the fact that, if we have not actually looked it up, our interpretation may be quite inadequate.

And we mumble!

This is all deplorable in any intercourse; in the purchasing office it can be all but fatal to effective operation. Except under the heading of "specifications," almost nothing is said in the text books and in the courses in purchasing about the great need for more clarity of expression. Usually, however, only the items of importance in cost or quantity, rate such a written specification. What about the great majority of items which the purchasing department is required to buy for which the "specification" is more likely to be a phone call asking that "another bunch of those thing-a-mabobs" be bought?

The other facet of the break-down of communication is that too often we listen with only a half an ear. We get only a faint impression of what is being said to us because we are so intent on our own thoughts and are so certain that we know just what the other fellow is about to say that all after the first five words are lost on us and wasted. Talk about your iron curtain; this "ego curtain" is really impenetrable!

Those extroverted free-wheeling operators to be found in almost any business organization who are impatient with routine and forms, will tell you that most of the material put into writing in the course of a business day is thereby embalmed. No one bothers to read instructions, they say, and the few who do don't understand them. The way to get things done, they say, is to pick up the phone, call Charlie, ask him about his family, his lumbago and his bowling score, and when he is placid tell him what you want. Well, mebbe so, mebbe so. At least it is the human side of the operation. Perhaps the more sure way to communicate is, after having called Charlie, to confirm the matter in writing, in language and terminology that even Charlie's Aunt could not misunderstand, and then keep a carbon copy.

And so, one of the first tasks of the manager of the purchasing department is to see to it that there is the least possible chance of failure to communicate. He should set the example by being lucid in his own speech and correspondence and by requiring the same of those who report to him. His buyers should be instructed not to let any instance pass unchallenged wherein they are in doubt as to exactly what is meant by any communication, oral or written, which comes to their official notice.

CREATIVE AND CONSTRUCTIVE MANAGEMENT

If the boss is a genius and knows more about the department and what it ought to be than all others put together, then no one around him need do other than just what he says to do. But if he is a normal human being with the normal quota of limitations and shortcomings, he will sometimes need help in deciding what he wants done. There is where the opportunity occurs for his associates to be creative and constructive, if they can.

A highly effective purchasing manager once said, "Don't go to the boss with problems, go to him with solutions." Good advice. Probably every manager has had the experience of having to deal with a subordinate who runs and jumps into his lap with every problem which arises. Perhaps the manager has invited this kind of behavior by having tried in the past to decide all questions both great and small, instead of encouraging others to assume some responsibility for decisions.

If a person in a subordinate position hopes to be considered for advancement to a prospective opening with greater responsibilities, the place for him to demonstrate his eligibility is in the position he currently holds. A trite observation, but how seldom does an awareness of its truth appear! The solving of operational snafu involves mental effort. Some operators seem not to have the mental equipment to cope with really tough problems, but in many cases it can be assumed that the failure to resolve a situation is attributable to mental laziness or other bad mental habits.

WANTED: IMAGINATION

Alex Osborne, writing on Applied Imagination, has the right idea; where there is a problem one should turn the imagination loose and see how many possible solutions he can think up. They can then be sifted down to the one or two that seem most likely to succeed. If one really needs the backing of higher authority he should go to the boss with his best judgment among the alternatives available, and ask his advice. With the advice he will probably receive a measure of increased respect and some sound support—handy things to have around. Conversely, to make it a practice to go to the boss with every jumbled-up headache and dump it in his lap, is bad psychology. It will not be too long before he will hate to see you coming.

People with limited insight frequently resent the fabulous paychecks that some managers are reputed to receive. Those managers get their king-sized salaries, if any, because of their demonstrated capacity to handle the big headaches. No one should permit himself the luxury of envying these managers unless there is also the comprehension of those giant economy headaches. One should not aspire to someone's else larger-size troubles until he has shown he can successfully treat his own modest cramps, for with bigger pay go ever more excruciating pains.

But, lest the earlier paragraphs of this opus have given the impression that the only place where initiative is called for is in the solving of those sneaky problems which come up behind us and kick us in the pants, let us hasten to affirm that effective management is not passive; it is dynamic. Many problems can be obviated by alert anticipation. Most of all, there is the opportunity to be creative in our approach to all of our functions.

POTENTIAL OF THE GROUP

Again, Alex Osborne is cooking on the front burner; there are new values waiting around every corner to be discovered by the alert manager who has imagination and who cultivates the creative potential in the members of his department. The periodic staff meeting and the staff conference are the "group dynamics" of modern business. Man is probably closest to being immortal when he is constructively creative.

This is not a plea for more democracy in business management. It still will be the responsibility of management to manage. The boss will have to give the word and make the decisions. In making decisions, management can not afford to forget that there are interests to be safeguarded other than the desires of the majority of the current employees. There is, for instance, the little matter of profits out of which dividends can be paid, and that other little matter of pleasing the customers so they will keep on buying.

And there is an evil of excess as well as the fault of deficiency in this business of making changes. Sometimes a newly appointed manager who is prone to confuse mere change with progress will feel called upon to change all of the tweedle-de-dums into tweedle-de-dees and vice versa, just to prove that something new has been added. Not so good!

For the most of us, being creative will not result in the discovery of some new theory of relativity or in the revelation of a universal touchstone. It will probably consist of finding a new and useful application of some old and familiar factors or in the making of new and potent combinations of existing elements.

KEEPING THE BOSS INFORMED

Question: How much should the boss be told? Answer: At least as much as you have reason to think he wants to hear. Maybe he can be made to want to hear more if what he is told is well told. The boss should undertake to give every one under his supervision an idea of how much he wants in the way of reports, and should guide them at first in the preparation of those reports. By all means he should have all of the information he asks for and nothing should be withheld which might be of use to him in making valid decisions and accurate evaluations.

Moreover, there are occasions when information should be proffered even when it is not called for in the report pattern provided. He is bound to "hear things about things" and it is simply good human relations, not to say public relations, to keep the boss informed on the significant facts of what is happening in the department and, perhaps, some of the things that are not happening which should happen.

Reports of routine operations can usually be tabulated and summarized and appropriate comparisons can be drawn with the help of charts and graphs. Matters other than routine should be made the subject of brief but accurate oral reports or written memos. Now and then an extensive study or analysis may be in order, and this should be compiled in concise and workmanlike style, omitting no essential detail. Such studies are usually made in the prospect of a possible change in policy or procedure; hence the presentation will be expected to provide a clean-cut conclusion or recommendation.

TEAM SPIRIT VS. OFFICE POLITICS

Unless the office is a dictatorship, everything possible should be done to establish a climate which is favorable to the team idea. Any department staff which lacks the team spirit is vulnerable to the usual tendency to divide up into factions or cliques. There tend to be those who are "with" the boss and others who are not. Everyone in the organization should have reason to feel that he is a member of the team in good standing and is expected to play a team game.

This also is no one-way street. The boss has to be team-minded too. His part is not only to call the signals but to listen to complaints, settle differences, and try to reconcile personality conflicts. Occasionally there will be a situation which can be properly resolved only by eliminating a chronic trouble-maker. Even a tough boss can be effective if he is able and fair. However, the boss who has genuine friendliness, consideration and self-restraint usually gets better voluntary cooperation than the hard-boiled one.

Most that is appealing about religion is devoted to the proposition that we all can do better than we do, that each person has rights to human dignity, and that mortal man should be given a second chance when he makes an honest mistake. We all make mistakes, mistakes of the head, of the heart and of the hand. Only a bigot will summarily condemn a contrite fellow-sinner without a hearing or will judge him unworthy of a second opportunity especially where there are extenuating circumstances.

It doesn't take much managerial ability for a boss to lie, as it were, in an ambush of managerial authority ready to pounce upon some hapless underling caught in a mistake, but it does require real breadth of character and positive foresight for the boss to help him to avoid that mistake in the first place. And it requires a genuine appreciation of people and their interdependence to be the kind of a boss who makes his people want to produce affirmative values for him to the extent of their ability. If he builds them up, they usually build him up. If he tries to tear others down in order to advance himself, he usually fails and finds he has built his future on sinking sand.

Questions on "The Human Side of Management"

1. What is the main idea of this selection?

   a. The skill of communication is the greatest need in management.

   b. The art of management lies in utilizing human relations to do its work creatively and constructively.

    c. Management should draw its practices from the arts as well as from the sciences.

    d. The way in which problems are handled reflects the difference between mediocre and creative, constructive management.

2. At what point does management most frequently fail?

    a. In its ability to delegate responsibility

    b. In its ability to communicate

    c. In not knowing just what it wants done

    d. In its willingness to listen to others

3. What does the author mean by the term "human relations"?

    a. Capacity for a genuine appreciation of people which promotes individual creativity

    b. Skill in attracting others to one's self

    c. Capacity to lead others in getting a job done without friction or stress

    d. Skill in implementing smoothly functioning procedures and policies

4. Creative imagination in the sense used here is best described as the:

    a. ability to create and institute changes in a service or product.

    b. ability to advance a new theory or create new services or product.

    c. ability to cooperate creatively in the approach to all functions.

    d. ability to lead and direct others toward creativity and efficiency.

5. Efficient communication in the business sense includes (choose as many as you need):

    a. interpersonal understanding without the need of written details.

    b. speaking clearly and carefully.

    c. listening with full attention.

    d. delegating responsibility clearly.

6. The team spirit in management fosters (choose as many as you need):

    a. creativity in subordinates.

    b. the formation of factions and cliques.

c. close personal supervision of each worker by the boss.

d. consideration of workers as distinct individuals.

Key: 1. b   2. b   3. a   4. c   5. b, c, d   6. a, d.

How did you read this 2800-word magazine article? Although it is not quite as fluent in its stream of ideas as Johnston's speech, it should be read rapidly. Since subheadings and more formal paragraphs are used, skimming is a possibility you should have recognized. Most of the facts demanded in the questions, and the real heart of the article would readily be found by skimming. Did you realize this? How did your rate compare with your earlier efforts?

Business Week [3]
330 West 42nd Street
New York 36, New York

Dear Sirs:

May I draw your attention to the steadily growing plight of a significant portion of our population—the Davy Crockett hat-makers?

As Business Week, with its extensive and up-to-date market coverage is well aware, prices on Davy Crockett hats have been plummetting, and an industry and way of life heretofore exuberantly expanding is now faced with the prospect of mass unemployment. Raccoons that have been encouraged to produce, now find that there is no market.

It is not necessary that this happen because several remedies are at hand that have had long and successful histories in other segments of our economy. Specifically, these remedies are:

1. That the Tariff Commission take off its rose-colored glasses and face up to the fact that the peril point has been reached in the Davy Crockett hat industry, that prohibitive duties be levied, that a quota be imposed to reassure the foreigners that we are still interested in some trade, and that all imported Davy Crockett hats be so identified, such as by being dyed bile green, so that American purchasers will know they are not purchasing skins from healthy well-fed American raccoons processed by healthy well-paid American workers. In addition, to prevent evasion of the intent of this regulation, its provisions should be extended to all hats made from raccoons that are not born in the U. S. or territories thereof.

[3] From a letter in "Readers Report," *Business Week,* November 26, 1955. Used by permission.

2. That a price support program be inaugurated perhaps under the jurisdiction of the Bureau of Wildlife and Fisheries but preferably under a brand new agency that will draw upon the staff of the aforementioned Bureau, of the Dept. of Agriculture, and of the Historical Division of the Smithsonian Institution. This agency should engage in a two-pronged attack on the problem.

It should support Davy Crockett hats at a full 100% of parity, the parity base period to be a time when the industry was in healthy condition, e.g., the first half of 1955. It is possible that surpluses may pile up, but this is a calculated risk. This program is essential if we are to maintain Davy Crockett hatmaking as a way of life in our society, a way of life that springs from the most deeply loved traditions and most inspiring history of our heritage. Where would our country be today if it weren't for Davy Crockett and men like him!

The other task of the agency should be to actively increase effective demand. Such means can be used as giving Davy Crockett hats to schools with underprivileged children, perhaps tying them in with the Free Lunch program. It should also arrange that a specified portion of our foreign aid or loans be spent to purchase hats; such a gift from us would indeed be twice blessed because it would not only be aid but would introduce foreigners to basic elements in the American spirit and to the foundations of the American standard of living.

We do not believe in paternal government, and therefore in addition to our legislative program we have a vast, industry-wide program under consideration. On our designing boards are thrilling plans that will, we feel sure, make every household a two—and maybe three—Davy Crockett hat household. In addition, we are in the process of preparing a communication to all magazines and newspapers that have carried pictures of people wearing live raccoons, pointing out the disadvantages of a live raccoon as compared to a bona fide Davy Crockett hat. . . .

Sincerely yours,

ELEANOR SHLIFER

How long did it take you to recognize that this letter was a satire—written with tongue in cheek? This should have been apparent after reading the first paragraph or two, if you were alert. Did you notice how often she inserted some of the propaganda clichés commonly used to bolster a weak argument? Did you recognize some of the old, reliable techniques in "American raccoons," "American workers," "way of life . . . deeply loved traditions . . . our heritage,"

"American spirit," "American standard of living," "underprivileged children," "bona fide Davy Crockett hat"?

What inconsistency often present in American business does she point up? Or, isn't there any contradiction in decrying paternalistic government on the one hand, and, at the same time, asking for protective tariffs, import quotas, a price support program, governmental disposal of surpluses, etc.?

Pitfalls of Collective Bargaining [4]

by Richard P. Doherty PRESIDENT, TELEVISION-RADIO MANAGEMENT CORPORATION, WASHINGTON, D.C.

The Author. An alumnus of Clark University and Brown University, Richard P. Doherty was Vice President of the National Association of Radio and Television Broadcasters from 1946 to 1954. In March, 1954, he became President of the Television-Radio Management Corporation and of the Doherty Labor Advisory Service, Washington, D.C. Previously Mr. Doherty had served as head of the Economics Department of Boston University and as Executive Director of the Industrial Relations Council in Boston; he was a management member of the National Wage Stabilization Board in 1951–52, and since 1949 has been a U. S. employer representative to the International Labor Organization in Geneva.

There is no simple, magic formula which will produce the clear-cut answer to successful labor-management relations. Nor are collective bargaining skills and techniques mastered by the simple process of reading a few books, listening to a few speeches, or dabbling in the process of giving advice to practitioners.

It is unfortunate that there are many immature and inexperienced persons who indirectly guide the actions of those management representatives who must hammer out practicable union contracts with union officials who "know" practical labor relations. Mature mastery of sound collective bargaining emerges from bargaining table experience and from a full knowledge and appreciation of the labor-management way of life. Practical experience soon teaches management that collective bargaining is quite different from the normal buyer-seller negotiations of the business world.

[4] Richard P. Doherty, "Pitfalls of Collective Bargaining," *Controls and Techniques for Better Management,* General Management Series No. 176, American Management Association, 1955, pp. 35-44. Used by permission of American Management Association, copyright owner.

All too often businessmen run into a variety of pitfalls along the collective bargaining road. As a guide to sounder and more constructive industrial relations, it is well to be aware of some of the more common pitfalls.

1. MAKING INNOCUOUS GRANTS AND CONCESSIONS

Union strategy often calls for the use of "foot in the door" techniques whereby seemingly unimportant demands are traded for issues which currently loom importantly on management's horizon. More than one businessman has applauded his own acumen when he has bought off certain union demands by the simple expedient of making concessions on issues which appeared to cost very little or meant very little to the company at the time.

Within given industries, it is common union practice to play one competitor against another. Concessions established in one case are generally transposed to other companies. In another year or so, the cumulative process of "innocuous" concessions winds itself back, and the strings on the total industry or area bag are tightened.

Also, many seemingly unimportant concessions involve very little, if any, money but do involve certain principles. Eventually, having established a beachhead, the union begins to put higher price tags on the established principle. This pitfall is particularly dangerous with regard to fringe issues and jurisdictional work clauses. Many "harmless" fringes and fringes of no apparent cost consequences, at the original instance, have grown and blossomed like the proverbial mustard seed.

2. AMBIGUOUS CONTRACT LANGUAGE

The typical union contract is complex enough to confuse both management and union officials at times. Ambiguous language adds confusion and provides operating pitfalls under the contract. Often, ambiguity of language is the result of sloppy thinking, of inexperience in contract construction. Efforts to impart a "legalistic" quality to contracts are quite certain to enhance ambiguity. However, ambiguous language is sometimes willful, deliberate, and intentional. On occasions, a union may purposely prefer loose contract language which, over the long haul, facilitates a difference in contract interpretation in its favor. Maybe the employer eventually can be made to concede a point or two in the face of a confused interpretation of the contract provision. If the provision and attendant problem go to arbitration, the arbitrator may accept the union's interpretation. There is always this chance, especially where evidence exists of pertinent discussions during earlier negotiations. At worst, the arbitrator won't do more than clear up the ambiguous language by an interpretive decision.

Unfortunately, also, there are a few unions which favor contract ambiguity because it promotes a steady flow of grievances. Some few unions use grievances as promotional services to members and as a chronic irritant to management.

When you and the union agree to certain provisions, be sure you are in accord as to meaning and then write the terms so that you both understand that they mean the same thing. Clear, straightforward language is always preferable to high-sounding "legal" phraseology.

3. THINKING ONLY OF YOUR OWN INTERESTS

Some employers, at times, think only of their own interests and turn a deaf ear to others. Worse is the employer who utilizes a union contract to do harm to his competitor. I am not addressing myself to the moral issues or to the concepts of so-called high-level competition. I am talking about the practical, realistic hazard which confronts many businessmen who dig a pit for themselves by disregarding the interests of other operators.

No union contract is negotiated without regard to intra-industry patterns. Various whipsawing tactics are used by unions to weave eventual total industry patterns. The long-range interests of each employer are best served by avoiding costly industry patterns because he must live within these patterns. As one example, an employer accepts A and B in his contract because, under the then existing circumstances, they don't affect him adversely. They may cover practices not then existent in his operation. But A and B are harmful to other employers who may accept C and D, which, at the same time, are harmful to the first employer but not the second. Thus agreements are reached which are disadvantageous to employers in general although not at the time of origin detrimental to the individual employers making the first concessions.

The only sound advice is to avoid provisions which have no current relation to your operation. Think of the other fellow—your competitor—and avoid adding fuel to the fire of intra-industry whipsawing of all employers, yourself included.

4. LACK OF ADEQUATE PREPARATION

One of the cardinal mistakes of management is to sit down at the bargaining table without adequate preparation. This is especially true among smaller businessmen.

The union representative is normally a skilled negotiator. In addition, he possesses a thorough knowledge of your union contract, and of other union contracts. Back at national headquarters, a research staff has supplied him with a substantial array of pertinent facts.

When the union representative makes such claims as, "We have this provision in the majority of contracts in the industry"; "There's no need to argue about holidays, we have seven holidays in 90 per cent of all contracts"; "We haven't signed a contract this year without sickness and health insurance"—many businessmen actually don't know the underlying truth and supporting facts.

No person's decisions can be better than the information upon which the decisions are based. An uninformed or poorly informed negotiator is practically certain to be a bad negotiator. He will often concede points without understanding their full significance and impact. Equally, he will often make mountains out of molehills and create needless impasses. Labor relations is a big job, a very complex job. It is difficult for most smaller businessmen to keep abreast of industry and area changes in union contracts. But the fact remains that the average negotiator is a lost lamb if he is not adequately informed.

It would be wise for every management negotiator to assemble all available information from his trade association, local chamber of commerce, local or regional employers association, or other pertinent agencies. Where readily available information doesn't exist, efforts should be made to secure facts from business colleagues and competitors. Then, when the union submits its demands, sufficient time should be taken to analyze completely every aspect of these demands. Discussions should be held with departmental and operating heads to ascertain fully the significance of each demand as applied to the company's operation. Pertinent and collateral facts should be collected.

Whenever you approach the bargaining table without having your case fully prepared, you invariably construct a very deep pitfall for yourself. It is virtually impossible to spend too much time analyzing, preparing, and reasoning out the information, arguments, and facts involved in the forthcoming negotiation.

On your own side of the case, don't depend on poker-playing bluff to take the place of strong, conclusive evidence. There is plenty of poker-playing in most negotiations, but you can always play a better hand of poker if you hold a few good cards of assembled information. If you yourself are going to make demands and claims, prepare your case so that you can prove it.

5. DANGERS OF THE BARGAINING TABLE

Bargaining table negotiations call for skill, fairness, firmness, and patience. There are no rules for this game, and the innocent generally pay a high price for their experience.

As a guide to successful conduct at the bargaining table, we would suggest the following:

a. Avoid negotiating against the clock. Negotiations should begin early enough to permit at least four to six reasonably long contract meetings before the expiration of the contract. A few brief exploratory sessions followed by one major push should be avoided. Do not negotiate all night. Negotiators generally get impatient in the wee hours of the morning and begin to make concessions to "get it over." Unions know this and they use their knowledge effectively. Generally it is businessmen who wear down first after long tedious hours of negotiating. Take lunch and dinner breaks with an all-day session. Do not make snap decisions. Don't be afraid to take a few minutes' recess to consider a proposal or an answer, and insist that negotiations shall "close for the day" by 8 P.M. or 10 P.M. at the latest, or after a normally full day of negotiations. Management seldom gains from extra-long overtime days at the bargaining table.

b. Be wary of "horse-trading." Having the union drop some economic demand in exchange for a clause that the union wants may result in a future restriction or curtailment of a management function such as layoffs or the setting of work standards, or loss of the right to consider skill and ability in promotions within the bargaining unit. "Horse-trading" is quite common at the bargaining table. Nevertheless, always "look a gift horse in the mouth." Even trades may be beneficial, yet there is always the potential hidden pitfall of the union giving up a "major" issue in return for a general concession on principles or policies or union rights. Don't be afraid to trade, but don't fail to understand the value of the items traded.

c. Beware of clauses which provide for "mutual" decisions or determinations—for example, "mutual" determination of layoff; "mutual" agreement on setting up shift schedules; "mutual" discussion on any disciplinary action; "mutual" agreement on discharges. These are management rights subject to certain grievance procedures, and management must retain its fundamental functions even in face of a strike. The right to set up work schedules, determine operating methods, decide crew sizes, and so on, generally means more to a company than granting a paid holiday or giving a few cents in wages. Too often, management will prefer to "take a strike" over various money matters rather than over more basic issues involving important management rights. Not infrequently, this proves to be short-sighted economics.

Incidentally, management must resist every effort by unions and also by government agencies to surround fundamental management functions and rights with "mutuality" concepts. If free American enterprise is to progress under the guidance of private management, there are certain policies and decisions which belong properly to the employer and should not be resolved on a mutual union-management basis.

I am indeed fearful of recent trends which would deprive management of unilateral policy-making decisions on such matters as employee stock purchase plans, bonus-profit sharing plans, and related subjects. If it is insisted that all such topics be regarded as coming within the purview of "mutual" decisions, American employer-employee relations will be seriously undermined, and progressive employer-employee relations will be retarded.

d. Do not think in terms of settling only the immediate contract. Precedents are hard to overcome, and contract errors are hard to rescind. Long-range effects must be considered—for example, seniority clauses, fee schedules, work jurisdiction, and shift differentials.

e. Don't treat each provision as a separate document. The interrelation of the various contract clauses must be watched and clearly understood. The union demands must be considered in their entire perspective and not treated piecemeal.

Very often, the union will insist on a settlement of each demand or issue by itself. In fact, you may run across the argument, "Let's go down the contract, section by section, and get things settled in order." All union demands should be considered *in toto* and treated as a "package deal." The very nature of contracts means that there are many interwoven sections; all provisions must be treated in relation to the total fabric.

Discuss all issues before getting down to the actual consideration of each. Don't be trapped by the apparent concession that offers, "If you will agree to this demand, we'll be glad to make concessions on later sections of the contract." It is naïve for management to "settle" specific issues on the strength of promises of later concessions.

When you "settle" one issue, be sure that you simultaneously "settle" related issues. Promised concessions are all too often forgotten, or bogged down, in the course of subsequent negotiations.

f. Don't negotiate a "blind" contract. Be sure all demands have been presented by the union when the first contract meeting takes place. Beware of such propositions as, "The union reserves the right to present further demands"; "Discussion of individual grievances will be presented to the company at a later meeting"; or, "We have only two major demands and will reserve the unimportant minor points until we have cleared up these few big issues."

g. Do not permit the union to introduce individual grievances during the course of general contract negotiations. The contract negotiation is not the vehicle by which individual grievances are to be aired "on the bargaining table." Personal problems can often muddy up negotiations. Their settlement often causes further contract changes.

h. Don't be perturbed by union contentions over "inequities" or "inequalities." Perorations about rank inequities and hardships under the existing contract, about unfair treatment of certain employees, or about unjust inequalities are designed to soften up management. If an employee negotiating committee sits in at the bargaining table, you may be sure that much of this kind of oratory is a "constituent selling" technique of the union representative.

Management should take one of two (or both) attitudes toward these "inequity" and "inequality" disclaimers: (1) insist on concrete proof and facts of proof, or (2) sit through them and let them wear off—as they always do.

i. Don't be alarmed by table-pounding and strong language. Some union leaders use "bruiser" tactics to throw management off guard and, possibly, even frighten inexperienced employers. If you are equally skilled at strong language, you may fight fire with fire—and put the fire out. If you lack the vocal vigor and rough diction of the union representative, remember that a "soft word turneth away wrath." In all probability, the latter is the better and more effective approach.

j. Never underestimate the basic significance of non-work provisions. All too many managements negotiate with their eye on the payroll consequences. Anything which costs money is major in their eyes. These money items are of top importance, but often the non-wage provisions can have far greater impact on the company's profit and loss statement and efficient operations. Pay the utmost attention to management rights, seniority clauses, work, scheduling, rest periods, transfers, disciplinary and discharge clauses, jurisdictional coverage, "no-strike" provisions, and so-called "employee protective" clauses. In the health-welfare-pensions field be absolutely sure you know what you are buying into, where the quicksand is, and on what road you are embarking. Very regrettably, "hidden" wages are too often hidden from the employer as well as the employee.

k. Don't lack competent advisers at the bargaining table. Few, if any, quarterbacks can call signals, pass, block, run, and receive. By the same token, few businessmen possess the all-around, complete ability to negotiate a fully successful contract. Competent advisers, at the bargaining table, are an essential part of management's negotiating strength.

Avoid the pitfall of playing the game all by yourself.

l. Don't rely on oral agreements or understandings. All items in the contract should be in writing, and clauses should be framed in clear, understandable language. When a section, or provision, is agreed upon, it should be spelled out. Don't "agree" orally on the various issues and postpone the writing task until negotiations have been concluded. Also, don't accept a statement that the union is willing to leave an issue for settlement at some future date if and when the problem arises. Have an understanding before there is a problem.

m. Don't make agreements with a negotiator who lacks binding authority. Sometimes the union representative must report back management's offers for final acceptance by an employees' committee or by regional or international union officials. In such cases, you are constantly "showing your hand" to the advantage of the union. The negotiators of the bargaining table must possess competent authority to make binding agreements. You have a justifiable right to insist on conclusive bargaining. Otherwise there is always the pitfall of exposing your full supply of ammunition to counterattack.

n. Don't be afraid of a strike. At some point in most negotiations there is a strike tension, probably even a concrete and definite strike threat. There are few negotiations without at least an implied strike inference by the union representative. Don't be stampeded; remember that—

(1) Any jackass may have a strike if he wants one, but it takes skill, patience, and bargaining strategy to avoid strikes.

(2) Only a very small percentage of strike threats ever materialize.

(3) Practically every union negotiator wants to avoid a strike because to strike means that he has failed to maneuver management into a settlement. The majority of international unions don't want strikes because they absorb union personnel, cost money, and always contain the threat of losing out.

(4) The vast majority of workers don't want a strike because it costs them money, imperils their jobs, and puts them on the defensive.

(5) Strikes rarely occur unless there are genuine strike issues—i.e., real impasses on issues of major significance. Only immature negotiators let bargaining unravel into a strike on issues which do not represent basic conflicts over labor and management goals.

In the final analysis, a union-management contract is essentially a working agreement by which two collaborators seek to blueprint their teamwork arrangements. Such agreements should avoid the pitfall of one-sided domination and punitive measures. Harmonious labor-management relations are built only upon mutuality of purpose and respect for the other party's rights, responsibilities, and functions.

Questions on "Pitfalls of Collective Bargaining"

PREVIEW QUESTIONS

1. Whom is the writer warning about collective bargaining pitfalls?
   a. Management
   b. Labor unions
   c. Employees
   d. Negotiators for both labor and management

2. From what background of experience does the author speak on this subject?
   a. Much of his work has been as negotiator for labor.
   b. Much of his experience has been as a representative for management.
   c. He has had a great deal of experience in radio and television management.
   d. His experience has been about evenly divided between management and labor.

3. The subject is apparently presented:
   a. quite superficially and written for the casual reader.
   b. in a highly technical fashion, suggesting specific behavior for specific situations.
   c. in a careful, fairly comprehensive manner, suggesting areas for caution in bargaining situations.
   d. as a list of rules for the negotiator.

4. The kinds of ideas presented apply mostly to collective bargaining in:

   a. small businesses.

   b. large businesses.

   c. both large and small businesses.

   d. factory or manufacturing enterprises.

COMPLETE READING

5. Collective bargaining between management and labor is:

   a. much like buyer-seller negotiations of the business world.

   b. relatively easy if the negotiator for management is a good speaker.

   c. a simple matter of agreement on steps for the common good.

   d. very different from normal buyer-seller negotiations.

6. What is the basic reason that management should beware of seemingly unimportant, nonmonetary concessions?

   a. Concessions create industry-wide precedents whose cumulative effect may later prove disastrous.

   b. By forcing management's hand for one concession, labor has management on the defense.

   c. A concession which seems harmless today may have unfortunate consequences as the business expands.

   d. No concession entered into can be unimportant.

7. What type of issues are most vulnerable to the danger of seemingly innocuous concessions?

   a. Wage disputes

   b. Working conditions

   c. Schedules

   d. Fringe issues and jurisdictional clauses

8. For what two reasons is contract language sometimes purposely written ambiguously?

   a. Ambiguity usually favors the union when put to arbitration.

   b. Ambiguity usually favors management when put to arbitration.

   c. Ambiguity promotes a steady flow of grievances.

   d. Ambiguity keeps legal staffs operating making interpretations.

9. What is the best defense against contract ambiguity?
   a. A consistent use of legal phraseology
   b. Interpretive clauses accompanying legally phrased contracts
   c. Straightforward, nonlegal phraseology
   d. Understanding the contract fully before it is written up

10. How can management best avoid abetting unions in their attempt to create eventual total industry patterns from minor, but precedent-granting concessions?
    a. Bargain with an industry-wide interest, but avoid provisions not relative to your own operation.
    b. Think primarily of your own interests, disregarding the interests of other operators and competitors.
    c. Allow provisions in your contract beneficial to the industry although not immediately related to your own operation.
    d. Bargain directly in relation to the immediate problem without allowing yourself to be drawn into a long-range view of the point under arbitration.

11. What is likely to happen if management's representative is technically uninformed as to the facts of the contract under discussion?
    a. A "poker-playing bluff" will probably see him through any technical discussions.
    b. He will concede important points and argue unimportant ones.
    c. He will see points of danger and will get the information before agreeing to the contract.
    d. It is understood that the representative cannot have available all the information, and thus he is given opportunity to gather information where necessary.

12. Extra-long bargaining sessions tend to work against:
    a. unions, because their negotiators want to "get it over with."
    b. unions, because they then have no time to re-examine their accumulating data.
    c. management, because the businessman is not used to the jargon and long, tedious sessions.
    d. management, because businessmen find it difficult to keep up their end of the discussion.

13. What does the writer think of agreements between unions and management on company policy-making decisions such as stock purchase plans, discipline, and the like?

    a. He is against them because unions are not as acquainted with these problems as is management.
    b. He believes concessions in this area are good for "trading."
    c. He believes they threaten free American enterprise.
    d. He believes it is union's right to function in such policy-making.

14. Should management treat union demands separately or jointly as a "package deal"?

    a. Separately, because the complexity of such demands can be understood only by a point-by-point approach
    b. Separately, because it is in the individual provisions that inequities arise
    c. Jointly, because the interrelation of contract clauses creates the total and thus true picture
    d. Separately, because each provision must be settled at the bargaining table in order

15. When unions introduce individual grievances dealing with "inequities" or "inequalities" during general contract negotiations, the representative for management should:

    a. immediately investigate the charges fully.
    b. attempt in every way to disclaim the charges.
    c. either insist on proof or forget about the charges.
    d. consider the charges as a part of the problem under negotiation.

16. What is the major reason that management should always insist that a fully authorized union negotiator with binding authority be present at every bargaining session?

    a. Much time can be lost in referring management's offers back to the union regional office.
    b. Misunderstanding and misquoting are likely where offers must pass through "channels."
    c. Nothing can be gained by either side when those with binding authority are not present.

d. Sessions not represented by a union official with binding authority simply expose management to a planned later counterattack.

17. How much real danger of a strike is there in the average collective bargaining situation?

   a. Union negotiators will push the situation to strike proportions if possible.
   b. A great many workers desire strikes because it is the quickest way to settle differences.
   c. Both the workers and the union would like to see negotiations end in strike.
   d. Neither workers or the union want a strike to happen in most instances.

   Key: 1. a   2. b   3. c   4. c   5. d   6. a   7. d   8. a, c
   9. c   10. a   11. b   12. c   13. c   14. c   15. c
   16. d   17. d.

This article was longer (3100 words) and more detailed than the previous ones. If you were sufficiently interested in it, you probably read it carefully and thoroughly. We assumed that you would first preview the article, and answer the preview questions. Then, if you wished to learn the details, you would read more slowly through the entire article and answer the questions based on a complete reading.

Even if you did reread in this fashion, your speed should be greater than in earlier articles. The previewing enabled you to gain an overview of the article and its organization. With the ideas in mind gained from previewing, your careful reading progressed more rapidly. Because of the previewing and skimming techniques, your rate of careful reading should be somewhat faster than it once was. Has it improved?

What Makes an Executive? [5]

by Paul Hencke

There's more room at the top than ever. Competent executive talent is one of this country's scarcest commodities. The growth of American business has been so rapid, and the problems of management have become so complex, that finding young men with executive potential, and developing them into mature and able leaders has become of major concern.

Partial solution of this problem lies in knowing: What makes an executive? How do you find him? How do you train him? Here are some of the answers.

Seventeen leaders in business and public affairs agree that a man must possess at least five qualities if he hopes to become an executive:

He must have strong, continuing drive or ambition.

He must have physical and emotional stamina.

He must be willing to make personal sacrifices.

He must be willing to take risks—to move from one place to another or to switch jobs in mid-career.

He should have a college education, although even without one he may be able to make the long pull to the top.

These qualities were isolated in the course of a Round Table on Executive Potential and Performance conducted by the Columbia University Graduate School of Business on a grant from the McKinsey Foundation for Management Research.

Those who participated in the eight sessions did so in the hope that, by drawing on their own experience as executives in business, government, military service, education, religion and medicine, they might add useful ideas to the already impressive pool of knowledge on management and human resources which Columbia's Business School has amassed under the leadership of Dean Courtney C. Brown.

The basic question which the Round Table sought to answer was "What Makes an Executive?" In the course of discussion, many subsidiary points were covered—origins of executive potential; value of college edu-

---

[5] Paul Hencke, "What Makes an Executive?" *Nation's Business,* Vol. 43, No. 6 (June, 1955), pp. 64-68. (Adapted.) Used by permission.

cation; how to identify potential executives; methods for evaluating executive performance.

The participants and their chairman, Dr. Eli Ginzberg, of the Columbia faculty, sensed as the discussion unfolded that they were venturing onto unmapped ground. While other business problems have been subjects of careful research, the selection and development of executives often has been left to instinct, hunch, or prejudice.

Dr. Ginzberg emphasized that the Round Table's work has been suspended and not terminated. In meetings this fall the group will explore five new areas of inquiry including an intensive examination of the careers of individual business leaders to determine what patterns, if any, exist in the development of, say, a General Electric board chairman and a Standard Oil president—and what these patterns mean.

In the following pages, *Nation's Business* presents a summary of the major subjects discussed. The Round Table members agree that their work produced only tentative answers, but important conclusions or areas of agreement did emerge which may serve as guides to those responsible for identifying and training executive talent.

EXECUTIVE REQUIREMENTS

Physical stamina is essential to a potential executive. Lacking this, Round Table members agreed, a person would be unable to maintain the grueling pace of executive leadership. They agreed, too, that emotional stamina—the ability to surmount the obstacles which accompany leadership—is essential to a person seeking an executive position.

The members agreed that the potential executive must have ambition, although this ambition may be complex or simple, embracing one or several goals. They conceded that not all people who possess ambition may want to be executives, and that the definition of success varies from person to person.

All insisted that a person who wishes to attain distinction today must be willing to make personal sacrifices—time with family, personal popularity, hobbies. The question whether Americans have become, in the past decade, frightened of risk-taking and conditioned to security, was not resolved. It was agreed, however, that individuals differ in their willingness to gamble on opportunities rather than seek security, and that these differences are important in executive performance.

Here are some views expressed in the course of this phase of the discussion:

"Plenty of men are willing to be good department heads and nothing more. They seem to know that, to go to the top, they must make sacrifices and they aren't willing to."

"We haven't been very gallant. We spoke about wives who hold their husbands back. But wisely ambitious wives have been a big help. They have been a strong factor in many a man's success."

"I ask why so many people assume that young men today want security. I think security is the last thing a person should desire. From a biological viewpoint, life in the full sense of the word is based upon the ability to adapt to many different types of environment. In terms of human qualities, security results in atrophy of the human spirit. Only in change, which is the antithesis of security, is there opportunity for spiritual and intellectual growth."

"Nearly everyone is willing to take a chance, to be daring. Each man seems eager not to get into an organization where there is little opportunity to progress. I think youth is daring if given a chance."

THE VALUE OF COLLEGE EDUCATION

The college degree is a logical preliminary screening device but, the Round Table warned, too much reliance on this approach may impede the discovery of many individuals of high potential.

Here are some comments:

James S. Schoff, president, Bloomingdale Brothers: "We have thrown out certain symbols of education as being useless. This applies to certain high-class schools of business. We have concluded that exposure to a liberal arts influence is the best possible preparation for meeting the future specialized demands in business. In my opinion, too much value is placed on the symbols of a formal education."

Roger Hull, executive vice president, The Mutual Life Insurance Company of New York: "We are looking not so much for technological skills as for skills in human relations. Therefore, we have paid most attention to men with liberal arts backgrounds. I want to add that I think there are important educational experiences aside from academic competence. Extracurricular activities, for example, show breadth of interests. This is easier to spot in the case of people who have gone to college. We do not look for the campus big shots, but for those who have tried to support themselves or do something similar while they went through college. We are not necessarily interested in men who win popularity contests. We are looking for those activities which indicate that a man has real drive."

Frank Pace, Jr., executive vice president, General Dynamics Corporation; former Secretary of the Army: "I would say that, as executives pay more attention to the evaluation of personnel, the opportunities for non-college people will increase, because a college degree is a formal rather than a personal method of evaluation. As I see it, top executives are increasingly concerned with putting the right men in the right places, irrespective of their backgrounds."

IDENTIFYING POTENTIAL EXECUTIVES

Testing, rating, volunteering and prediction are desirable instruments to distinguish early between individual degrees of potential leadership, but few such instruments exist now, the Round Table found. Members also questioned whether any reliable evidence short of actual trial in the working world would reveal significant difference between individuals. There was agreement, however, that when a man has reached his late 20's or early 30's some differentiation can be made.

Discussion of the usefulness and limitations of tests was heated. The tentative conclusion was that, although tests are in many ways limited because of inadequate knowledge of what we are testing for, test procedures do contribute to a systematic and objective promotion system.

Similarly, in the case of rating systems, no one denied that superiors are likely to rate men working for them with some degree of bias whenever a high evaluation of subordinates constitutes a threat to themselves. On the other hand, a considerable movement toward group judgment has developed and the Round Table felt that multiple raters produce more objective ratings.

Members agreed that, although opportunities to volunteer for advancements still exist, selection by superiors rather than self-selection now predominates.

Frank Pace, Jr., stated that "A great number of cases came to my attention (while Secretary of the Army) where officers thought they had been treated unfairly in being evaluated and in 90 per cent of the cases I agreed with them."

"So many people think selling themselves means thinking along the same lines as their superiors. It is important to get across to an organization that the boss knows what he thinks; what he wants to know is what the other man thinks."

DEVELOPING FUTURE EXECUTIVES

Companies using courses in advanced management should be careful in selecting the men who attend and in handling these men upon their return. The danger in singling out a group of men, the Round Table members agreed, is that this may give the impression that those not chosen have a less promising future.

The members agreed that responsibility of selecting personnel for advanced training should rest with the company without reliance upon volunteers.

Some felt that executive development programs place too much emphasis on promotion and not enough on doing one's present work better. Since men frequently have to remain in the same post a long time, they will become restless if they pay too much attention to promotion. It was pointed out that, although formal courses may be useful, probably the single most important contribution to the training of a future executive is made by his boss, particularly his first boss.

It also was agreed that no executive development system can work successfully unless the company establishes a fixed retirement age. Without this, top jobs will not open up often enough to permit the system to work. The members emphasized that, if individuals are given important responsibilities and permitted to operate with little interference, most will develop their full potential. But, if the company is centralized and specialized, it is improbable that any formal teaching system or other device can overcome the deficiencies narrow assignments impose.

Among the views expressed were these:

"I think there is a danger in selection (for training courses) but if you are put on guard you can do something about it. You can send men to these courses who are moving from one department to another or from one region to another. Our biggest fear is that the man may begin to look upon himself as a fair-haired boy. We also have to be sure that others feel their chance is still to come."

"I would say that we should not think about executive development until a man is 45 or 50. The best development program is for a man to be a foreman or a squad leader. I do not think any development program is as good as actually being a boss and knowing what the problems are. For the first 15 years of a man's business life, I would say that the most important thing is that he have enough minor jobs to test his strengths. When a man is 50, you might go into a somewhat more formal program. It would seem that these programs have many pitfalls and that, on the whole, relatively few people would come through with a clean profit."

"There is a middle ground between telling a 21 year old that he can be president at 49 and in giving one's employees no indication of the opportunities open to them. A bright young man will be able to see how far he can go."

"You must convince your top men that, unless they take an interest in the individuals coming along and broaden them as they get assigned and reassigned, nothing else they may try to do to strengthen the personnel of the organization will work. Failure to do this will be interpreted as the top man's fear that, if he trains the second man, he will be displaced. You must convince executives that it is smart to train the people under them because they can then go on to bigger things."

EVALUATING EXECUTIVE PERFORMANCE

Many companies have tried to introduce some form of rating system in the hope of improving their methods of evaluating executive performance. The Round Table emphasized the difficulties of making any type of rating system work effectively, but agreed that a rating system turns a spotlight on organizational problems and on personnel.

The members stressed the advantages of periodically having the performance of executives reviewed by their superiors. This is especially valuable if done at the same time companies make their important decisions regarding budget, personnel, research and development, and related matters.

The discussion ended with a return to the question of the personal qualities needed by successful executives—particularly the ability to make decisions and the ability not to let personal feelings govern judgment of associates and subordinates.

Some comments:

"Profits over a five year period are not necessarily a good measure of executive performance. I think the best measure of an executive is how he trains his successor, how good he is in human relations, and whether he is good enough to be promoted. It might be 15 or 20 years before the man at the top can be judged. Some men gain in stature, some shrink."

Roger Hull: "If I had to choose between an executive who surrounds himself with good people and listens to them as against a more brilliant fellow who listens to no one, I would definitely choose the first. The lone eagle, however brilliant, sooner or later trips himself up. But if a fellow has the good sense to get good people around him, listen to them, and form judgments based upon their viewpoints, it seems to me he's certain to come out ahead of the others.

Dr. Ginsburg, psychiatrist, Vanderbilt Clinic, College of Physicians and Surgeons, Columbia University: "If I had to pick a single psychological characteristic of a good executive, I would say that it is a sense of inner security. He can be venturesome when necessary, he is not unduly threatened by competition, and he is not punitive to individuals who bring in ideas and plans he has not thought about himself. I would say that he had a good enough self-image so that he will be able to take care of himself, even in a tight situation."

THE EXECUTIVE AND THE ORGANIZATION

Do different types of organizations require different types of executives or can a good executive perform effectively in any type of organization? Round Table members found this a complex question with few definite answers.

Several members pointed out that, in some cases, well qualified people missed deserved promotions because of chance events—for example, a sudden change in the top leadership and the fact that the new man promoted his own associates.

A discussion of seniority brought the suggestion that a seniority system be modified by promoting some men on the basis of outstanding merit rather than age. The Army has adopted this practice.

The opportunities for advancement in government and business were compared. Some members argued that the chances are greater in government, since it is relatively easy to move from one department to another. This means that a comparatively large number of top posts are open to an ambitious person, while fewer top positions are available in a business concern. Others insisted that a large number of important positions in a private organization do not carry top titles but still offer the individual ample scope for his abilities.

Comments:

"You have to have movement in an organization. If you have turnover every ten years, or preferably faster, a fellow knows he does not have to wait until someone dies to advance. Then he will be interested in the job. When we talk about retirement we make the mistake of always talking about the person who will retire but seldom about all those underneath who will have more important work to do."

"I think we have different types of executives. You put a certain type of man in charge of a new store; when the business gets on its feet, you often have to remove him and get a different kind of person. I have seen this many times in our company and elsewhere. The man who builds up a company frequently is not capable of running it after it gets established!"

"I do not think there is the same competition for good men in industry as in government. In government the way is open to a greater extent than in business where the company president is eager to hoard all the good men he can. I suppose this is also true of a cabinet member or head of a department, but not to the same degree. I admit, though, that a man must be willing to take risks—leave civil service protection and strike out for himself. I think it is done more often in government than in business, and I raise the question whether there is anything that business can do to avoid hoarding top executive potential."

Questions on "What Makes an Executive?"

1. In which areas are these conclusions about executive development valuable?
   - a. Government and the military
   - b. Education and business
   - c. Religion and medicine
   - d. All of the above

2. How much research time has been given to the study of executive potential?
   - a. Almost none
   - b. About as much as to other business problems
   - c. More than to many other business problems
   - d. Enough to chart executive development programs rather completely

3. What view did certain members of the panel hold regarding youth's willingness to accept risks in its drive to success?
   - a. Few people today are willing to accept risks.
   - b. Risks not involved with security are the only ones considered.
   - c. Young people are willing to accept risks if given a chance.
   - d. Youth has learned to find success without any basic risks.

4. According to the panel, what value has a college education to potential executives?
   - a. It is an adequate screening device.
   - b. It is useless.
   - c. Its value is relative to its emphasis on human relations.
   - d. Its value is relative to its emphasis on technological skills.

5. How early can potential executive leadership be identified?
   - a. Not until after the individual has had considerable business experience

   b. As early as the late twenties or early thirties
   c. When the individual is about forty-five or fifty
   d. After at least fifteen years of business experience

6. With which of these points on developing future executives would
   the panel agree?
   a. Executive development programs place too much emphasis on
      promotion.
   b. Volunteers, rather than selected personnel, should be given
      executive training.
   c. Executive development systems can work only in companies
      having a fixed retirement age.
   d. Training given by one's superiors is apt to be more valuable
      than formal courses in executive development.

7. According to the panel, which of these are desirable qualities of
   the executive?
   a. Physical stamina
   b. Willingness to make personal sacrifices
   c. Strong drive and ambition
   d. Strong desire for security
   e. Willingness to take risks in job changes
   f. Skill in training subordinates
   g. Willingness to wait for advancement

   Key: 1. d   2. a   3. c   4. c   5. b   6. a, c, d   7. a, b, c, e.

   In our opinion, this 3000-word article is simple enough to be
read by skimming. It is concerned largely with the desirable characteristics of executives, and the problems of identifying and developing potential executives. These three ideas are developed in a
rather loose framework because of the insertion of quotations from
various members of the panel. However, the major portion of the
article does lend itself to skimming or rapid reading. Did you read
it in this fashion? How fast did you read the article? How does this
rate compare with your earlier rate scores?

11

Improving Other Communication Skills

Can You Listen Effectively?

What You Will Do
   Discover some facts about listening skills

What You Will Learn
   How to make your listening more efficient

WHY TRY TO IMPROVE LISTENING?

Much more time is spent in listening in the average business day than most of us commonly realize. This has been shown by time studies of the communication activities of business people. For about two months, Paul T. Rankin, director of research and adjustment for the Detroit Public Schools, studied the daily routines of 68 individuals engaged in business. He found that they spent 9 per cent of their communicating time writing, 16 per cent reading, 30 per cent talking, and 45 per cent listening. Other studies at the University of Minnesota, Florida State University, and Michigan State College substantially agree with Rankin's results in indicating that about 40 per cent of the day of the average businessman is spent in listening.

Despite the amount of time spent in this type of communication, effectiveness of listening is decidedly poor for most individuals. Dr. Ralph G. Nichols, who has pioneered in training work in listening, points out that immediately after the average person listens to another he remembers only about half of what he has heard—no matter how carefully he listened. Other surveys show that only about a fourth of an audience understands clearly even the main theme of a speaker. Are you willing to continue to function with about 50 per cent effectiveness? Can you afford to waste time and money by getting only half of what the other person says, when you could listen more effectively?

Numerous studies of learning indicate that listening is probably a more effective medium than reading. Delayed recall of facts has been found better after auditory presentation than after reading in many experiments. Thus listening effectively seems to be one of the easiest ways of acquiring information. Can you use this simple way of getting facts efficiently?

WHY IS OUR LISTENING SO POOR?

There are a number of causes for the ineffectual listening of the average person. Some of these are due to the peculiar nature of the situation, others are the result of bad habits of listening or lack of training. Listening is an instantaneous process with no opportunity for rereading or backtracking. Without asking the speaker to repeat, which you often cannot do, you have no second chance to understand the thought, as you would in reading or writing. Secondly, most individuals think at a faster rate than the speaker can talk. Speed of thinking is easily 500-600 words per minute while speed of speech is seldom greater than 125 words per minute. As a consequence, the untrained or undisciplined listener is far ahead of, and often far afield from, the ideas of the speaker.

A common poor listening habit is attending to the facts rather than the main ideas. When a series of facts is being presented, the untrained listener soon becomes lost trying to recapitulate the ideas of the speaker. By the time a half-dozen facts are presented, the listener has dropped far behind because of his attempts to catalogue or memorize the separate facts rather than to understand the central theme.

In everyday conversations, how often have you jumped to conclusions after someone has spoken only a few sentences? You decide what he is going to say before he has said half of it. This quick reaction is particularly harmful to good understanding if it is accompanied by an emotional reaction to an idea you thought was present. Most persons react too quickly to such symbolic words as *red tape, sex, Communist, unionism, Republicans,* etc. Without waiting to hear what the speaker really has to say, you are off in a blaze of emotion. You stop listening until you cool off and, of course, seldom learn what it was the speaker intended to tell you.

The same blocking occurs when the speaker is uninteresting. You close your mind to him and mentally wander off to more personal thoughts, while he continues to drone on. Some of us have perfected this ability to seem to be listening intently, so that even in face-to-face conversations the other person is never aware of our inattention. This little bit of acting only succeeds in hurting the listener, who has lost whatever of value could have been gained from the situation, and merely wasted his own time.

HOW CAN YOU BECOME A BETTER LISTENER?

Here are the components of effective listening as drawn from the experiences of James I. Brown and Ralph G. Nichols of the University of Minnesota. These principles have shown their practical values in listening training of many businessmen and businesswomen.

1. *Get ready to listen.* Listening is an active, not a passive process. To profit from listening, assume a listening posture, focus on the speaker, attend to him. If possible, maintain eye contact with the speaker. Force yourself to be interested, if necessary, for without interest you will gain very little.

2. *Switch off your emotional attitudes.* Try to identify your own sore points, the ideas to which you overreact. Probe the reasons for these touchy areas, and try to introduce some clear, logical thinking into your prejudices. Learn to suspend reaction when the speaker steps on your mental toes. Listen as calmly as possible to his complete idea, not by simply waiting to inject your answer as soon as he stops for breath, but to understand completely.

3. *Start listening immediately.* How many times have you been introduced to someone, and then been unable to recall his

name a few minutes later? This is a common indication of the tendency to fail to listen to the first few sentences of a conversation or speech. In listening to a speech, avoid this mistake by beginning active listening as soon as the speaker begins. He will often offer his main idea in an explanatory introduction. Speakers frequently feel obliged to justify themselves by such an explanation, or to prepare their audience for better comprehension by a statement of the central purpose of their remarks. Failing to hear the speaker's opening remarks may leave you wondering about his point through most of the speech.

4. *Get the central idea.* It is not practical or even desirable to attempt to remember the many individual facts offered in a formal speech. Listen for the central theme or purpose of the speaker. If you have this clearly in mind, his explanations and illustrations will fall into place and be meaningful.

5. *Listen for chief supporting ideas.* Many speakers signal the major sections of a speech by various types of cues. They change their pitch or volume, use cue words or phrases such as *in the first place, therefore, in conclusion, first, second,* etc. Listen for these emphases that mark off the important ideas supporting the central theme.

If the material is formal or technical, or you are anxious to retain it, try to outline as the speaker progresses. Keep your outline simple, consisting mainly of the central idea and the major supporting points. You can fill in the blanks later on, if you need to. Simple note-taking is less effective than outlining when listening to factual presentations. In addition to being less effective, note-taking is actually more difficult and less profitable because of its random nature. The organized arrangement of outlining is easy to use when listening to formal or difficult material since it lends itself to the structure of the speaker's remarks. Moreover, it provides a more comprehensive coverage of such materials than note-taking does, in the hands of most listeners.

6. *Listen critically.* As the speaker offers his main points, weigh and consider his proofs. Evaluate his competence to make such assertions. Watch for the common propaganda appeals: emotionally toned language, the Bandwagon, Plain Folks. Judge his logic and look for fallacies in his thinking. Keeping his central theme

and major supporting ideas in mind, anticipate his probable conclusions. These attitudes of critical listening are necessary to combat the tendency for the prestige of the speaker to influence you in accepting his premises.

7. *Avoid tangential thinking.* Since you can think so much faster than the speaker can talk, there is a very strong possibility of distracting yourself by flights of thought. As we have suggested earlier, one means of preventing this self-distraction is by maintaining eye contact with the speaker. Another method of controlling your attention is achieved by developing a thought pattern for your listening. Try to cultivate the habit of anticipating the speaker's points, of mentally summarizing or rephrasing his arguments. Practice critical listening and listening "between the lines" to the meanings given by facial expressions, changes in voice, and gestures.

These seven elements of effective listening will of course not be acquired without practice. They will not become part of your skills in dealing with people unless you make a distinct effort to apply them. Look for situations in which you can practice good listening, such as the radio, TV, public lectures, etc. The experiences of those who have practiced these seven elements show that with a little effort they can be readily acquired, and that they result in marked improvement of listening efficiency.

Here are the titles of several articles on listening effectively that you may find helpful.

Brown, James I., "How teachable is listening?" *Educational Research Bulletin,* Vol. 33, April, 1954, pp. 85-93.

Chase, Stuart, *Power of Words.* New York: Harcourt, Brace, 1954. Chapter 15.

Nichols, R. G., "How well do you listen?" *Education,* Vol. 75, January, 1955, p. 302.

Nichols, R. G., and Stevens, L. A., "You don't know how to listen," *Collier's,* Vol. 132, July 25, 1953, pp. 16-19.

"Rules for good listening," *Science Digest,* Vol. 38, August, 1955, p. 34.

Strong, Lydia, "Do you know how to listen?" *Management Review,* Vol. 44, August, 1955, pp. 530-35.

Zelko, H. P., "Art of listening," *Rotarian,* Vol. 87, December, 1955, p. 27.

Do You Write Effectively?

What You Will Do
Look critically at current writing practices

What You Will Learn
How to make your writing more effective

There has been a growing recognition in business and government of the need for improving communications with the public, particularly in the medium of writing. Letters, announcements, annual reports, and all sorts of matter being offered to the public are now being examined critically. Company newspapers and magazines, public relations materials, and even financial statements are evaluated for readability and reader appeal. The standards of technical accuracy, and completeness are rapidly giving way to new ideals of clarity and warmth.

WHAT'S WRONG WITH BUSINESS WRITING?

From the viewpoint of the public, it has taken business and government a long time to realize that much of its proffered material is almost unreadable. Picture, if you will, the reactions of a policyholder who received this reply to his inquiry about surrendering his policy:

Dear Mr. Blane,
Surrender of the policy is permissible only within the days attendant the grace period on compliance with the citation relevant options accruing to the policy so we are estopped from acquiescing to a surrender prior to the policy's anniversary date. We are confident that an investigation relevant to the incorporation of this feature will substantiate that the policy is not at variance with policies of other companies.[1]

This is not a particularly horrible example. Rather, it has the undesirable characteristics found in many business letters. Its

[1] "Throw Away Your Business Grammar," *Nation's Business,* Vol. 43, August, 1955, pp. 35-37.

phraseology is ponderous and almost unreadable. It covers its meaning in polysyllabic words, or abstract, complex terms when these are really not needed.

Edgar Dale tells an amusing story of the typical inability of technicians to communicate with the public. It seems that a plumber wrote to a research bureau regarding his use of hydrochloric acid in cleaning sewer pipes. The first reply was as follows: "The efficacy of hydrochloric acid is indisputable, but the corrosive residue is incompatible with metallic permanence." The plumber then thanked them for the information approving his procedure. The dismayed research bureau tried again, saying, "We cannot assume responsibility for the production of toxic and noxious residue with hydrochloric acid and suggest you use an alternative procedure." Once more the plumber thanked them for their approval. Finally, the bureau, worried about the New York sewers, called in a third scientist who wrote: "Don't use hydrochloric acid. It eats hell out of the pipes." [2]

The inability of management to express itself so that the public can understand is quite apparent. As James E. McCarthy puts it: [3]

Management, it is true, is increasingly aware of the necessity of telling its story. What it has lacked is the proper approach. Our management reports win high praise from management men. They are written with the rhetorical flourishes of management language. But they might as well be written in classic Greek, insofar as the public is concerned. They are honest enough, but many of them are also dull, and clothed in an excessively involved language that causes the man in the street, whom it should enlighten, to read the comics instead.

HOW CAN BUSINESS WRITING BE IMPROVED?

The New York Life Insurance Company made a four-year study of ways in which it could make its letters to clients more effective. The greatest weakness, it found, was that the language of its letters was a combination of technical terms and commercialese. Some of the letters intended to clarify matters for policyholders were as diffi-

---

[2] Dale, Edgar, "Clear Only if Known," *The News Letter,* Bureau of Educational Research, Ohio State University, Columbus, Ohio.

[3] McCarthy, James E., "The Blackout on Economic Facts," *New York Sun,* January 10, 1949.

cult to read as the policy itself, in all probability.

The findings of the New York Life survey suggest four principles of communication that can be adopted in any type of business.[4] These principles are:

1. Use your own language—forget formal business English and technical terms. Try to express the idea in simple, informal ways. Among the terms and expressions the business letter-writer should avoid are:

acknowledge receipt of	hereby advise
answering yours of	pursuant to
beg to acknowledge	regret to advise
deem	take the liberty of
for your files	under separate cover

2. Write your own way—stop trying to imitate a real or imaginary model. Develop your own style of writing, rather than the legalistic or technical style of contracts and specifications. Say it in your own way, rather than in the phraseology or clichés so commonly used. Let your personality show in your writing.

There is a tendency in business to coin terms, such as *roadability, do-gooder, know-how, swivel-chair-it,* which are meaningful only in the jargon of the office. Advertising men are held responsible for the current practice of adding *-wise* to almost any noun to convert it to an adverbial use, as in business-wise, financial-wise, policy-wise, etc. This is scarcely an improvement upon the former use of such expressions as *in regard to, in terms of, with respect to,* and the like.

In government, letter-writers and memo-scribblers have created a whole stream of meaningless phrases. A plan or direction is never carried out, it is always *implemented;* an answer becomes a letter of transmittal; facts become *substantiating data;* a letter that can't be answered is "referred for appropriate action." Some of the humorous aspects of this Pentagon Dictionary, as it has been called, are given in these cynical definitions:

To activate—To make carbons and add more names to the memo.

[4] *Nation's Business, op. cit.*

Note and initial—Let's spread the responsibility for this.

Will advise you in due course—If we figure it out, we'll let you know.

Further substantiating data is necessary—We've lost your stuff. Send it again.

To clarify—To fill in the background with so many details that the foreground goes underground.[5]

Avoid this technical jargon. Write to your client as directly and simply as you might if you were talking to him face to face or on the telephone.

3. Don't worry too much about grammar. A great deal of the formality of business writing is due to the concern about grammatical structure. The fear of incomplete or run-on sentences, or nonagreement of verb and subject, or lack of agreement between pronoun and antecedent is very real to some writers. They forget that language is a vehicle for expressing ideas and treat it as though it were a strait jacket for restraining spontaneity. Grammar is a matter of common usage rather than rigid principles. As such, it reflects the ways in which people express themselves, as much as it actually guides their manner of expression. Write your material as clearly as you can, then try it aloud on yourself before sending it. If you avoid obvious slang and strive for simplicity, you needn't worry about your grammar.

4. Cultivate the qualities of clarity, force, and warmth. Many firms and government agencies have submitted their materials to the test of readability. Various formulas for estimating this quality are available.[6] Basically they include measures of the number of polysyllabic words, and the length of sentences. These two characteristics are the chief components of reading difficulty. The use of short, simple sentences not more than 15-20 words in length is one method of insuring readability for the average respondent. Eliminating technical terms and lengthy phrases is another step toward simplification. The use of polysyllabic words such as *multifarious, cerebration,*

---

[5] Hicks, George R., "More Federalese," *Word Study*, 31, May, 1956. Copyright 1956 by G. and C. Merriam Co., Springfield, Mass. By permission.

[6] For example, Dale, Edgar, and Chall, Jeanne, *A Formula for Predicting Readability*, Bureau of Educational Research, Ohio State University, 1948.

desideratum, and *contemporaneous,* when simple words would do, marks the writer as pedantic rather than intelligent. The use of connectives to string ideas together in a long, complicated sentence only serves to leave the average reader floundering for meaning. Clarity, then, can be achieved by two simple practices—giving only one idea at a time and avoiding lengthy, complex sentences.

Force is acquired by directness. Answer the client directly. Tell him who does what, or who did what, or exactly why you cannot do what he asks. Avoid circumlocutions such as a "tea containing cup" or "iron containing globules" and unnecessary abstractions such as, "because of the sphericity of the retinal surface" for "because the surface of the retina is round." [7]

Warmth comes through, as suggested earlier, by using your own informal style of writing. Express your personality through your use of spontaneous explanations rather than the hackneyed clichés of business gobbledygook.

WRITING REPORTS AND SPEECHES

In broader types of material than letter writing, a number of suggestions have been offered by Klare and Buck.[8]

1. "Before you begin writing, define your purpose, not vaguely, somewhere in the back of your mind, but out in the open in words," they say. Defining purpose permits you to look at it objectively, to define it as needed, to clarify it for better writing. A clearly stated purpose enables you to evaluate ideas that might be included in the text. Do they strengthen or contribute to your goal? Finally, an objective should help you to keep in mind the kind of audience for which you are writing. Can they understand this? Does it tell them what you wish them to know? How can you illustrate this point to make it clearer to this particular audience?

[7] Examples from Baker, John R., "English Style in Scientific Papers," *Nature,* Vol. 176, 1955, p. 851.

[8] Klare, George R., and Buck, Byron, *Know Your Reader.* New York: Hermitage House, 1954.

2. Outline your ideas, not I, A, a, b, c, necessarily, but in the rough. This helps plan the length of the material and promotes easier, better organized writing. Outlining ideas helps you to work for unity and to avoid going off on tangents. It aids you in tying the material together and in offering a smooth flow in transition of ideas from one group to the next.

WRITING DIRECTIONS

Edgar Dale, one of the country's authorities on readability, offers cogent principles for writing directions.[9]

1. Appreciate the complexity of what you are saying. How many times have you tried to follow the street directions of a native when seeking a certain place, only to find that you couldn't comprehend or follow them a few minutes later? When writing directions, realize that the reader may know literally nothing about the thing or situation you are trying to explain. Remember that time you tried to assemble Jim's Christmas present from the printed directions? Be as simple, detailed, and direct as possible. Leave little or nothing to the imagination of the reader.

2. Eliminate any elements not absolutely necessary. Extraneous details are confusing and distracting. You are not discussing the merits of the thing, or its characteristics, but simply trying to tell your reader how to do something. Tell him that, and nothing else for the time being.

3. Try for reader identification. Make your writing seem pertinent, or even personal to the reader. Try to anticipate his reactions, by putting yourself in his place and appealing to his probable interests. Make your explanations and illustrations understandable. For example, if the American public spends 300 million on something, the reader will understand the point better if it is presented in the fact that this costs the average American about two dollars.

[9] Dale, Edgar, and Chall, Jeanne, "Developing Readable Materials," *Adult Reading,* Fifty-fifth Yearbook of the National Society for the Study of Education, Part II. University of Chicago Press: Chicago, 1956, pp. 218-250.

WRITING AN EFFECTIVE MEMO

In his book *Effective Letters in Business,*[10] Robert L. Shurter points out the main purposes of memoranda as (1) maintaining a continuous flow of information and (2) forming a reminder or permanent record. The flow of information to which he refers must exist both horizontally across levels and vertically through the ranks of an organization. These purposes must be accomplished by the memos of the staff of any modern complex business if it is to achieve lasting success. Such success can be achieved only by those individuals or concerns that maintain a continuous flow of accurate, readable internal communications.

Perfection in internal communications is seldom accomplished. If you don't think so, take out the last three or four memos you received and examine them for the faults discussed below.

Common Faults in Memo Writing

Some of the common faults or dangers in memo writing are:

1. Being too long-winded. Don't try to impress the reader with all that you know about the subject. Or, don't try to show him all the work that you've done on this question. The reader doesn't care how much trouble you've had collecting the facts, or carrying out your assignment. He is not concerned with your personal doubts or feelings regarding the significance of the question you are trying to answer.

Do try to sum up the situation, reduce it to the essential facts, and express your reactions or contribution concisely.

2. Hedging your answer with provisos. Don't equivocate or cloud your memo with *ifs, buts,* and *howevers.*

Do face the question squarely and give your answer briefly. If it is necessary to show the reasons for your answer, give only the essential reasons.

3. Using a double standard in writing. Don't attempt to handle internal communications and those with the public by two styles of

[10] New York: McGraw-Hill, 1954.

writing. Don't save your force, clarity, and warmth for only one type of writing.

Do try to write as clearly to other employees as you would to a stranger. Do write as well as you can every time you write.

Writing carelessly, or in a telegraphic style in one situation will ruin your writing skill in most attempts to write.

4. Failing to communicate with the reader. Don't sprinkle your writing with private or technical terms known only to you or your own group. Don't assume that the purpose of the memo is obvious.

Do tell the reader what the memo deals with. Give him some facts to help him understand why you wrote it. Do use language he can understand in the form or style he prefers. Or, if form or style are dictated by company policy, follow that dictate.

5. Failing to organize your ideas. Don't write lengthy memos right off the cuff. Don't treat a memo like a short story which gradually builds up through many minor incidents to a climax.

Do identify your main point early in the memo. De-emphasize minor details and eliminate superfluous matter by planning or outlining. You are not telling a story but supplying or asking for definite facts.

6. Overcommunicating. Many businessmen write too many memos to too many people. They exercise little or no selection of their readers. Don't contract the disease of memoitis—the distribution of too many memos of little significance to the readers. Unorganized, fragmentary, or isolated ideas or bits of news, or grapevine information about the company or its personnel, are not suitable for memos or any other kind of internal communications.

Do remember that the purpose of memos is not to keep everyone informed about everything. This is virtually impossible in business as it is everywhere else. Think about the material you are about to write. Will it be significant to all those to whom you are sending it? Could or should the reader do anything about the facts you offer? If not, don't write the memo.

Further suggestions for improving the style of business letters may be found in the following books and articles:

Barzun, Jacques, "Not gobbledygook but plain words: federal government's pamphlet on plain letters," *New York Times Magazine,* August 21, 1955, p. 25.

Chase, Stuart, *Power of Words.* New York: Harcourt, Brace, 1954, Chapter 23.

Grady, James F., and Hall, Milton, *How to Dictate Better Letters.* New York: Harper, 1942.

Hall, Milton, *Getting Your Ideas Across Through Writing,* Washington, D. C.: Federal Security Agency, Training Manual 7, 1950.

Janis, J. H., "What your letters reveal about you," *American,* Vol. 159, June, 1955, pp. 159-160.

Janis, J. H., "Ways to write better letters," *Reader's Digest,* Vol. 67, September, 1955, pp. 116-118.

"Making It Plain," *Newsweek,* Vol. 45, January 17, 1955, p. 24.

Morton, Herbert C., "Better business writing: company programs pay off," *Management Review,* Vol. 44, November, 1955, pp. 790-798.

"Simplified letter saves money," *Nation's Business,* Vol. 44, January, 1956, p. 93.

Thurber, James, "The psychosemanticist will see you now, Mr. Thurber," *The New Yorker,* Vol. 28, May, 1955, pp. 28-31.

Whyte, Wm. F., Jr. *Is Anybody Listening?* New York: Simon and Schuster, 1952.

Wyden, Peter, "She hates gobbledygook: government correspondence," *Coronet,* Vol. 39, March, 1956, pp. 70-72.

12

How Much Have You Improved?

What You Will Do
  Re-evaluate your reading skills

What You Will Learn
  How much your reading skills have improved

This chapter, containing two tests similar to those you took when you first began to use the book, offers a final opportunity for formal evaluation of your reading skills. We suggest that you give yourself these tests and compare your present performances with the earlier ones.

Follow the directions carefully; otherwise you cannot compare your results with the standards.

The first test, General Reading, is a measure of rate and comprehension in continuous material of moderate difficulty. The second test, Reading Flexibility, determines your speed and accuracy in skimming, scanning, and thorough reading. As before, the content of these tests is drawn from common business materials to make them as realistic as possible. You may read more rapidly in literary materials than in these tests. But we think it is more practical to measure your skills in the kind of material you ordinarily read in the course of your work. The purpose of this entire book has been to promote improvement of your reading in work-type materials, rather than in recreational materials. Therefore, this final evaluation of your reading is measured in business reading matter.

GENERAL READING TEST

Directions.   This is a test of your skill in general reading. Read the short article in this test in the same way that you ordinarily read any interesting article. Read as rapidly as you can and still understand what you read. When you finish reading, you will be asked to answer questions on the material you have read.

You will need to make an accurate record of the time you take to read this selection. Write the time you begin to read on the first line "Begun" next to the title of the article. As soon as you finish reading, before answering the questions, write down the time you finish on line "Ended."

Then begin to answer the questions. Do *not* look back at the article again.

What Makes Salesmen Tick? [1]   Begun_____

by Dr. Charles L. Lapp   ASSOCIATE   Ended_____
PROFESSOR OF MARKETING AT WASH-
INGTON UNIVERSITY, ST. LOUIS, MISSOURI.

There are four levels of motivation under which the salesman operates: the level of self-interest, the level of mediocrity, the level of aspiration, and the level of commitment. Motivation is the art of inspiring and energizing a salesman for the purpose of obtaining a better sales performance.

THE LEVEL OF SELF-INTEREST

At the level of self-interest very little motivation is provided. The salesman is given neither job nor income security. Sales executives assume no responsibility for his success. Only those salesmen are retained who are capable of self-motivation.

Self-motivation in a salesman is an admirable characteristic; but very few men can develop this trait without help. The salesman takes a job, is given a sample case, and told to go out and sell. Further direction or motivation is not provided. Responsibility is not assumed by such companies for the basic satisfactions desired by a salesman.

[1] Adapted from *Systems,* 15, No. 10, October, 1951, pp. 21-22. Copyright 1951 by Remington Rand. Used by permission.

Very few companies can succeed under these conditions. The greater number of salesmen quit. The philosophy of these companies is to show no concern about manpower turnover and little concern for the man. The practice is to exploit the man as long as he will stand for it.

THE LEVEL OF MEDIOCRITY

The motivation goal of many other sales supervisors is merely at the level of mediocrity. A salesman is not developed to make decisions. Overemphasis on mechanical sales control without an accompanying program of developmental motivation leads to a mechanized type of selling.

The salesman is merely an automaton—a "Charlie McCarthy" type —that moves on a string and echoes the voices of top management in a soulless and uninspired manner. Very little wage of psychic incentive is provided to encourage better performance. All that is expected of the salesman is that he does what he is told, in return for the security of a definite weekly or monthly wage.

Salesmen at this level must feel that their working conditions are satisfactory, or the motivation provided takes on the aspects of the level of self-interest. The salesman should understand the method of compensation and feel that it's fair.

Opinion surveys showed that the major reason salesmen think a compensation plan is unfair is that it hasn't been explained to them.

The salesman may feel that his company is not providing him with adequate sales equipment. In many companies, the desired sales equipment could be supplied with very little additional cost or effort.

A supervisor's goal at this level of mediocrity is to obtain a minimum of so many calls per week, so many new customers, and so much sales volume. Motivation at this level is termed mediocre. It is not sufficiently broad and comprehensive to provide a way of life.

Certain basic urges that could be used in motivating a salesman are not stressed. The details for making sales are given primacy over the "why" of making sales. The salesman as a human being is forgotten, with the exception of giving him security and somewhat favorable working conditions.

THE LEVEL OF ASPIRATION

The next higher level of motivation is that of aspiration. At this level, sales supervisors recognize, in addition to the salesman's desire for security, certain basic desires that can be used to energize the salesman to a higher level than one of a relatively routinized performance. At this point, the sales supervisor is beginning to utilize developmental motivation.

The provision for some form of money incentive may or may not stimulate a salesman. For example, a salesman may be making four hundred dollars a month. Even though he could make more, he will not always try to do so. The salesman may be given continued training to make it possible for him to make more money if he worked the same number of hours. But the salesman may be satisfied with his four hundred dollars a month and react to this training by putting in fewer hours. At the aspirational level of motivation, the sales supervisor attempts to energize a salesman by means of prestige, praise, power and opportunity.

The basic urges having the greatest effect on a salesman are prestige and power. It is true money helps to satisfy these two urges. However, the supervisor desiring to motivate a salesman on this level, may have to create a further desire within the salesman for a different way of life. The salesman is shown how, through better sales performance, this new way of life can be acquired. This desire for prestige must be of a permanent nature. It must make the salesman seek a permanent higher level of living.

Praise is another means of seeing that a salesman receives prestige. If a salesman does not get it in his own organization he will seek it elsewhere.

The idea of power is closely tied to prestige. The properly motivated salesman will not feel like a puppet on a string. He will want the satisfaction of making more decisions for himself, and having increased authority and responsibility.

Sometimes it is costly to develop a salesman to the point where responsibility and authority can be given to him. But when a salesman has developed to this point, a company then has a man motivated to turn in a much higher level of performance. The reason some salesman are willing to remain in mediocrity is that they have never been made to desire power and prestige.

The salesman must feel that he has a future within his present company. College graduates and others just starting to sell are at first primarily concerned with security. As these recruit salesmen become more confident, they become dissatisfied with having just security and want greater opportunity.

At the level of aspiration, the salesman should be made to feel that he has an opportunity to grow in his organization. If a salesman does not feel that his opportunity with his company is exceptionally good, there is the greater probability he will leave his job to seek employment elsewhere.

To provide opportunity does not mean that every salesman must aspire to be a sales executive. The salesman can be made to feel, through recognition, rewards in the form of greater power, and commensurate pay increase with more efficient and effective performances, that he has an unlimited opportunity in his company.

THE LEVEL OF COMMITMENT

The top level for motivating salesmen is one which takes into account not only the factors described at the levels of mediocrity and aspiration, but in addition those basic factors that go into making a completely motivated individual. One factor is loyalty toward his company, inwardly felt or expressed by the salesman in his attitude.

A salesman must feel he is working for a company better than all others to reach peak performance. A salesman must feel that the company's policies and procedures are fair and properly administered. It is false to assume that because a salesman stays on the payroll he is fully committed to his company. Such reasoning simply is not borne out by actual experience.

If salesmen are to have complete loyalty, sales executives must conduct themselves in a manner to justify it. Even a company's fair, practical, and economically sound policies must still be "sold" to the sales force.

A second factor in motivating a salesman at the level of commitment is to make him feel that he is of service to humanity. He may put forth the necessary effort, but if he feels selling is not worthwhile, beneath him, or does not provide an outlet for his abilities and interest, this man will not be satisfied, and consequently will not do his best work.

The salesman must be made to feel that his job is creating something important. He must feel his job is basic, not a stop-gap until some other job comes along.

Many salesmen lose confidence in the products they sell. They feel their company's competitors have more to offer. This aspect of motivation is closely tied up with continued training. Salesmen must constantly be assured that their products have distinct advantages over those of competitors. Salesmen must be convinced their products are the best buy relative to price.

Salesmen may be loyal to their company, but still lack confidence in their immediate superior. To reach the highest level of commitment, salesmen must not only be motivated so that they are committed to loyalty toward their company, to their job of selling, and the products they sell, but to those who are their leaders. Salesmen must have complete confidence in this leadership.

THE SUPERVISOR SETS THE PACE.

In opinion surveys, salesmen suggested that these were the qualities they wanted in their supervisors:

1. Understanding Attitude (expressed by an interest in them as a human being); 2. Leadership Ability (i.e., to plan, organize and control their operations); 3. Good Personality; 4. Sales Ability; 5. Product Knowledge; 6. Aggressiveness; 7. Integrity and Honesty.

The sales supervisor who has these basic qualities is the supervisor who is going to command the confidence of his salesmen, and thus will be able to motivate them to a higher level of performance.

The sales supervisor can quickly gain or lose the confidence of his salesmen by the example he sets. As a leader, he must set a standard for sound and temperate personal habits, for efficient business habits, and good mental habits—through his own confidence, cheerfulness, emotional tranquility and self-discipline. He must create a working relationship in which mutual respect and confidence exist between him and his salesmen.

A sales supervisor must give a salesman special consideration when personal difficulties arise.

The salesman that is well motivated has been provided with job security, satisfactory working conditions, prestige, power, opportunity, loyalty for his company, respect for selling, high regard for the products or service sold, and confidence in his supervisor.

It is through providing these nine basic demands that a sales force can be motivated—a stimulated and energized sales force that will reach new levels of selling efficiency.

Write down the time you finished reading.

Questions on "What Makes Salesmen Tick?"

1. The major reason salesmen think that the method of compensation used by their company is unfair is that:

   a. it has never been explained to them.

   b. as a matter of fact it usually is unfair.

   c. most companies operate on a flat salary without a commission incentive.

   d. the salesman is usually one of the company's poorest-paid employees.

2. In order to furnish a salesman with adequate sales equipment, most companies:

    a. would find it an expensive and time-consuming task.

    b. rely on the salesman's ingenuity to collect and arrange it effectively.

    c. could do it with little added cost or effort.

    d. require the salesmen to pay for it, at least in part.

3. At the "level of mediocrity," stress in selling is directed to:

    a. the "why" rather than the "how" of making sales.

    b. the basic drives of the individual.

    c. a fairly high commission bonus as the goal.

    d. the details of making sales.

4. The "level of self-interest" is so named because:

    a. interest is maintained only by monetary considerations.

    b. all motivation is left up to the salesman.

    c. the salesman is primarily selfish in his attitudes toward the company.

    d. only the basic desires of the salesman are motivated by the company.

5. What basic urges have the greatest effect on a salesman?

    a. Prestige and power

    b. Praise and esteem

    c. Opportunity and monetary gain

    d. Responsibility and monetary gain

6. The factor or factors of motivation provided at the "level of commitment" not present at any other level is or are:

    a. loyalty to one's company.

    b. prestige and power.

    c. belief in his future with the company.

    d. praise and esteem.

7. The fact that a salesman continues with a company indicates:

    a. he has passed the level of self-interest.

    b. he is fully committed to his company.

    c. very little about his true feelings toward the company.

    d. he is completely satisfied with his working conditions.

8. The level of mediocrity is superior to the level of self-interest in that:

   a. the salesman's loyalty to the company has been stimulated.
   b. the emphasis is placed on the mechanics of selling.
   c. greater security and better working conditions are offered.
   d. certain basic desires and aspirations of the salesman are recognized.

9. The salesman just beginning to sell is probably the most interested in:

   a. security.
   b. opportunity.
   c. prestige.
   d. praise.

10. The "level of aspiration" is characterized by:

    a. strong appeal to monetary incentives.
    b. praise and esteem.
    c. appeal to the salesman's needs for prestige, power, and opportunity.
    d. emphasis upon the salesman's identification with the company.

11. The apparent purpose of the author in writing this selection was to:

    a. stress the importance of motivational factors in employing salesmen.
    b. illustrate various motivational devices.
    c. emphasize the significance of supervisor-salesman relationships.
    d. disparage the values of monetary incentives for salesmen.

12. We could conclude from this article that the most important element in a salesman's success is:

    a. the motivational devices used by the sales supervisor.
    b. the supervisor's skill in arousing higher types of motivation in his sales force.
    c. the attitudes of a salesman toward his supervisor and the company.
    d. the incentives offered by the supervisor to his sales force.

13. The author uses the term *motivation* in the sense of:

 a. the salesman's attitudes toward the task of selling.
 b. the salesman's feelings and attitudes that enter into his success and continuation on the job.
 c. the incentives offered by the supervisor and the company.
 d. the level at which the salesmen of a company exist.

14. The "level of commitment" is characterized by:

 a. loyalty toward the company.
 b. ability for high self-motivation.
 c. complete feeling of security.
 d. unlimited opportunity.

15. Another important element present at the "level of commitment" is that the salesman feels that he:

 a. is of signal service to his company.
 b. has ability for a sales executive's position.
 c. is of real service to others.
 d. can do the job better than any other salesman.

16. Turnover among salesman is probably greatest:

 a. at the level of mediocrity.
 b. among those working at a self-interest level.
 c. among those working with small companies.
 d. in companies having the largest sales forces.

To determine your rate in the General Reading Test, divide the number of minutes you needed to read the article into 1,500, the number of words. Your rate may then be compared with the standards given below.

RATE

Better than 300	Excellent
250 to 300	Very good
200 to 250	Good
150 to 200	Fair
Below 150	Poor

Now compare your answers with the following correct answers to the sixteen questions.

Answers on "What Makes Salesmen Tick?"

1. a.	5. a.	9. a.	13. b.
2. c.	6. a.	10. c.	14. a.
3. d.	7. c.	11. a.	15. c.
4. b.	8. c.	12. b.	16. b.

COMPREHENSION

Above 13	Excellent
12 or 13	Very good
10 or 11	Good
7 to 9	Fair
Below 7	Poor

WHAT DO YOUR SCORES MEAN?

The comparison of your rate scores in this test and the General Reading test in chapter 2 should give some indication of your progress in learning to read more rapidly. If you have overcome the habit of slow reading, and really learned to read for ideas, your rate undoubtedly has increased.

Your comprehension score should probably be somewhat better in the second test, although the two tests are relatively equal in difficulty. Increase in comprehension is, of course, the most favorable type of performance in the second test. But even achieving merely a similar degree of comprehension, at a faster speed of reading, is real progress. Being able to read somewhat more rapidly than formerly and still maintain a constant degree of comprehension is no simple accomplishment. For those of you who were slow readers in the first test, this achievement may well represent permanent change in your reading habits. Being able to read faster opens new opportunities for the slow reader. It helps take some of the feeling of pressure off his shoulders, and relieves the feelings of frustration that come from attempting to cope with the mass of reading matter demanded by his work. With faster speed in reading, the slow reader finds time to finish his required materials, and some opportunity to do recreational reading. Reading itself becomes easier, more profitable, and even a pleasant pastime.

There is, of course, the possibility that your rate and comprehension scores in the second test may not have improved greatly. Some individuals tighten up as soon as they know they are taking a test. They may not do as well in the second test as they have been doing in previous exercises. Some other persons find it very difficult to read as rapidly as they really can when they know their performance will be evaluated. Finally, there is a small group of inflexible readers who seem to be unable to vary their rate at will. Habit is so strong for these individuals that increase in reading rate is difficult to achieve.

Any single measure of rate and comprehension is not highly reliable and your performances may be disturbed by any of a number of factors. The second article, for example, may have been more difficult for you than the first. If so, even though you read it as well or even better than the first, your scores do not appear to show progress. Other factors such as concentration, interest in the article, and familiarity of the content may affect your reading performances. If your scores in the second test do not seem to reflect growth, review your performances in the articles in the last few chapters. If your average rate in the last four or five selections is higher than in the first test, you have shown progress in learning to read more rapidly and effectively.

Now try this second Test of Reading Flexibility to see whether you have learned to skim, to scan, and to read thoroughly. Remember to follow the directions carefully. You will need about an hour of uninterrupted time to complete this test. As before, you will also need the assistance of a timer or some person to help you time the First Reading, which must be completed in exactly three minutes.

Test of Reading Flexibility [2]

This is a test to discover your ability to read for different purposes. Three different reading situations are suggested for the same selection, "Business Insurance." Work through each of the following plans before going on to the next one.

[2] By Paul C. Berg and George D. Spache, Reading Laboratory and Clinic, University of Florida, Gainesville, Florida. Copyright 1956 by Paul C. Berg and George D. Spache.

FIRST READING

Suppose that you found this article "Business Insurance" while looking through a magazine and wished to gain a general idea about the kinds of information it contained. Allow yourself *only three* (3) minutes to look or read through the entire selection, beginning on page 285. Then answer questions 1 through 10 without checking back to the selection. These questions deal with the general ideas or the main points the article presents. You will not be asked any very detailed questions after this brief reading. Remember, you have only *three minutes* to cover the *whole* article.

(*Do not read further on this page until you have completed the* FIRST READING.)

SECOND READING

Presume now that you have several specific questions about business insurance that you would like to have answered. As you turn again to the article, questions 11 to 20 come to your mind. Before you read the first of these questions, you will need to make an accurate record of the time. Write down the time you begin answering question 11 and again when you finish question 20. Write these, times right above question 11. Now answer questions 11 to 20, finding the answers from the reading as quickly as you can. As soon as you have found all of the answers, again make a record of the time.

(*Do not read further on this page until you have completed the* SECOND READING.)

THIRD READING

Now read the entire selection as you would to answer detailed questions. As soon as you have completed the reading, answer questions 21 to 42, without referring back to the article. Write down the time you begin this reading and again when you finish. Do *not* include the time for answering the questions.

Questions on "Business Insurance"

FIRST READING

1. This selection deals with:

    a. all types of business insurance.
    b. fidelity, forgery, and surety bonds only.
    c. burglary insurance and several types of bonds.
    d. ways of protecting your business against fraud.

2. A fidelity bond:

    a. protects against employee dishonesty.
    b. guarantees the performance of an obligation or contract.
    c. protects against theft, forgery, or similar crimes.
    d. insures the honesty and sincerity of employees.

3. A surety bond:

    a. protects against fraud or deceit in a contract.
    b. guarantees performance of an obligation or contract.
    c. protects against fraud or deceit by employees.
    d. insures against breach of contract.

4. A forgery bond:

    a. provides protection against embezzlement and similar crimes.
    b. protects against theft or forgery by employees.
    c. guarantees against loss by dishonesty.
    d. covers loss caused by forged or altered checks.

5. Burglary insurance protects the businessman mainly from:

    a. unlawful, forceful entry into his premises.
    b. shoplifting and other petty thievery.
    c. such crimes as theft, larceny, robbery, etc.
    d. all of these.

6. The purpose of this selection is to:

    a. show businessmen how to guarantee the reliability of human beings.
    b. inform businessmen regarding certain types of business insurance.

   c. protect business from common crimes and fraudulent practices.

   d. introduce the reader to the more uncommon types of business insurance.

7. It is apparent from one quick reading of this selection that:

   a. there are only one or two basic types of fidelity, surety, and forgery bonds.

   b. fidelity, surety, and forgery bonds have the same basic purpose of protection of the businessman from loss.

   c. a few general types of insurance would suffice for most situations.

   d. most types of burglary insurance have the common purpose of protection against theft of merchandise.

8. If an employee is found to have misappropriated property or funds from his employer, which general type of coverage will recover this loss for the employer?

   a. Fidelity bond

   b. Forgery bond

   c. Surety bond

   d. Money and securities broad form policy

9. A contractor, hired to build an office building, goes bankrupt during the period of the contract and the work is left incomplete. What general type of protection must the employing agency have if it is to recover for this loss?

   a. Fidelity bond

   b. Forgery bond

   c. Surety bond

   d. Burglary insurance

10. While transporting the day's receipts to the bank, a messenger for a business is attacked and forced to relinquish cash and securities. Which type of protection must the employer have if he is to recover the loss through insurance?

   a. Fidelity bond

   b. Forgery bond

c. Surety bond
d. Burglary insurance

Begun_____

Ended_____

SECOND READING

11. Approximately how much money is lost each year to the American public through forgery?
    a. $300,000,000
    b. $400,000,000
    c. $500,000,000
    d. $600,000,000

12. What is the approximate amount of money lost to business each year by employee dishonesty?
    a. $200,000,000
    b. $300,000,000
    c. $400,000,000
    d. $500,000,000

13. How many types of surety bonds are discussed in this article?
    a. Four
    b. Five
    c. Six
    d. Seven

14. Which of the following sources are suggested as specialists in giving information concerning insurance and insurance coverage?
    a. Insurance agent, broker, company representative
    b. Insurance agent, broker, lawyer
    c. Insurance agent, Defense Plants Administration, company representative
    d. Company representative, lawyer, Insurance Research Department

15. Paymaster robbery policies cover:
    a. loss of payroll inside the premises.
    b. loss of payroll outside the premises.

    c. loss of payroll both inside and outside, and robbery loss **and** damage to property.

    d. loss of payroll, property loss and damage, and injury to messenger.

16. What kind of burglary insurance policy covers the loss of securities consigned to a safe deposit box?

    a. Valuable papers and record policy

    b. Money and securities broad form policy

    c. Comprehensive dishonesty, disappearance, and destruction policy

    d. Securities insurance policy

17. What is the name of the bond that insures the federal government's receipt of taxes and duties levied on certain imported merchandise?

    a. Performance bond

    b. Internal revenue bond

    c. Payment bond

    d. Customs bond

18. What is the purpose of fidelity and surety bonds?

    a. To guarantee the loss resulting from unauthorized alteration of securities

    b. To guarantee the reliability of another in business relationships

    c. To protect against loss from the larceny of unprotected property

    d. To protect against loss of valuable papers and records

19. In the 1950 study, how many places (in round numbers) were robbed each day in the 359 cities above 25,000 population?

    a. 100

    b. 500

    c. 1100

    d. 2000

20. What type of bond insures against the dishonesty of a person holding a specific position: teller, cashier, etc?

a. Blanket position bonds
b. Individual or name schedule bonds
c. Securities bonds
d. Position schedule bonds

Begun_____

Ended_____

THIRD READING

21. The general purpose of a bond is to:

    a. protect the businessman in his contractual obligations to others.
    b. insure the performance of certain obligations by employees or by the other party to a contract.
    c. protect the businessman from the illegal actions of others.
    d. insure the businessman against loss resulting from a contract.

22. The word *fidelity* is used here to mean:

    a. the loyalty of the two parties to a contract.
    b. the dependability of human beings in business relationships.
    c. the trustworthiness of employees.
    d. a type of protection against dishonesty.

23. Fidelity and surety bonds differ from other types of insurance in that they involve:

    a. two parties—the person who is bonded and the insuring company.
    b. three parties—the businessman who is bonded, the insuring company, and the customer.
    c. three parties—the bonded party, the insured party, and the insuring company.
    d. three parties—the two parties to a contract and the insuring company.

24. The chief difference between the primary commercial blanket and blanket position fidelity bonds is:

    a. in the extent of retroactive coverage.
    b. in the number of employees covered.

   c. the extent of the coverage in thefts involving more than one employee.

   d. the first covers all employees; the second, those in certain positions.

25. Of the amount lost by American employers by employee dishonesty, what per cent is covered by insurance?

   a. About 50 per cent

   b. About 10 per cent

   c. About 5 per cent

   d. Less than one per cent

26. Which type of employee most often causes the greatest losses through dishonesty?

   a. The "trusted" employee

   b. The short-term or part-time employee

   c. The underpaid "white collar" worker

   d. The known suspects

27. Good business management would require which employees to be covered by fidelity bonds?

   a. Personnel handling money and securities

   b. New and thus unknown employees

   c. All officers and employees

   d. All officers, and employees handling money and securities

28. For what purpose is the position schedule bond especially designed?

   a. Bonding of designated employees in a specific position

   b. Bonding retroactively to the employee's original date of employment

   c. Covers each employee found in collusion

   d. Specific positions where there is high employee turnover

29. Depositors' forgery bonds are available to:

   a. any individual or association desiring such bonding.

   b. individuals and business establishments, except savings and loan associations.

   c. associations only.

   d. individuals only.

30. In doing business with a bank, you can be sure of protection against loss by forgery:

    a. because all banks are legally liable for forged checks if they honor them.
    b. if you are covered by an incoming check rider bond.
    c. only if you have a depositors' forgery bond.
    d. if you are covered by a securities bond.

31. Which type of surety bond guarantees that the bonded person will furnish the merchandise purchased by another?

    a. Supply contract bond
    b. Customs bond
    c. Performance bond
    d. Payment bond

32. Which bond guarantees the faithful performance of a contract, such as constructing or remodeling a building?

    a. Supply contract bond
    b. Payment bond
    c. Customs bond
    d. Performance bond

33. Which bond guarantees that the finished structure or product of a building contract will be turned over to the owner free of material and labor costs incurred by mechanics and subcontractors?

    a. Supply contract bond
    b. Payment bond
    c. Customs bond
    d. Performance bond

34. Which of these means the carrying off of goods by forcible entry?

    a. Stealing
    b. Burglary
    c. Robbery
    d. Theft and larceny

35. Which of these means the taking of property by violence or threat?

    a. Stealing
    b. Burglary

   c. Robbery
   d. Theft and larceny

36. Which of these means the taking of unprotected property?
   a. Stealing
   b. Burglary
   c. Robbery
   d. Theft and larceny

37. More than half of the burglaries committed are committed against:
   a. stores and offices.
   b. individuals.
   c. gas stations.
   d. homes.

38. Which type of burglary insurance is most attractive to the small businessman?
   a. Office burglary and robbery policy
   b. Mercantile safe burglary policy
   c. Mercantile open stock burglary policy
   d. Storekeepers' burglary and robbery policy

39. The mercantile safe burglary policy pays for damages or loss from safe deposit vaults:
   a. only when visible marks of forcible entry are present.
   b. for all types of incurred damage or loss to the contents of the safe.
   c. for all types of damage to the contents of the vault, the premises, and the fixtures.
   d. whether or not the contents consigned to the safe were within the safe at the moment of burglary.

40. The interior robbery policy covers the loss of goods from a show window when:
   a. the glass is left intact and the merchandise is taken from within the window of the establishment.
   b. the glass is broken from outside during business hours.
   c. the glass is broken from outside after the business is closed for the day.

d. the glass is broken and personal violence to the storekeeper or clerk is involved.

41. We might conclude from this discussion of bonds and burglary insurance that:

   a. the average businessman should carry almost all the different kinds of insurance.
   b. one or two policies will cover most situations.
   c. the businessman is likely to need expert advice in selecting policies.
   d. most businessmen don't carry policies with sufficiently broad coverage.

42. Even if you are not actually concerned with the insurance aspect of a business, what general conclusions might you learn from this article? (Choose as many answers as you need.)

   a. Losses to business through employee dishonesty could be materially reduced through adequate insurance coverage.
   b. Employee dishonesty could be eradicated by appropriate business insurance.
   c. It is advisable to anticipate the dishonest actions of any and all employees by insurance protection.
   d. A business may be protected against financial loss in any contractual obligation by appropriate bonding.
   e. It probably would not be wise for the average businessman to plan his insurance program without professional assistance.

Business Insurance [3]

Fidelity, Forgery, and Surety Bonds

Fidelity and surety bonds are important to the businessman because they deal with guaranteeing the reliability of human beings in business relationships. Forgery bonds are important because they protect the businessman against loss resulting from forgery or alteration of checks and other securities.

[3] From *Management Aids for Small Business, Annual No. 1,* edited by Edward L. Anthony. Small Business Administration, Washington, D.C., January, 1955.

Fidelity and surety bonds differ from other insurance contracts in that they involve three parties: (1) the *principal,* or bonded party, who promises to fulfill certain obligations; (2) the *beneficiary,* or insured, who requires the bond, and (3) the *surety,* or insuring company, which reimburses the beneficiary if the principal defaults on his promise. In the case of forgery bonds, only two parties are involved: The person to whom the bond is issued and the insuring company.

FIDELITY BONDS

A fidelity bond protects the businessman against loss caused by employee dishonesty. Although the average employer finds it hard to believe that any of his employees could be dishonest, losses from employee dishonesty cost American business more than $400,000,000 each year, according to the estimate of some authorities.

Only about one-eighteenth of the loss is covered by insurance. Losses by individual firms sometimes have been large enough to force the firms into bankruptcy. Good business management requires that every officer and employee of an enterprise be covered under a fidelity bond, regardless of whether he handles money, securities, or merchandise as a part of his duties. Fidelity bonds serve to deter employees who are tempted to dishonesty and, if the employees are dishonest, enable the businessman to recover his loss.

The following types of fidelity bonds are available to the businessman:

1. *Primary commercial blanket bonds.* This form is used to bond all a businessman's employees, making it unnecessary to select certain ones to be covered. This is particularly useful if a business has considerable employee turnover. Coverage of all employees is important, also, because "trusted" (and therefore often uninsured) employees usually cause the losses. When two or more dishonest employees work together in stealing from a business, this bond reimburses only up to the limit of the bond. Since losses under these circumstances may be very substantial, it is important to carry a bond that gives adequate coverage.

2. *Blanket position bonds.* This form is broader than the primary commercial blanket bond in that it automatically covers each employee up to the limit of the bond. In a case of collusion (where two or more employees work together to steal from the business) each employee who can be shown to have contributed to the loss is covered up to the full amount of the bond. Thus, if an employer carries a $5,000 bond, and 2

employees are found responsible for a $10,000 loss, the insurance company will pay the full $10,000.

3. *Individual or name schedule bonds.* This type of bond is used to cover one or more designated employees. The employees can be insured for different amounts.

4. *Position schedule bonds.* This form covers specific positions, rather than specific individuals. Each position is covered for a stipulated amount, and the person holding the position is automatically covered. This bond is especially designed for businesses which have high employee turnover.

5. *Discovery bonds.* This type of bond is similar to the name schedule and position schedule form of bonds but applied retroactively to the original date of employment of the bonded employee. It is a particularly desirable type for employers who, in the past, have carried inadequate fidelity insurance or none at all.

FORGERY BONDS

A forgery bond covers loss caused by forged or altered checks and other securities. Businessmen are constantly exposed to losses of this kind because of the tremendous volume of checks, drafts, notes, securities, and other written instruments used in modern business. No one knows the total dollar loss suffered each year by commercial and industrial organizations and individuals through forgery, but crime authorities estimate it at some $300,000,000. The following types of forgery bonds are available:

1. *Depositors' forgery bonds.* This form of bond is available to both individuals and businesses, with the exception of savings banks and loan associations. It is the principal form of forgery bond used by business concerns. Under the terms of the bond, the insured and his bank are reimbursed for forgery losses which occur and are discovered while the bond is in force. Coverage for the businessman's bank is important, because in many instances a bank is not legally liable for forged checks which it honors. The bond protects against loss from forged or altered checks, drafts, and similar instruments issued by the insured or his agent. The depositor's forgery bond concerns itself with outgoing checks, drafts, and other instruments.

2. *Incoming check rider.* This rider is attachable to the depositor's forgery bond and protects the insured against loss from forged or altered

instruments he receives as payment for personal property sold and delivered, or for services rendered.

3. *Securities bonds.* This type of bond is particularly valuable for banks, investment houses, and other financial institutions which are their own transfer agents. Two forms are available. One form applies to persons engaged in buying securities for themselves or who buy or sell securities for others. The second form covers persons who act as issuing agents, transfer agents, or registrars for corporations.

SURETY BONDS

A surety bond guarantees performance of an obligation or contract. The premise underlying surety bonds is that no losses are expected, and the premium amounts to a service charge to compensate the insurance company for pledging its credit. Many surety bonds are in the nature of financial guarantees. When applying for a bond of this type, the businessman must be prepared to furnish the insurance company with financial information and possibly collateral security to support his application.

In most cases, the purpose of a surety bond is not to protect the businessman; rather, it is legally required of him, as a means of protecting others. In turn, surety bonds make it possible for the businessman to operate his business, pursue an action or defense in litigation, or obtain benefits for himself which would not otherwise be possible.

The following are among the many types of surety bonds which are of interest to the businessman:

1. *License and permit bonds.* These are required by Federal, State, and local governments in the case of certain types of businesses. They guarantee that the bonded person will comply with the law or ordinance governing the types of operation for which the license or permit is issued. They enable the bonded person to engage in a certain line of activity and enjoy certain privileges and, at the same time, protect the public from any loss resulting from noncompliance with the law.

2. *Supply contract bonds.* These usually are required by Federal and State purchasing offices, and guarantee that the bonded person will fulfill the conditions of a contract for furnishing supplies. If the supplier defaults, the insurance company reimburses the buyer.

3. *Customs bonds.* These bonds are required by the Federal Government to insure compliance with regulations governing importation of certain merchandise. They guarantee that the owner of the merchandise will pay any required taxes or duties and will comply with the applicable

Federal statutes, thereby enabling him to obtain immediate possession of the merchandise.

4. *Internal revenue bonds.* The Federal Government requires these bonds in order to insure compliance with specific regulations or payment of certain Federal taxes.

5. *Court bonds.* Various courts require individuals engaged in lawsuits to post these bonds.

6. *Performance bonds.* This form of bond guarantees that the principal or bonded person will faithfully perform the terms of a contract, such as for constructing or remodeling a building. The insurance company assumes responsibility if the bonded person defaults on his obligation.

7. *Payment bonds.* A payment bond is a supplementary agreement to a performance bond, usually in connection with a building contract, and guarantees to the insured that the finished structure or product will be turned over to him free of labor and material costs incurred by the mechanics and subcontractors. This bond, like the performance bond, is particularly important to a business firm which is planning to expand its facilities by constructing new buildings or remodeling existing plants.

Burglary Insurance

To understand the protection which burglary insurance offers a business, it is important to know that this insurance includes protection against loss resulting from the following crimes:

Burglary, which requires forcible entry. For example, your safe is broken open or a person breaks into your place of business after it is closed, with all doors and windows securely locked, and carries off your merchandise or office equipment.

Robbery, which means taking your property by violence or threat of violence. A person enters your place of business, for example, and holds you up at gun point while he cleans out your cash register or safe.

Theft and larceny, which mean stealing property while it is unprotected. For example, a person finds the door of your business establishment open and steals your property.

While no one can guarantee that you won't fall victim to one of these crimes, you can protect yourself against the resulting financial loss through proper insurance.

Need for insurance.   A casual examination of any daily newspaper should bring home to the businessman the need for burglary insurance. Scores of such crimes are committed daily. The Federal Bureau of Investigation reported, for example, that in 1950, in 359 cities above 25,000 population, a total of at least 146 persons were robbed and 1,129 places were entered by burglars every day. Almost one-third of the robberies were committed against some type of commercial establishment and more than half of the burglaries reported were of stores and offices.

Without insurance, many small businesses could not sustain a sudden loss, such as loss of the week's payroll, or of the funds kept in a safe on the premises, and still remain solvent. Insurance not only protects an owner against the immediate loss from a robbery, theft or burglary, but it also guards against his having to close his shop as a result and accept a possible business failure.

Also important to the average businessman is the speed with which insurance companies usually settle claims. Prompt settlement means continued operation of the business.

THE COVERAGE IN BRIEF

A brief description of each of the various burglary insurance coverages follows:

Storekeepers' burglary and robbery policy.   This policy is attractive to the small retail storekeeper and other businessmen who are exposed to a number of kinds of possible loss but which are not large enough to warrant the purchase of appropriate individual forms of coverage. The basic "package policy" provides up to $250 for each of the following types of loss: (1) robbery within the premises, (2) robbery outside the premises, (3) kidnapping, (4) burglary of a sale, (5) burglars taking money or securities after forcible entry into the night depository of a bank or a custodian's home, (6) burglars making forcible entry into the premises and taking merchandise and equipment, and (7) damage to property and premises due to any of the foregoing sources of loss.

Office burglary and robbery policy.   This policy is especially useful for professional and business men who do not sell merchandise or keep it in stock, but who need insurance protection for their office equipment and supplies. Coverage is the same as the Storekeepers' Burglary and Robbery Policy except that there is no coverage on merchandise and there is $50 of insurance covering loss of money taken from the premises by burglars.

Paymaster robbery policy.   In many businesses, the payroll is the only large amount of cash that is handled. It is exposed from the time that the paymaster leaves the bank until the employees leave the premises with their pay. This policy covers loss of payroll money and checks by robbery occurring either *inside* or *outside* the insured's premises. It also covers resulting loss of, or damage to, the container holding the money and to the furniture, fixtures, or property in the premises of the insured.

Paymaster broad form policy. Upon payment of an additional premium, the Paymaster Robbery Policy is extended to cover all losses of payroll money and checks caused by destruction, disappearance, or wrongful abstraction (any form of illegal removal).

Mercantile safe burglary policy. This policy covers loss of money, securities, and other property due to a burglary from insured safes or vaults, when the safes have been properly closed and locked and entry is made by means of tools, explosives, electricity, gas or chemicals. There must be visible marks of forcible entry. The policy, in addition to covering loss of contents of the safe, covers all damage (except by fire) to the safe, premises, furniture and fixtures caused by a burglary or by an attempted burglary.

Mercantile open stock burglary policy. This policy provides protection against loss by burglary of merchandise, furniture, fixtures and equipment from stores, lofts, and warehouses and also all damage (except by fire) to the merchandise and premises, including furniture and fixtures, caused by burglary. For an additional premium, the policy may be extended to cover theft.

Interior robbery policy. This policy covers loss of, or damage to, money, securities and other property, within the premises of the insured, under the following circumstances: (1) when robbers enter the premises, which are open for business, and forcibly take the property, which is in the care of a custodian; (2) when the custodian or messenger is kidnaped while outside the premises and compelled by violence or threat of violence to admit a person into the premises after they are closed, but before they are next open for business; and (3) when property is stolen from within a show window, while the premises are open for business, by a person who has broken the glass from outside the premises.

Messenger robbery policy. This policy covers loss or damage to money, securities, or other property in the custody of a messenger while *outside* the premises of the insured. The property must be forcibly taken from the messenger through violence or threat of violence.

Valuable papers and records policy. This policy covers all loss or destruction of, or damage to, valuable papers, which are defined as written, or printed, or otherwise inscribed documents including books, maps, films, drawings, abstracts, deeds, mortgages, manuscripts (but not money or securities) used by the insured in his business.

Accounts receivable policy. This policy covers direct loss resulting from the inability of a business institution or individual to collect due accounts, because of destruction of or damage to the accounts receivable while within the premises, or during or after removal to a place of safety, if done to preserve the records from imminent destruction.

Securities insurance policy. This is a broad-scope policy for lessees of safe deposit boxes and primarily covers all losses of securities in safe deposit boxes. Loss of securities within the premises while temporarily outside the safe deposit box, whether by burglary, robbery, or theft, is also covered.

Money and securities broad form policy. This policy protects the insured against loss of money and securities, whether by destruction through fire, water damage, rodents, or other causes. If carelessness results in disappearance—for example, if a strong wind whisks money or valuable securities off a desk and out a window—the policy holder is protected against loss.

Comprehensive dishonesty, disappearance, and destruction policy. This combination policy consists of five insuring clauses, all optional, and covers: (1) loss through employees' dishonest acts, (2) loss of money and securities occurring within the premises, (3) loss of money and securities outside the premises, (4) loss of securities within leased safe deposit boxes, and (5) loss through forgery of the firm's checks, drafts, promissory notes and similar instruments. This policy may be expanded by endorsement to include other forms of insurance.

Obtaining Proper Insurance Protection

The only way in which you can be certain that your business is properly protected by insurance is to see an insurance agent, broker, or company representative. Just as you are a specialist in manufacturing or some other line of business, so he is a specialist in insurance. His services are available to you without charge. Ask him to survey the insurance needs of your business establishment. Since there are many types of coverage, the burglary, theft, and robbery protection he suggests for you will depend upon your type of business. He will tailor your insurance program to meet the particular needs of your business.

Answers on "Business Insurance"

First Reading	Second Reading	Third Reading	
1. c.	11. a.	21. b.	32. d.
2. a.	12. c.	22. c.	33. b.
3. b.	13. d.	23. c.	34. b.
4. d.	14. a.	24. c.	35. c.
5. c.	15. c.	25. c.	36. d.
6. b.	16. d.	26. a.	37. a.
7. b.	17. d.	27. c.	38. d.
8. a.	18. b.	28. d.	39. a.
9. c.	19. c.	29. b.	40. b.
10. d.	20. d.	30. c.	41. c.

Number right_____ Number right_____ 31. a. 42. a., c., e.
(Possible score 10) (Possible score 10) Number right_____
(Possible score 24)

STANDARDS

	First Score	Second Score	Third Score	Time in Minutes	
				Second	Third
Excellent	Above 9	Above 9	Above 20	Below 5	Below 9
Very Good	8-9	9	18-20	5-5.5	9-12
Good	7	8	15-17	6-7.5	12.5-14.5
Fair	5-6	7	13-14	8.0-10.00	15-19
Poor	Below 5	Below 7	Below 13	Above 10	Above 19

WHAT DO YOUR SCORES MEAN?

There are a number of possible comparisons between the results of this Test of Reading Flexibility and the one in chapter 2. These various comparisons may help you to determine your progress in several different reading techniques.

Skimming. The score on the First Reading is indicative of your ability to skim in an effective manner. You may remember your reaction to this task the first time you took the Flexibility Test. Most slow readers are amazed at the suggestion that they attempt to cover a whole article in three minutes. Their only concept of reading is to read straight through something, line by line, to the bitter end. By this time, you certainly have learned other approaches and should be able to skim without struggling. A gain in the score on the First Reading reflects learning to skim as contrasted with a one-track idea of how to read. If you have learned to skim, your score in this section of the test will probably rise at least one step, as from Poor to Fair, or Fair to Good.

Scanning. The second part of the Flexibility Test is a measure of your ability to scan—to find specific, detailed facts quickly. Of course, the correct facts should be found if this is to be an effective effort. Your score in the Second Reading indicates your accuracy in finding the correct facts. But even more significant than the score is the time you needed to do the task. The time for the Second Reading should decrease if you have learned to scan. Real improvement in scanning is shown by an increase of at least one step in the ratings.

Complete Reading. The third section of the Flexibility Test measures both rate and detailed comprehension. Here again you may compare your results directly with the corresponding scores on the earlier test. You may find improvement either in rate or comprehension or both. Ideally, you should find both, but a gain of at least one step in the ratings in either rate or comprehension also shows real improvement.

If you now read somewhat faster, with about the same comprehension as before, you can feel proud of your ability to handle materials of moderate difficulty with greater speed. You have probably accomplished one of the aims for which you undertook this effort.

If you now read with better comprehension than before, at about the same rate as earlier, this is a highly desirable improvement. If you continue to try for greater rate, you may also achieve that goal in a reasonable time.

One other evidence of your growth in Flexibility may be found in the results of this test. You may compare your rate of reading in the General Reading and the Flexibility tests. If you are learning to adjust your rate to different reading situations, the rates of reading in these two selections should differ somewhat. Most persons find the "Business Insurance" selection to be more difficult reading than

"What Makes Salesmen Tick?" Hence, they tend to read it more slowly and carefully. If this was true in your case, your rate of reading in the article on business insurance should have been slower. Your rate of reading in "Business Insurance" may be found by dividing the number of minutes for the Third Reading into 2000, the number of words in the article. If your speeds in the two articles differed by as much as fifty words per minute, you have shown flexibility in adjusting rate' of reading to the nature of the material read.

These two tests need not be the final evaluation of your progress in improving your reading. With the skills and knowledge you have gained in using this book, continued progress is possible. If you continue to make the effort, you will be able to increase your reading speeds in various types of reading materials and improve your comprehension and retention. Your skill in handling different reading materials by skimming, scanning, previewing, or other reading techniques will also grow and yield dividends in economy of time and greater reading efficiency.

Your writing and speaking vocabularies, and hence, your ability to communicate effectively with others, will constantly improve, if you continue to show interest in words. Your competence in reading critically and intelligently in persuasive writing and in interpreting statistical matter will be augmented and intensified. You will learn to enjoy matching wits with a writer and the thrill of being able to analyze and evaluate the ideas he offers. You will find time for pleasure reading—for exploring the many interesting fields of thinking about which you would like to know more. Best of all, you will continue to grow in self-confidence, in your respect for your ability to understand and to use words and ideas.

Have your attitudes, beliefs, and reading practices changed while working with this book? Take the Inventory of Reading Habits and Attitudes below and compare your present answers with those you gave earlier, in chapter 2.

INVENTORY OF READING HABITS AND ATTITUDES

Indicate whether you A—agree, D—disagree or ?—are doubtful about each of these items.

A D ?   1. One may determine whether he is a flexible reader by comparing his rate of reading different materials.

A D ?   2. Fast readers generally have better comprehension than very slow readers.

A D ?   3. The basic characteristic of all efficient readers is reading with a purpose.

A D ?   4. Learning to read for ideas rather than reading words more quickly is the only sound way of increasing rate.

A D ?   5. The major difference between the effective and the ineffective reader is skill in various reading approaches.

A D ?   6. A good reader can read a group of three or four words in a fraction of a second.

A D ?   7. The most important way to increase reading efficiency substantially is to increase rate of reading.

A D ?   8. If the reader really tries, meanings of unknown words may often be found by careful reading of the context.

A D ?   9. Vocabulary improvement can be achieved only by cultivating an active interest in words and their characteristics.

A D ? 10. Most adults have a much greater reading vocabulary than what they use in speaking or writing.

A D ? 11. The efficient reader reads to remember all the details and main ideas in the material.

A D ? 12. Difficulties with concentration are usually due to lack of planning or lack of interest in the reading.

A D ? 13. Vocabulary increases almost as rapidly during adulthood as during childhood.

A D ? 14. The average person listens to another with only about 50 per cent effectiveness.

A D ? 15. If used effectively, listening is an easier and better way of acquiring information than reading.

A D ? 16. Reading improvement can only be achieved by conscientious practice of new methods and approaches.

A D ? 17. A shelf of general and special dictionaries and other aids to word study is essential to growth in vocabulary and word usage.

A D ? 18. The reading of facts presented in graphic, tabular, or other mathematical forms is difficult for many otherwise well-educated adults.

Indicate whether you follow these practices A—always, S—sometimes, N—never.

A S N 19. I try to make my business writing natural and personal but forceful.

A S N 20. When reading rapidly, I am able to read for ideas, skipping unimportant words.

A S N 21. Before reading any important material, I preview or look over its content thoroughly to decide how to read.

A S N 22. When trying to find a specific fact, I look over the material very rapidly rather than reading line by line.

A S N 23. I deliberately change my rate from one selection to another according to the way I think it best to read.

A S N 24. When reading materials of only moderate difficulty, I skim selectively rather than read line by line.

A S N 25. I read a wide variety of printed materials with equal ease and enjoyment.

A S N 26. I tend to say or think each word as I read in order to get good comprehension.

A S N 27. I try to get the meaning of an unknown word by pronouncing it to myself.

A S N 28. When reading persuasive or propaganda material, I am apt to react to the author's attitude before reading the entire selection.

A   S   N   29. I consciously analyze parts of a word to discover its meaning, if I do not recognize its meaning immediately.

A   S   N   30. Whenever I read, I read for some definite purpose and this purpose influences the way I read.

A   S   N   31. I pay little or no attention to new words other than to secure a temporarily satisfactory meaning.

A   S   N   32. I find it difficult to read statistical material intelligently and critically.

A   S   N   33. I tend to use my usual rate of reading when looking for a single fact, name, or number.

A   S   N   34. I try to think along with the writer to recognize his facts and evaluate his beliefs and attitudes.

A   S   N   35. I use the dictionary for much more than the meanings of words I need to know temporarily.

Answers to the Inventory

The first eighteen statements refer to attitudes and beliefs. The correct answers are:

1. A	7. D	13. D
2. A	8. A	14. A
3. A	9. A	15. A
4. A	10. A	16. A
5. A	11. D	17. A
6. A	12. A	18. A

The next group of statements refer to habits and practices. The correct answers are:

19. A	25. A	31. N
20. A	26. S or N	32. N
21. A	27. N	33. N
22. A	28. N	34. A
23. A	29. S	35. A
24. A	30. A	

If your answers still disagree with those given here, it would be well to review our detailed discussion of the Inventory, following the answers in chapter 2.